DramaContemporary

SCANDINAVIA

THE DRAMACONTEMPORARY SERIES

DramaContemporary is a series specializing in the publication of new foreign plays in translation, organized by country or region. The series developed in response to the increasing internationalism of our age that now links world societies more closely, not only economically, but culturally as well. The last twenty years, in particular, is characterized by cross-cultural references in writing and performance, East and West and throughout the Americas. The new drama series is designed to partake of this movement in world patterns of culture, specifically in the area of our specialty, theatre.

Each volume of DramaContemporary features a selection of recent plays that reflects current social, cultural, and artistic values in individual countries. Plays are chosen for their significance in the larger perspective of a culture, as a measure of the concerns of its artists and public. At times, these plays may find their way into the American theatrical repertoire; in other instances, this may not be possible. Nevertheless, at all times the American public can have the opportunity to learn about other cultures —the speech, gestures, rhythms and attitudes that shape a society—in the dramatic life of their plays.

The Publishers

IN PRINT:

DramaContemporary: Czechoslovakia
DramaContemporary: Spain
DramaContemporary: France
DramaContemporary: Latin America
DramaContemporary: Scandinavia

IN PREPARATION:

DramaContemporary: Hungary
DramaContemporary: Poland
DramaContemporary: Germany
DramaContemporary: Russia
DramaContemporary: India

DRAMACONTEMPORARY

SCANDINAVIA

plays by

Olafur Haukur Simonarson
Tor Åge Bringsvaerd
Ulla Ryum
Margareta Garpe
Jussi Kylätasku

Edited, with an Introduction, by
Per Brask

PAJ PUBLICATIONS
NEW YORK

For my parents, Inge and Olaf Brask
and for Rebecca, Aaron, and Justin

Library of Congress Cataloging in Publication Data
DramaContemporary: Scandinavia
CONTENTS: *Under Your Skin; The Glass Mountain; And The Birds Are Singing Again; For Julia; Mary Bloom*
ISBN: 1-55554-050-3 (cloth)
ISBN: 1-55554-051-1 (paper)

Printed in the United States of America

Publication of this book has been made possible in part by grants received from the National Endowment for the Arts, Washington, D.C., a federal agency, and the New York State Council on the Arts.

The publication of *DramaContemporary: Scandinavia* was made possible by a generous grant from the Nordic Cultural Fund, Copenhagen, Denmark, whose support is gratefully acknowledged.

Additional grants were made available by The Reed Foundation, Inc., whose support is gratefully acknowledged.

General Editors of the DramaContemporary Series:
    Bonnie Marranca and Gautam Dasgupta

Contents

Preface

by

Per Brask

"IT DOESN'T MATTER WHO WE VOTE FOR OR WHAT THE RESULT IS, because we're all Social Democrats." This statement by a conservative journalist at the 1982 election party opens Hans Magnus Enzensberger's essay on Sweden in his 1987 book *Ach Europa!* (translated as *Europe, Europe* when it recently appeared in the U.S.). I am quoting it here because there is some small truth in that sentiment which might well apply to all of the five Nordic countries. Enzensberger goes on to suggest that the culture he is observing is under the sway of a social democratic hegemony, one which it is becoming increasingly costly to maintain. Again, with a large grain of salt thrown in to temper the statement, this could be said to apply to Iceland, Norway, Denmark and Finland, as well. The five countries of *Norden* [the North] do have a great deal in common and a North American traveler would find that in spite of the obvious scenic differences—ranging from the volcanic fields of Iceland, the fjords of Norway, the woods of Sweden, the Finnish lake district, to the rolling hills of Denmark—people living in these diverse surroundings share some basic attitudes.

What is at the root of these attitudes is often hard to discern; certainly part of it is an environment where "goodness" is defined in social categories, as opposed to the North American categories of "individual freedom." Of course, individual freedom is valued there, but it does not hold the dominating position on the cultural list of priorities that it does in North America. In the Nordic countries the balancing act between freedom and equality looks quite different from here. As a consequence, the traveler will encounter a lot less poverty than he/she is used to accepting as normal and also a lot less individual wealth. Of course there are poor people and wealthy people in the Nordic countries, but the middle range seems to include a much larger percentage of the population than it does here. Taxes are very high, there are many social services, a massive bureaucracy, a wealth of rules and regulations, an extremely well-educated population, a basic trust that the state is there to do good for all citizens, and a massive indebtedness.

Democracy in the Nordic countries is an old concept, starting with the Viking *ting*, solidified in Iceland with the establishment of the *Althing* in 930 C.E., which founded perhaps the first democratic parliament. Considering the physical setting of the five countries, with their paucity of resources and scattered population (except for Denmark which has one of the highest population densities in Europe though it is one of its smallest countries), it begins to make sense that cooperative systems would be necessary for comfortable survival. The social democratic features of the Nordic countries, however, are rooted in the changes which took place during the Industrial Revolution in all of Europe in the middle of the last century. The new methods of production and economic organization demanded fundamental changes in the Nordic countries, as elsewhere, changes which led to the creation of cooperative farm movements and education movements. During the 1920s the first social democratic governments started the processes which led to the welfare states of the post-World War II era, reaching a climax in the early 1970s when the oil embargoes dealt the economies of the Nordic countries particularly harsh blows. Now, in the 1980s/90s, these countries, along with the rest of Europe are being subjected to some of the neo-conservative winds blowing across the Western world. Their indebtedness and a mounting resistance to the ever-increasing tax burden is resulting in a growing sense of dissatisfaction, expressed by people from the left as well as the right, with the previously so beloved state.

What exactly the future will bring is naturally always difficult to speculate, but in the case of the Nordic countries an important factor in the development will be what will happen in Europe after 1992 when the free trade agreement between the EEC countries comes into full effect. Of the Nordic countries only Denmark is a member, a fact which undoubtedly will have effects on the ways they have cooperated in the past both culturally and economically.

* * *

The theatre history of the Nordic countries varies greatly from country to country but suffice it here to state that the development of professional national theatres, as we define them today, via their different routes began in

Denmark in the early 1700s, in Sweden in the late 1700s, in Norway and Finland in the mid to late 1800s, and in Iceland in this century.

The sheer quantity of professional theatrical activity in these countries in the 1980s is astonishing, and it is probably without likeness when their very small population base is taken into consideration. Iceland is the smallest of the countries with 244,099 (1986) people, then follows Norway with its 4.2 million (1986) people, Finland with its population of 4.93 million (1986), Denmark with 5.12 million (1987), and Sweden with a population of 8.4 million (1985). That these countries are also among those with the highest standards of living in the world is perhaps discernible from the figures below, which show the amount of public funding given (by state and local governments) in the five countries in 1986. The figures are given in millions of dollars and they have been collected by Professor Jørn Langsted, Institut for Dramaturgi, Aarhus Universitet, Denmark:

	Denmark State/Local	Finland State/Local	Iceland State/Local	Norway State/Local	Sweden State/Local
National theatres	22.0/—	6.2/1.6	1.6/—	14.8/2.8	33.9/—
Regional/City theatres	8.1/9.4	6.3/28.5	0.1/1.9	12.6/8.4	14.7/25.8
County theatres	2.2/2.2	4.0/7.0	0.1/0.3	3.7/1.3	6.3/15.7
National touring theatres	1.9/1.8	—/—	—/—	6.5/—	17.5/—
Free groups	2.2/0.4	1.4/0.7	0.1/—	0.7/*	3.5/3.5
Amateur groups	0.1/—	0.1/*	0.1/—	0.4/*	0.1/—
Ticket marketing schemes	3.5/3.2	—/*	—/—	—/—	0.9/1.2
Other	0.7/—	1.2/*	—/—	0.7/—	—/—
Subtotals	40.7/17.0	19.2/37.8	2.0/2.2	39.4/12.5	76.9/46.2
TOTAL	57.7	57.0	4.2	51.9	123.1

*Information not available

(Free groups are most often theatre groups whose histories date back to the late 1960s and who tend to be organized along democratic lines and to develop their own plays, as opposed to the decision making processes and creative processes of institutional theatres.)

Jonna Oulund of Nordisk Teaterkomité (The Nordic Theatre Committee) reports the following number of theatres in the Nordic countries in 1988 (the figures for the free groups are reported as approximate):

	Dance Theatres	Institutional Theatres	Private Theatres	Free Groups
Denmark	10	15	1	52
Sweden	26	38	9	116
Norway	5	13	1	19
Finland	16	35	—	5
Iceland	1	4	—	8

It is clear that in countries with this amount of activity and support the number of new plays presented every year, particularly by the free groups, but also, substantially, by the regional and city theatres, is quite impressive. An anthology containing a play from each country, and selected from a repertoire written since the mid-1970s, can in no measure claim to be representative of the variety of work done in these countries. In choosing the plays I've been biased towards works written by playwrights who have made significant contributions to the drama of their countries, who have created a body of work, and whose work is not conventional, yet is accessible to an English-speaking readership without needing specialized information concerning unique political or cultural histories. The plays selected, naturally, also reflect my personal tastes.

In order to avoid suggesting a thematic relationship between the plays, or a chronological development between them, I have chosen to present them in what could be termed a geographic order from west to east: Iceland, Norway, Denmark, Sweden, and Finland (left to right on the map). I have, thus, put the plays in a "spatial" relationship to one another rather than a sequential one, so that the "gap" between them would not need to be "filled" by interpretation.

* * *

Under Your Skin (first produced by the National Theatre of Iceland in 1984) is the first play in a trilogy about the life of a fisherman's family in contemporary Reykjavik. Olafur Haukur Simonarson (b. 1947) was known as a novelist and poet before he turned to playwriting with *Blómarósir (Lovely Girls)* in 1979. Since then his plays have become an important part of the Icelandic repertoire. Where this first play of the trilogy introduces us to the whole family, the following two plays focus more particularly on the stories of the younger and the elder sons, respectively. This first part of the trilogy was also produced as a separate play on West German radio. Though *Under Your Skin* bears witness to Simonarson's effective and lively handling of a neo-realist universe, his writing is by no means limited to this form. In 1980, he co-wrote a musical, *Grettir,* based on the saga of Grettir the

Strong; 1985 saw his comedy *Astin sigrar* (*Love Conquers All*). The same year his dramatization of Kipling's "The Cat Who Walked by Himself" was produced. And, in 1987, his thriller *Bilarverkstaedi Badda* (*Baddi's Garage*) was staged.

* * *

Tor Åge Bringsvaerd (b. 1939), who holds degrees in Religious Studies and in Folklore, made his debut as an anthologist, with Jon Bing, in 1967 with a book of fantastical stories. (They also published a collection of short stories that year.) In 1969 Det Norske Teater (Norway's National Theatre) produced their play *Å miste et romskip* (*To Loose a Spaceship*). Since then Bringsvaerd has produced a body of work which includes over fifty titles, featuring novels, short story collections, anthologies, plays, radio and television dramas, children's books, and plays. *The Glass Mountain* (first produced by Det Norske Teater in 1975) well represents Bringsvaerd's unique combination of fairy tale fantasy and social criticism. The play is based on the medieval tale "The Princess on the Glass Mountain" which tells the story of knights attempting to ride over/conquer the Glass Mountain to receive a gold apple (a symbol of wisdom) from the Princess who sits at the top of the mountain. Bringsvaerd has received several prizes for his work, including the prestigious Ashehoug Prize which he received in 1979 in acknowledgement of his work till then.

* * *

Ulla Ryum (b. 1937) has produced an *oeuvre* of amazing variety since her debut as a novelist in 1962. She has published four novels, three collections of short stories, and two collections of essays. She has had eleven plays produced, several radio dramas, ballet scenarios, operas, and TV dramas. Many of these she has directed herself for different theatres, including the Royal Theatre in Copenhagen. She is also active as a teacher of dramaturgy and directing, and she is well-established as a theorist of the drama. *And the Birds Are Singing Again* is a radio drama which was first produced, in 1980, by Danish Radio who submitted it as Denmark's entry to the Prix Italia in 1981. (It was subsequently produced in a staged reading at the Intiman Theatre, Seattle, in a different translation, in 1982.) The fact that a radio drama has been selected for this collection pays tribute to the significance of this medium for dramatic writing in the Nordic countries, as well as to the very high quality of work being written for radio. *And the Birds Are Singing Again* is part of a larger group of works set in "the not too distant future," after some major devastation (ecological, nuclear, etc.) has secured the power of a totalitarian regime over its dehumanized and "peaceful" subjects. Making use of radio, stage and prose, Ryum's investigation into the death of democracy and Western civilization began in 1971 with the radio drama *Den bedrøvede bugtaler* (The Sorrowful Ventriloquist) and has so far culminated in the novel *Jeg er den I tror* (*I Am Who You Think I Am*), published in 1986.

* * *

Margareta Garpe (b. 1944) is a playwright, director of stage and film, and a journalist. During the 1970s she co-wrote a series of plays, with Suzanne Osten, committed to the women's movement and radical social change, beginning with *Tjejsnack* (*Girl Talk*), in 1971. In all of her plays, Garpe is concerned with the conditions for women's liberation, and through that the liberation of children and men, as well. But whereas the plays of the early seventies could be described as taking a sociological point of departure, some of her later plays, such as *For Julia* (first produced at Stockholm's Royal Dramatic Theatre, Dramaten, in 1987, and directed by herself) take a more psychological approach. About this change in aesthetic direction she stated in the program to *For Julia:* "I don't see any contradictions between the psychological theatre, which deals with the liberation of the individual, and the political theatre, which deals with collective liberation." The specific concerns addressed in this play, such as the relationship between mothers and daughters, and the status of children, she began approaching directly in the late seventies with the play *Barnet* (*Child in Our Time*), produced in 1978. ("I am . . . preoccupied with the questions of why children are born and what position they are given in the world.")

* * *

Mary Bloom was first produced as a radio drama in 1980, and adapted for the stage the following year. Its author, Jussi Kylätasku (b. 1943) has written several collections of poetry, novels, filmscripts, as well as drama for the stage, radio, and television. Kylätasku has gained a reputation as an experimental and challenging writer, as he treats large political themes in formally inventive ways. *Mary Bloom,* dealing with the issues of faith and belief in a world awaiting disaster, and evoking a revival meeting, is a good example of this. In another play, *Gracchuskan pojat* (*The Brothers Gracchus*), 1981, he uses history to deal with loss of faith in democracy expressed by such phenomena as terrorism and incipient fascism in Europe. In an interview with the magazine *Samtiden* in 1981, he stated in relation to both of those plays: "The new fascism is trying to find an acceptable form. Many people have lost their faith in the democratic system, they are longing for something which is simple and easy to understand, they long for strong leaders and hard systems. Democracy goes through crisis after crisis. Our view of human beings is changing to a point where the model of the 'ideal' person is growing ever harder and colder, more efficient and more demanding. Despite the fact that we know that such a development leads us into disaster. And exactly because the disaster is predictable people attempt to create leaders who will exempt them from responsibility.''

* * *

Given the Nordic countries' more than thousand-year history of cultural interconnectedness, the fact that four of them developed their languages from the same Old Norse roots (the Finnish language is Finno-Ugric in origin), and given the prevailing social outlook, it should come as no surprise that the plays in an anthology containing a very different kind of play from each country have something in common despite all differences. All of the writers presented here are from their different perspectives working confidently from the position that an artist is an integral part of the culture, one who engages in and can effect the social environment in which he/she works. Certainly very strong characters are at work in these plays, characters with highly individual concerns and desires. But, within the context of each play, it is the social significance of their actions which is of concern to the playwright; the background morality of all the plays, the ''mechanism'' which focuses the action of each play, is clearly social in character rather than individualistic.

* * *

I would like to express my gratitude to Nordisk Kulturfond which awarded a special grant for this publication, and to the publishers, the playwrights, and the translators, without whose generosity this anthology never would have appeared. In addition, I would like to thank some of the many people whose assistance was crucial during the research stage of this project: Sigrún Valbergsdóttir of the Icelandic Centre of the ITI, Sigudur A. Magnússon, Liv Kern of Norske Dramatikeres Forbund, Prof. Jørn Langsted of Aarhus Universitet, Jonna Oulund of Nordisk Teaterkomite, Kate Hegelund of Det Danske Selskab, Hanne Jørna, Birte Fischer, and Kirsten Proschowsky of Danske Dramatikeres Forbund, Gerd Widestedt-Ericson of Folmer Hansen Teaterförlag, Anneli Suur-Kujala of the Finnish Centre of the ITI, and last, but certainly not least, my wife Carol Matas.

Under Your Skin

a play in 19 scenes

by

Olafur Haukur Simonarson

Translated from the Icelandic by Inga Birna Jónsdóttir

CHARACTERS:

Sigurd
Asta
Bodvar
Haddi
Gogo
Gudmund
Halla
Jona

Scene 1

(*Asta and Halla. Asta is putting curlers in Halla's hair. Yet, they are in two different worlds.*)

HALLA: I guess dad has been very ill. I though he'd be taking his last breath this morning. When I called his voice rattled heavily on the phone.

ASTA: His rattle always gets worse when he's talking to you. He never rattles when he talks to me.

HALLA: Strange how long it's taking. It's unlikely he'll last much longer. Stubborn, that's what he is. And how is Loa feeling?

ASTA: She's about the same, I think.

HALLA: Yeah, her father's finally dead.

ASTA: (*Irritated.*) Sure as you're here.

HALLA: There are so many people one knows who are dying. Oh, I don't know. It's so depressing. Heart attack, arteriosclerosis, stroke, all kinds of cancer: bone, vaginal, stomach, breast, kidney . . .

ASTA: (*Quite irritated.*) Please, Halla, let's talk about something else!

HALLA: How is Bodvar doing at the University? He doesn't have to be afraid of unemployment, more and more people are going crazy. Has his kid recovered from eczema?

ASTA: It was only an allergy.

HALLA: Well, I thought it was eczema. There's so much eczema in our family. Have you looked at my legs?

ASTA: Do you want another shot in your coffee? (*Pours into Halla's cup.*)

HALLA: Oh, I don't know. Everything gives me gas. I wouldn't be surprised if I have an ulcer.

ASTA: And how is Gudmund doing?

HALLA: I've been begging him for months to go to a specialist. Yesterday I had to go with him all the way into the examining room at the clinic.

They're thinking about admitting him to the hospital. For a check-up, they say, but you know what that means. He's a workaholic, that man. Suicidal.

ASTA: Can't he slow down for a while?

HALLA: Oh dear, that's what I keep telling him every day. I say: Darling, you're buying yourself a oneway ticket out of this world. But it's easier said than done for someone with his own business. He's just ordered a new truck because that's the only thing he really cares about. And how is Sigurd doing? He looked exhausted the last time I saw him.

ASTA: I think the fishing is bad these days.

HALLA: Yeah, he seemed to be very upset. Do you think he's sick?

ASTA: I think he's going to sell the boat. But he doesn't bother to tell me anything.

HALLA: He should really quit the sea and try to get an easier job.

ASTA: Having him home all the time wouldn't make things better.

HALLA: But then you couldn't say he was never home. And old Kate's dead. She really deserved the rest, dear old soul. She was buried in the family plot, wasn't she?

ASTA: (*Looks straight at her sister for the first time.*) Halla, I'm thinking of getting a job.

HALLA: (*Eyes her sister almost aggressively.*) What does Siggi have to say about that? And Haddi? What about the taxes? Gudmund doesn't want me to work at the fish factory. He'd rather I spend my time on our home. (*Halla takes a few steps backwards, as if there were a threat in Asta's speech.*)

GOGO: (*Enters.*) Hi, is Haddi back?

ASTA: (*Demanding.*) No, he isn't.

GOGO: (*Embarrassed.*) Can I take a bath?

ASTA: (*Milder.*) A bath? Yes, of course, you may take a bath.

GOGO: Listen, could you spare a cigarette? (*Takes the whole packet.*) I'll get them back to you on payday.

ASTA: Yes, Gogo dear, I'm sure you will. (*Gogo exits to bathroom.*)

HALLA: Well, Haddi has found himself a girl. I'm looking forward to seeing him. Who's her family?

ASTA: People don't pay attention to things like that nowadays. I think they're from the West fjords.

HALLA: Does she go to school?

ASTA: She says she's going to be a nurse. And that's probably for the best since the poor guy takes after his father.

HALLA: You have to go to college for that now, don't you?

ASTA: To take after one's father?

HALLA: (*She suddenly realizes Asta's state of mind.*) Dear, dear Asta . . . (*Backs away immediately.*) You remember Gunna Henriks? She's got vaginal cancer.

ASTA: (*Turns away.*)

HALLA: They gave her chemotherapy. It didn't help. Then they cut her open, but sewed her up right away. Her poor husband and children.

ASTA: (*Turns smiling toward Halla.*) Do they have cancer too?

HALLA: Some people are known to recover. (*A sound from the hall. Sigurd enters.*)

HALLA: Hi, Siggi dear. What's up?

SIGURD: (*Obviously coming from the sea.*) What's up?

HALLA: Yeah, you must have something nice to say? Say something cheerful.

SIGURD: Something cheerful? Do you think you're speaking to Johnny Carson?

HALLA: How was the fishing?

SIGURD: Is this a quiz?

HALLA: Now come on, you must have some news.

SIGURD: Call NBC, they're the news people.

ASTA: Do you want coffee?

SIGURD: (*Searches in drawers.*) Where's the evening paper?

ASTA: It's not here yet.

SIGURD: What about the morning paper?

ASTA: That didn't come either.

HALLA: Come and join us.

SIGURD: Join you?

HALLA: You don't get to see your dear sister-in-law every day, do you?

SIGURD: No, luckily you haven't started hunting me down out on the deep blue sea.

HALLA: You guys would love having some sweet things with you at sea.

SIGURD: How would you know?

HALLA: Oh, I know my family.

SIGURD: Is the boy home?

ASTA: No, he's working at the construction site.

HALLA: Poor boy, in this awful cold.

SIGURD: He won't get any sympathy from me. No problem with the heat there.

ASTA: Are you saying I forced him to quit?

SIGURD: You know the answer to that. I guess that female inspired him.

HALLA: Is there any harm done. He's just trying to figure out what he wants to be, what he wants to do.

SIGURD: Taking a bath is for sure what he'd prefer to do.

HALLA: Taking a bath?

SIGURD: Yeah, their main interest is playing in the bathtub together, isn't it?

ASTA: What's wrong with the poor kids taking a bath together?

HALLA: Why are they taking a bath together?

SIGURD: (*Points at Asta.*) Ask her. I never join them in the bath. Ask her what they do.

ASTA: Wash—what else?

HALLA: Together?

ASTA: Saves water. Have a cup of cofee, Siggi dear.

SIGURD: I don't want to disturb your conference. (*Goes into the living room.*)

HALLA: Siggi doesn't look healthy. It's terrible to see him like this.

ASTA: I don't see anything different about him.

HALLA: Where's he going?

ASTA: To watch soccer. He wouldn't miss it even on Doomsday . . . (*A car honks.*)

HALLA: Jesus, is it that late? It must be Gudmund. (*The car honks again.*)

ASTA: Won't he come in? (*The car honks again.*)

HALLA: (*While putting her coat on.*) He's got ants in his pants. Men can be so boring. Well, see you tonight. (*They kiss.*) Thanks for fixing my hair, dear. (*Car honks.*) Yeah, yeah, chauvinist pig. I'm coming. (*Says goodbye and runs.*) Okay, dear, bye-bye! Bye Siggi boy! (*Siggi doesn't answer.*)

SIGURD: (*Enters the kitchen.*) Coffee?

ASTA: You had the offer a moment ago.

SIGURD: I can't stand that woman.

ASTA: And you never try to hide it.

SIGURD: Any reason I should?

ASTA: Because she is my sister, you know.

SIGURD: That doesn't make her any more tolerable.

ASTA: But you're going to have to behave tonight because they're coming over.

SIGURD: I just asked if there's any coffee.

ASTA: The thermos is on the table right under your nose. You might try to unscrew the lid.

Scene 2

(Asta and Haddi. He is returning from work. Rips off his dirty clothes and throws them on the floor. Asta picks them up.)

ASTA: Were you cold, darling?

HADDI: Not at all. We sat in the shed all day long.

ASTA: Not working?

HADDI: We filled up the ditch we dug yesterday. It wasn't where it was supposed to be. We waited four hours to get new measurements.

ASTA: That's a strange way to do things.

HADDI: That's okay. Adequately loony.

ASTA: Did you eat the sandwiches I made?

HADDI: *What?* Yeah, yeah, I think so. Is Gogo here?

ASTA: Yes, she is taking a bath. Are you going out tonight?

HADDI: Yes, why do you ask?

ASTA: You might stay home.

HADDI: In the bosom of the family.

ASTA: You have not been home a single night all week. You could give it a try.

HADDI: And do what? *(Gets himself a glass of milk.)*

ASTA: You could watch TV.

HADDI: With the old man at home to keep things cheerful.

ASTA: Gudmund and Auntie Halla are coming for a visit. They'll be going back east tomorrow. Halla is dying to see you.

HADDI: That's a damned lie!

ASTA: Relax. *(Tries to give him a hug, but he turns her down.)* They have come all the way from the East fjords.

HADDI: That's a long and winding road. Did they come all this way just to see me?

ASTA: No, not just to see you. Gudmund had to see a doctor.

HADDI: I thought work horses like him never got sick. They usually just drop dead one day to everyone's genuine relief.

ASTA: Why do you always talk like that?

HADDI: Like what?

ASTA: You don't have to imitate your father.

HADDI: *(Silence.)* Is Bodvar in some kind of trouble?

ASTA: Not that I know.

HADDI: Why couldn't I see his letter?

ASTA: What letter?

HADDI: The one you wouldn't let me see.

ASTA: There's no such letter.

HADDI: I saw it.

ASTA: Is that so?

HADDI: And I read it.

ASTA: Then why do you ask?

HADDI: Is he on his way home?

ASTA: Dunno.

HADDI: Why are he and Gugga splitting up?

ASTA: You read the letter. I don't know any more than you.

HADDI: You're lying!

ASTA: Don't call me a liar, you. . . !

HADDI: You're maybe plain stupid.

ASTA: That's more like it. I know nothing.

HADDI: (*Searches in the refrigerator.*) Any peanut butter?

ASTA: I've quit buying it. It's fattening.

HADDI: Y entonces?

ASTA: I don't understand foreign languages.

HADDI: You never understand anything.

ASTA: Please stay home tonight. Halla wants so much to see you. I told her that you're growing fuzz in some new places. Please let me show you off to her. Please, just this once.

HADDI: It'll take a bribe to keep me home.

ASTA: (*Laughs.*) You are mine. You're flesh of my flesh, blood of my blood.

HADDI: Disgusting all this crap about flesh and blood. You're like cannibals!

ASTA: You are my flesh.

HADDI: The hell I am! Leave me alone!

ASTA: I'm no pariah while I've got you. (*She laughs and tries to embrace him.*)

HADDI: Let go! You don't own a thing. You are nothing but a piece of shit! (*Runs naked with a towel in front of him into the bathroom.*)

Scene 3

(*Asta and Sigurd.*)

SIGURD: (*His head in the refrigerator.*) Isn't there anything to eat?

ASTA: To eat?

SIGURD: Yeah, that's what I said—eat.

ASTA: See for yourself. Use your eyes. You must know what you've bought.

SIGURD: (*Turns around.*) What I've bought. Did I go shopping?

ASTA: Yes, didn't you? Didn't you go shopping?

SIGURD: Very funny. (*Turns to the refrigerator again.*)

ASTA: I can't believe that someone who is constantly hungry would forget to buy food. Wouldn't that be something? (*Sigurd doesn't answer but takes a package of sausages from the refrigerator.*)

SIGURD: What's this?

ASTA: Hot dogs.

SIGURD: Yes, that's what I thought. Why did you say there was nothing to eat?

ASTA: Those hot dogs are not mine.

SIGURD: Whose are they? The president's?

ASTA: Who here eats nothing but hot dogs?

SIGURD: Why doesn't he eat anything but hot dogs? (*Haddi appears in the doorway with a towel around his middle.*)

ASTA: Ask him.

SIGURD: Why don't you eat anything but hot dogs? (*Haddi doesn't answer, but goes straight to the refrigerator.*)

ASTA: Are you hungry, Haddi dear?

HADDI: What!

ASTA: Do you need a hearing aid? (*Haddi sees the hot dogs in his father's hand, pretends he hasn't noticed, takes a bottle of coke from the refrigerator.*)

HADDI: Where are my hot dogs?

ASTA: Your father has them.

HADDI: (*Pretends to be surprised.*) What's he doing with them?

ASTA: Ask him.

HADDI: Why can't my hot dogs be left in peace?

SIGURD: Why can't you eat anything but hot dogs?

HADDI: Why worry about that?

SIGURD: Answer me, why can't you eat anything but hot dogs?

HADDI: Why can't one steal a decent bottle of whiskey from you? Why is it that you can't drink anything but your bloody stinking home brew?

ASTA: You two are arguing like Satan and his ex-wife.

SIGURD: Okay, tell me why can't you eat anything but damned hot dogs. Is that the only food you ever devoured in your whole life?

HADDI: Don't fuck with other people's hot dogs. Give me my hot dogs!

SIGURD: You won't get any hot dogs unless you give me a good explanation. Why don't you ever eat what's on the table?

HADDI: Stick it up yours with mustard and ketchup and chopped onions.

SIGURD: (*Lifts his fist.*) Want a knuckle sandwich?

HADDI: (*Takes the wet towel off.*) You just try! (*Makes a weapon out*

of the towel.)
ASTA: Get out of my sight—both of you!

Scene 4

(*Asta and Gogo in the kitchen. Gogo is wrapped in a towel.*)

ASTA: You should try and influence him.
GOGO: (*Combs her wet hair.*) He's just so selfish. There's no point in me talking to him.
ASTA: Do you know his plans? Is he going to school this fall?
GOGO: I dunno. He's so tight-lipped. He never tells me anything.
ASTA: It scares me how money just runs through his hands like water. He'll be just as broke when he starts school again. Couldn't you try to get him to stay home a bit more? You're never here.
GOGO: He doesn't listen to me. Not really.
ASTA: There's no family life when nobody's ever home. I don't know what one's doing here. How is it at your place?
GOGO: I don't know.
ASTA: Are your sisters and brothers never home?.
GOGO: No.
ASTA: When I was growing up people stayed at home at nights, even though there was no TV.
GOGO: Doing what?
ASTA: All kinds of things—reading, talking, playing cards . . .
GOGO: Playing cards?
ASTA: Whist and bridge.
GOGO: Really . . .
ASTA: We played games . . .
GOGO: It's different now.
ASTA: I don't understand people going to the movies five nights a week . . . It's beyond my comprehension.
GOGO: What else is there to do? There's nowhere else to go. Do you have any clear nail polish? My nails keep cracking.
ASTA: (*Explodes.*) No, I don't have any damned clear nail polish. Do you think I'm Cleopatra or something?
GOGO: (*Hurt.*) Sorry. (*Rises. Exits.*)

Scene 5

(*Sigurd in front of Haddi's room. The stereo is at its loudest.*)

SIGURD: Turn the sound down, will you? Do you hear, *down*!

HADDI: Doesn't it turn you on?

SIGURD: If you don't turn it down I'll have the police remove all that blood junk from my house!

HADDI: (*Descriptively.*) Tomorrow's headline. He had often threatened to use violence. Son of the accused tells true story of his hardships. Then there's a great picture of me and a terrible one of you.

SIGURD: You must be deaf.

HADDI: And so what! Aren't the deaf entitled to listening to music just as others?

SIGURD: People like you need to have their ears cleaned.

HADDI: You're talking to me in the third person plural. Are you already seeing double?

SIGURD: Yes, I had thought that The Association for the Deaf and Dumb was here.

HADDI: Yeah, listen, we still haven't got a chairman, are you going to run for office? One thing's for sure, you won't get my vote.

SIGURD: If only you could play something that sounded like the human voice.

HADDI: Like Placido Domingo?

SIGURD: Why does that person bark like that? Has she got rabies?

HADDI: Just relax, dad. We're not on your wave length. Why don't you go downtown and listen to the Salvation Army.

SIGURD: Someone should take that woman to the vet.

HADDI: We, the members of The Association for The Deaf and Dumb, would like to be left in peace.

SIGURD: If you don't turn down that blasted machine I'll have the police come and confiscate it.

HADDI: (*Descriptively.*) Scoop! He didn't love his kids. The Daily Paper uncovers a cruel dad. Yeah, yeah, I'll turn it down now. (*Sigurd takes a seat in the living room, watches TV for a while, starts snoring.*)

Scene 6

(*Jona and Asta.*)

ASTA: *Jona*, you old hag, you startled me!

JONA: Oh, sorry dear, the door was open. I realized I was out of potatoes. Isn't Siggi home?

ASTA: He's in the living room.

JONA: In the dark?

ASTA: He's got a bad headache. (*Puts some potatoes in a bag.*)

JONA: Just enough for dinner, Asta dear. Not too many. How's Haddi feeling about his job?

ASTA: I suppose one always gets the same kind of pleasure digging ditches in the stiff, frozen ground.

JONA: Any news from Bodvar?

ASTA: Why do you ask?

JONA: Well, I just saw that there was a letter from Denmark in the mail yesterday. (*Asta shows Jona into the kitchen away from Sigurd.*) Is everything okay?

ASTA: As far as I know.

JONA: No, someone told me—who was it now—yeah, according to Magnus, Ibbie and Bjarne's son, he's studying in Copenhagen too. Bodvar's now working at the Carlsberg Brewery.

ASTA: I guess he's working to stretch the student loan.

JONA: He also said, I was told, that Bodvar and Gugga don't live together anymore.

ASTA: Then you and Magnus know more than I do.

JONA: And that they're getting a divorce.

ASTA: You're really bringing news.

JONA: (*Rises from the chair.*) Oh dear, I must be going out of my mind. Everything must be boiling over downstairs.

ASTA: Probably your potatoes, too.

JONA: (*Laughs aloud.*) Oh, Asta, you know me!

ASTA: Yes, you're nobody's fool.

Scene 7

(*Haddi and Gogo. Haddi's room.*)

GOGO: You don't have any money?

HADDI: (*Sulky.*) Me? Do you think I've got a money tree in the backyard. Why is it that you're always broke?

GOGO: Dad has become so stingy. I don't know why. Mom too.

HADDI: You've got a job but you never have a dime. Are you building a house or something?

GOGO: Do you know how much I make? You know what they pay for working in a kiosk?

HADDI: I know you take your pay in cigarettes and candy. It's not normal how little you get on payday.

GOGO: It's none of your business.

HADDI: Okay, okay, I've got plenty of damned money.

GOGO: (*Relieved.*) Were you lying when you told me you didn't have any money?

HADDI: Do you love me?

GOGO: Not madly.

HADDI: You're nuts about me! Don't you think I've noticed your rolling eyes? (*She nudges his hair which is in a new wave-like style.*) Don't touch my duck's ass! I'm shaping it. (*Combs his hair.*)

GOGO: Where should we go?

HADDI: Do you mind if we stay home tonight?

GOGO: Here!? In this loony bin!

HADDI: Mom says you steal all our shampoo, conditioner, rinse, body lotion, just everything.

GOGO: The bitch!

HADDI: She says you leave a messy trail behind you like a drunken sailor. (*She tears the newspaper to pieces.*)

GOGO: The damned bitch!

HADDI: You don't have to ruin the magazine. She says that just to say something. What else could she say?

GOGO: I don't fucking care. I'm never going to speak to that bitch again. I hate her!

HADDI: Not when she gives us money.

GOGO: She never gives me any goddamned money. I'm out of here. (*Haddi grabs her, throws her down on her back, holds her down.*) Let go! Let go of me! Leave me alone! Get off me, you bastard! (*He lies on top of her.*)

HADDI: I'll buy you a dress.

GOGO: I'm not speaking to you. (*Pause.*) I need a pair of white slacks, not a dress.

HADDI: And a pair of shoes.

GOGO: You haven't got any money. When are you going to do it?

HADDI: After the weekend, when I get paid.

GOGO: Promise?

HADDI: If you say: I love you, admire you, and worship you.

GOGO: You're a fool.(*She tries to mess his hair.*)

HADDI: Stop messing my hair or I'll beat you up. Say: I love you . . .

GOGO: (*Repeats after him.*) I love you.

HADDI: Admire you.

GOGO: Admire you and worship you.

HADDI: And we're going to stay at the loony bin tonight.

GOGO: And we're going to stay at the loony bin tonight.

HADDI: And then we'll go to bed and fuck.

GOGO: And then we'll go to bed . . . asshole!

HADDI: *That's* it, then we'll go to bed and fuck like assholes!

Scene 8

(*Sigurd, Asta, Haddi. Noise from the stereo.*)

SIGURD: (*Rubs his eyes.*) This is like living in a trench.

ASTA: I live in no-man's-land. Why can't the poor kids play music?

SIGURD: Never before were man-size loudspeakers necessary in ordinary homes. You can hardly get into the room because of those monster boxes.

ASTA: Why should you want to go into that room? Just to yell at him?

SIGURD: And if you do make it inside, the smoke is so thick you can't see a thing.

ASTA: Do you think it's better chain-smoking on the roof? Like we used to?

SIGURD: I don't want him to smoke in my house.

ASTA: This is his home too. They do as they please. But if you always want to fight . . .

SIGURD: Where's the newspaper I bought?

ASTA: Didn't you take it with you to the bathroom?

SIGURD: I didn't go to the bathroom, woman! When do I have the chance to go to the washroom with those dignitaries here. Don't they have a bath at the girl's home.

ASTA: She comes here straight from work. Is there any reason she shouldn't use the bath?

SIGURD: I shall never be able to understand what the devil people can be doing in the same bathwater for three hours. Unless they're dead.

ASTA: Do you want gravy on your meatballs?

SIGURD: Don't people usually eat meatballs with gravy?

ASTA: Depends.

SIGURD: Depends on what? For god's sake. (*A hiccough.*) Have you checked the mailbox?

ASTA: This morning, yes.

SIGURD: I didn't ask you if you checked it this morning, I asked if you checked it today?

ASTA: Yes. I checked it today. The paper wasn't there. Why are you so restless?

SIGURD: Whether I'm restless or not has nothing to do with this.

SIGURD: If it affects everyone around you. Potatoes or rice?

SIGURD: Rice, is that food?

ASTA: Well, I haven't got any anyway.

SIGURD: What kind of nonsense is this. You offer rice and then you say you don't have any.

ASTA: Your niece Maggie is planning a trip to Italy this year.

SIGURD: Don't you think the boy's got the paper?

ASTA: The travel agency's been a second home to her for two months. Doesn't talk about anything but Italian food.

SIGURD: I hope the spaghetti winds into knots in her intestines. (*Asta giggles. The telephone rings.*) Probably for his highness! (*Grabs the receiver from Asta.*) Yes, he is home. No, I'm not sure he can make it to the phone.

ASTA: Now be polite to the kids.

SIGURD: (*On the phone.*) I'll try to pull him out of the loudspeakers. (*Puts the receiver down, walks to Haddi's door and whispers.*) Telephone, telephone.

HADDI: I've got it.

SIGURD: Now he's a part of the family. He hears when it suits him, when he's called to the phone. I'm going to have the telephone disconnected, my boy.

HADDI: Quiet, dad.

SIGURD: That's what I said, I'll have the telephone disconnected.

HADDI: Dad!

SIGURD: There's a three-hour conference call each time you wanna go to the movies and that is not a rare event. You know how much I pay per minute? Do you?

HADDI: (*In the receiver.*) Sorry, I have to answer an unscheduled question. (*To Sigurd.*) Did you ask me how much each unit is?

SIGURD: Yeah.

HADDI: Local or long distance?

SIGURD: Don't you need a switchboard operator?

HADDI: Not while I have you. But thanks for the offer. (*On the phone.*) Yes, dad was just asking how much it costs to use the phone. Yes, he's in a great mood. He's attached a meter to me. No, no, not the movies tonight. Gogo and me are going to spend the evening on the road. Yeah, dad was just offering me the car. Yeah, yeah, of course my dear Haddi, he said, it's no problem, go for a long ride. Yeah, smiling from one ear to the other. Yeah, your best regards to my dad. I'll tell him. (*Puts the receiver down.*) Mummi said to give you his best regards and ask if you want to be his dad too and lend him your car tomorrow.

SIGURD: Wouldn't you like to have a butler? And what have you done with my newspaper?

HADDI: I wiped my ass with it. (*Sigurd pushes Haddi.*) What's going on? Are you hallucinating? What have you been smoking?

SIGURD: It's in bits and pieces?

HADDI: Hey, the news is starting on TV! First it comes in sign language, then it's read to you. Next, you get it in a secret language and then in picture language; then there's a summary before they give you an overview. Finally, a tiny little newsman walks out of the set and gives you your own personal newsgram.

ASTA: Dinner is on the table.

HADDI: I don't want any.

SIGURD: You can just eat like other people.

HADDI: Is "not eating" forbidden?

SIGURD: You are to eat at mealtimes. Not all these snacks in the evening and during the nights. You are to eat at mealtimes.

HADDI: Mealtime is when you eat.

SIGURD: Mealtime is when there's food on the table.

HADDI: Okay. You win. You're the boss. Heavy moccasin wins. Mealtime is when there's food on the table, not when you eat.

ASTA: Don't you want anything at all, Haddi?

HADDI: I'm not hungry.

ASTA: Ask your girlfriend if she wants something.

HADDI: She isn't hungry.

ASTA: How do you know?

HADDI: I just know she isn't hungry.

ASTA: Tell her to come and have a bite. I've made some delicious meatballs in gravy.

SIGURD: No, no, just eat each other's ear lobes.

ASTA: Come on, leave the poor things alone.

HADDI: I want to be left alone.

SIGURD: Yeah, go into your room and blast the speakers so your hair stands on end.

HADDI: Laughter extends life.

ASTA: I made curry sauce for the meatballs.

SIGURD: Curry sauce?

ASTA: You love variety, don't you? Why are you looking at me like that? Do you think I'm trying to poison you?

Scene 9

(Gudmund, Haddi, Halla, Asta, Sigurd, and Gogo watching TV in the living room.)

HALLA: What a good picture you have. Your reception is so much better than at home.

ASTA: Really, the picture's not clear?

HALLA: It's because of the mountains. And then, the colors aren't the same as here.

SIGURD: (*To Gudmund.*) How's the road?

GUDMUND: (*Absentmindedly.*) Some places good, some places bad.

ASTA: We've just got us a new set.

HALLA: It's just as if the colors are a lot duller in the east.

GUDMUND: They've traveled a long way. (*Looks up.*) The colors, I mean.

SIGURD: You didn't get caught in a sandstorm, did you?

GUDMUND: What? No, no.

ASTA: Old Lilla didn't have the strength to come along?

HALLA: She can't handle traveling anymore.

ASTA: What about flying?

HALLA: She's afraid of flying. She's never flown, poor thing.

ASTA: It's about time she starts practicing if she's going to become an angel.

SIGURD: Do you use radial tires?

GUDMUND: Yeah, I'm on radials.

SIGURD: They're hard as hell. You can't use them on dirt roads. I wouldn't want them.

GUDMUND: Is he married to the dark one? (*Points at the TV.*)

GOGO: No, he's married to the other one, the blond.

HADDI: She is definitely wearing a wig.

GUDMUND: Then why is he kissing the black one?

HALLA: He's just stepping out.

HADDI: Such bad taste.

GOGO: I think she's cute.

HADDI: It's like kissing a whole chemical factory.

HALLA: She looks quite loose to me.

SIGURD: Well, isn't that what she's supposed to be?

HALLA: Somehow the other one seems to be a much better sort of person, to me at least.

GOGO: I can't see anything special at all about the guy.

HADDI: He's got a tough car, that's what counts.

GUDMUND: Cars like that wouldn't last long on our back roads.

HADDI: It's good for racing around. The cops would never catch you in a car like that, Gudmund. And in case they corner you there are wings in the side panels and a laser gun in the dashboard.

GUDMUND: A laser gun. What am I supposed to do with a laser gun?

ASTA: I'll go and make some coffee.

HALLA: Oh honey, don't make a fuss over us.

ASTA: No trouble at all. (*Rises, goes to the kitchen.*)

SIGURD: How's the weather been out east?

GUDMUND: Not too bad.

SIGURD: And the fishing?

GUDMUND: The trawlers have been landing respectable catches.

HALLA: (*Watching TV.*) Now she got what she deserved.

HADDI: This is pure dribble.

HALLA: That's life, dear hearts. Men can't cope with more than one woman at a time. It always ends in disaster.

HADDI: Now he's apologizing. This is ridiculous. He should have given her one on the jaw. Then she'd have said ''how high'' if he'd told her to jump.

HALLA: Probably.

HADDI: Women want to get beaten up.

GOGO: Is that so!

HADDI: The ones I know.

HALLA: Some do, not all.

HADDI: All of them.

GOGO: An educational program. I don't want to watch this.

SIGURD: I don't know where the hell they dig up all those educational programs about insects. You'd think this station was run by spiders.

HALLA: They're talking about reducing broadcasting hours.

SIGURD: They should cut out all this bullshit and let people watch what they want to watch. Show the news in Icelandic and switch over to Sky.

HALLA: You don't really mean that, Sigurd dear.

SIGURD: Of course I mean it. (*Rises to his feet. Takes out a bottle.*) Wouldn't you like a drink, Gudmund?

GUDMUND: What d'you have?

SIGURD: I hope you haven't become too good for basement based industrial products.

GUDMUND: Then I would be someone else.

SIGURD: (*Pours into glasses.*) It goes down, no problem.

HALLA: (*Rises to her feet as she is not offered a drink.*) I'll go and help Asta, Gudmund dear. You're driving later, remember.

SIGURD: Yes, go on out and be of some use.

GUDMUND: (*Tastes.*) How strong is it?

SIGURD: Oh, about 150 proof. Cheers!

GUDMUND: Cheers!

SIGURD: (*After a short pause.*) Is it true what I hear, that you're going to buy a Mazda?

GUDMUND: They're said to be good.

SIGURD: The price of Japanese cars has gone sky high.

GUDMUND: They keep their resale value.

SIGURD: They still cost more than they're worth.

GUDMUND: I'm not so sure about that.

SIGURD: There are no cars like American cars.

GUDMUND: Yet they're taking over the American market.

SIGURD: They're made of much thinner material than American cars.

GUDMUND: Who says?

SIGURD: It's a fact.

GUDMUND: That's rubbish.

SIGURD: You'll know when it starts falling apart under your ass.

GUDMUND: (*Hurt.*) There's quite a difference in gas mileage between a Japanese car and an American car.

SIGURD: Time will tell what'll end up costing you the most in the long run. (*Fills the glasses.*) I've heard the paint on Japanese cars peels off.

GUDMUND: Why does everybody buy them then?

SIGURD: Advertising confuses people.

GUDMUND: I haven't noticed them advertising more than anybody else.

SIGURD: I wouldn't even look at a Japanese car.

GUDMUND: (*Agitated.*) This is one of the best-selling cars in the world.

SIGURD: People will buy anything as long as its been advertised long enough. It's just a trend.

GUDMUND: (*Angry.*) Well, have it your way.

SIGURD: I'm not having anything my way. Those are the plain facts. You don't have to get upset over it. I just know that many guys will come to painfully regret having put their faith in Japanese cars.

Scene 10

(*Halla and Asta.*)

HALLA: I really do think Gudmund is seriously ill. He's become so depressed. One can't get a word out of him. I called the doctor this morning, but of course he didn't want to admit anything. Asta, it's about time you visit us out east. That could be fun. We've got plenty of room.

ASTA: (*First time face to face with Halla.*) Don't you get bored staying alone in that big house all day long?

HALLA: Gudmund comes both for lunch and for afternoon coffee. Then I have to keep everything clean. There's so much dust everywhere, always.

ASTA: Dust? What dust? The streets in your village are all paved now.

HALLA: (*Excited.*) That doesn't seem to have made any difference. Asta, do you think you'll come east this summer?

ASTA: Why aren't we swimming in the sea someplace where it's warm?

HALLA: In the sea?

ASTA: Go to a beach. The breeze is warm. And us completely naked.

HALLA: Without men?

ASTA: There's no point in having them around then. We can swim far out because the ocean is smooth as a mirror.

HALLA: I can't swim.

ASTA: (*Strangely aggressive.*) You just let yourself float. (*Seizes Halla by the arm.*) Halla! Let's go. Let's do it!

HALLA: (*Frees herself.*) We'll think about this when you come to visit.

ASTA: You mean we're not going to swim in the warm sea?

HALLA: Gudmund would be happy if Siggi turned up. They could talk about everything under the sun.

ASTA: I can't swim either.

HALLA: We would send the men out to do the shopping. Then we could sit comfortably by the window and watch the plane come in from the south. I've got binoculars so we can watch who's coming. Sometimes the plane circles and can't land. It's always kind of exciting; it could crash right in front of our eyes, Asta!

Scene 11

(*Bodvar enters the house. He's obviously returning from a trip. Noise from Haddi's stereo.*)

BODVAR: (*Imitates his father.*) Haddi, turn down that damned noise, boy!

HADDI: Yeah, yeah, I'll turn it down!

BODVAR: And do it right now, damn it, I said!

HADDI: What's the matter?! (*Surprised and pleased.*) Oh, it's you? Did you just arrive?

BODVAR: Do you have guests?

HADDI: Halla and Gudmund.

BODVAR: Aren't they leaving soon?

HADDI: Dunno. Aren't you going to say hi.

BODVAR: That can wait. (*He sees Gogo.*) So you've got a chick with you? I'm just making a pit stop. (*Studies Haddi.*) I can see you're old enough to get into the saddle. The last time I saw you you were sucking on a pacifier.

HADDI: That's plain crap!

BODVAR: That's right, you were sucking on a pacifier.

HADDI: Are you crazy or something. Do you really think I was sucking on a pacifier four years ago?

BODVAR: Well, some people keep sucking on their pacifiers for a long time.

HADDI: Is Gugga with you?

BODVAR: (*To Gogo.*) He doesn't suck on a pacifier,does he?

HADDI: Are you staying for a while?

BODVAR: It's not quite clear yet.

HADDI: Something wrong?

BODVAR: With whom?

HADDI: No, I just thought . . .

BODVAR: (*Grabs Gogo's hair.*) This is a fine pacifier.

HADDI: Let go of her!

BODVAR: (*Starts filling his pipe.*) And the old man is gonna sell the boat. What's he going to do, deliver newspapers?

HADDI: I dunno.

BODVAR: Work at the aluminum smelter?

HADDI: Ask him.

BODVAR: I don't care.

HADDI: Then why are you asking?

BODVAR: Maybe he's going to run this house. Take care of his highly cherished fruits of love.

HADDI: Who knows.

BODVAR: You said it. (*Inhales the smoke from his pipe. Gives it to Haddi.*) I wonder if you can get a bad conscience by killing cod.

HADDI: I don't think so.

BODVAR: You think maybe he doesn't know what a bad conscience is?

HADDI: Ask him.

BODVAR: You're not unlike someone I know.

HADDI: Why should I be?

BODVAR: Sometimes I really do think that cod are superior to us. At least they talk about things that matter.

HADDI: What matters?

BODVAR: The temperature, food, breeding. Doesn't this girl ever say anything?

HADDI: It's up to her if and when she talks.

BODVAR: Are you just going to keep on stroking her expanding belly?

HADDI: Do you have to be like this?

BODVAR: Say something, you little filly.

HADDI: Shut up!

BODVAR: (*Giggles.*) You don't know what kind of predator you've let into

your fish tank, litle brother. But I know what those teeth can do, they
can gnaw every bit of meat off your bones.

HADDI: You're crazy.

BODVAR: Why've you got that expression on your face, a kid your age?

HADDI: What damned expression?

BODVAR: Our Father in Heaven, Holy be thy Name, thine shalt be
the Power, both on Land and Sea, forever, Amen. (*They both giggle.*)

HADDI: Oh, yeah, that expression! "Eat your horsemeat, leave the table
and turn down that damned noise."

BODVAR: Horsemeat!

HADDI: Turn it down!

(*They repeat the last words again and again and laugh uncontrollably. Gogo
has turned her back to them and covered herself with the blanket.*)

Scene 12

(*In the living room.*)

HALLA: Yes, I said cod liver oil. You don't have to shake your head, Siggi
dear, because it's been tested scientifically. But you have to take a good
sip from the bottle, then the cod liver oil goes straight into your
bloodstream and prevents arthritis.

SIGURD: I have a greater belief in black coffee, preferably on an empty
stomach.

ASTA: Yes, if you want to kill yourself.

SIGURD: I'm not dead yet.

ASTA: Just you wait.

SIGURD: Sorry to disappoint you, but I'm not on my way to the cemetery.

HALLA: It's been proven scientifically, so you might just as well believe it,
Sigurd.

SIGURD: Is that so? Well, you just don't know what's going on. Why is
everyone talking about fat being unhealthy for you? Because it is
unhealthy. And what is cod liver oil—fat!

HALLA: That's quite different, Siggi dear.

SIGURD: Just try and drink four cups of cod liver oil. See if it's good for
you. I drink six cups of coffee after dinner and I feel like a king. Try and
drink six cups of cod liver oil in a row.

ASTA: (*Tries to change the subject.*) How are your flowers, Halla?

SIGURD: I guess you feed them with cod liver oil too.

ASTA: Stop it, Siggi!

HALLA: What's on TV now?

ASTA: It must be some film. You want another drink, dear?

SIGURD: Give her a double cod liver oil.

ASTA: Are you drunk or something?

HALLA: Can't you hold your liquor, boys?

SIGURD: Have some more, Gudmund. It'll be good for you on top of cod liver oil, especially if you're going to rattle all the way to the east in a Mazda.

GUDMUND: Just a weak one, Siggi boy, I'm driving.

Scene 13

(Bodvar, Haddi, and Gogo. Haddi's room.)

BODVAR: The family is the placenta you feed on after you leave your mother's womb. Dad, mom, grandpa, grandma, aunts, uncles, all the way back to the red asshole of time. Eat us, they plead. Eat us and absorb our images into your being. Improve them. And you, you little monster, think: okay, okay, and you go on eating thoughtlessly and you get bloated and fat and you start hating yourself and at the same time you see your carte blanche turn into a developing picture reflecting their cowardice, their narrowmindedness and failures. But you cannot do a thing. The ghosts of the past have settled in you. All the while your body and your mind cry for nourishment. You grab whatever comes your way and stuff yourself, you little cuckoo. You keep evolving the increasingly deformed picture of yourself and there's no way back. You can't say anything. You whine and regurgitate some words. People think you're saying something nice about everyday matters. Because the words you've been feeding on are not food for human consumption, they are stones, poor little things, stones, without any nutrients. You are dumb even if you keep talking, unable to bridge the gap with words. What's sadder than a speechless man who speaks fluently?

HADDI: Turn down this horsemeat.

BODVAR: But perhaps—some day—because you have had more than your fill—who knows—then a pressure forms in your belly and you shit it all out—the stones rush out of your anus together with blood and entrails.

HADDI: Oh! Oh!

BODVAR: And there you are, hollow and empty, but at least you may have the chance to start all over.

HADDI: Or I may be torn to pieces from head to foot and die. Or I'll be sewn together? I may not recognize myself in the mirror. Hi, Mr. Frankenstein. Hi. I think I'm about to vomit.

BODVAR: Are you losing control, my boy? Vomit, boy, throw it all up, everything I've told you. Throw up! *(Haddi vomits.)*

Scene 14

(Gudmund, Halla, Asta, Sigurd, Bodvar. The living room. The TV is on.)

GUDMUND: Well now, I hear you're selling the boat. How much will you get for it?

SIGURD: I'm going to sink it.

GUDMUND: What?!

SIGURD: Do you want to buy her? She's a nice little vessel.

GUDMUND: I have enough to do with my trucking business.

SIGURD: Yeah, yeah, you just go ahead and drive your classy trucks loaded with rotten codheads, a man who has never pissed in the salt water.

ASTA: It wouldn't do you any harm to mix the drinks.

GUDMUND: What are you going to do when you quit the sea?

SIGURD: I think I'll allow myself to read the papers in peace on the toilet at the old folks' home.

HALLA: What a long and boring film!

SIGURD: Yeah, it is long and boring, what about it?

HALLA: I don't know why they have to show you such misery.

SIGURD: Just you give them a few cups of cod liver oil. Then they'll be better off.

GUDMUND: Isn't your brother Henrik working at the military base?

SIGURD: Henrik is dead.

ASTA: Cut the crap, Sigurd.

SIGURD: Okay, Henrik isn't dead. He's just shrunk so much that you can fit him into one of the waste baskets he's supposed to empty.

HALLA: Well, I'm a bit sleepy. And we haven't really spoken much of anything.

ASTA: We'll talk next summer, Halla dear, if we come east.

HALLA: Yeah, let's have a good chat then. We'll send the old guys out somewhere and we'll just sit by ourselves the whole day and talk.

GUDMUND: People make good money building power plants, I'm told. Have you thought of getting a job at one of them?

SIGURD: Hell, I look like I'm thirty?

GUDMUND: I just mentioned it as a possibility.

HALLA: You're being so serious, boys.

ASTA: They're beginning to understand that life is serious business.

SIGURD: Who told you?

ASTA: I've got ears and eyes.

GUDMUND: Well, I think we'll have to be pushing off.

HALLA: It's been so very nice, dear. *(They are on their way out. Halla has nearly fallen over Bodvar, who is lying in the hall.)*

ASTA: (*Stoops down. Embraces Bodvar.*) Is that you, my little darling? Are you hungry?

BODVAR: No.

ASTA: Gudmund and Halla are here.

BODVAR: (*Still sitting on the floor.*) Hi there.

GUDMUND: How are you, Bodvar?

HALLA: It's been a long time since I last saw you. How was it out there?

ASTA: I'll get you something to eat.

BODVAR: I'm not hungry, mom.

ASTA: You must be hungry. I made some wonderful meatballs for dinner.

SIGURD: (*Stubbornly but controlled.*) Why are you home, if I may ask?

BODVAR: Doesn't he know how to say hello anymore?

ASTA: Now, don't you two start.

SIGURD: I greet those who I have reason to.

BODVAR: Is he intoxicated, the young man?

HALLA: (*Tries to sound relaxed.*) They take a drink now and then, the dear old boys.

SIGURD: I just don't understand why they keep giving these people all kinds of stipends.

ASTA: Student loans, Sigurd.

SIGURD: Most of the time they squander it all over the place.

BODVAR: Isn't he ever going to grow up?

SIGURD: (*Excitedly.*) And then they come up here, nothing but a craving mentality and demand that society keeps on providing for them. The state is expected to open up ten new offices each day where this kind of scum can settle in at the cost of the working part of the population.

BODVAR: Stop nagging.

SIGURD: And half of them never finish their studies, they can't even wipe their asses, not to mention cut fish after twenty years on the school bench.

BODVAR: And don't forget the architects.

SIGURD: No, for sure I'm not going to forget them. The roofs on the houses in this country didn't start to leak until those damned halfwits swarmed the place.

BODVAR: Isn't it time for your bunk watch, old bum?

SIGURD: No advice needed from you, I do as I please.

HALLA: (*To Bodvar.*) Are you staying for a while?

BODVAR: I just don't know.

HALLA: How's Gugga and the kid.

BODVAR: Fine, everything's okay with them.

HALLA: Didn't they come with you?

BODVAR: —We're divorced.

HALLA: Oh. (*Pause.*) Little Siggi could have come with you. It would have been nice to see him.

BODVAR: His mother wouldn't let him go.

HALLA: I can understand that, but his grandparents would have treated him to soemthing nice.

GUDMUND: But you're going abroad again, aren't you?

BODVAR: Who knows.

GUDMUND: You haven't quit your studies, have you?

BODVAR: They've decided to bomb the world back to the stone age. I guess we won't need any diplomas in hell. But you never know.

SIGURD: You're full of bullshit.

BODVAR: Shut up!

SIGURD: Are you telling me to shut up?

BODVAR: Yes, try to use your brains for once. You're not out at sea now with all your great admirers.

ASTA: Now Bodvar, that's enough! Stop it!

SIGURD: You damned miserable rat.

ASTA: Go to bed, Sigurd!

SIGURD: Damned, damned, damned!

ASTA: Yes, you will be if you say it often enough.

HALLA: Well dear, I think it's time for us to take off.

BODVAR: No, please stay, take part in this little play of ours all the way through. Don't miss the last and the most interesting scene.

GUDMUND: No, it's so late. (*They leave.*)

BODVAR: (*Begging, low voice.*) Dad . . . (*Sigurd walks to him. Their eyes meet. Sigurd gives Bodvar a heavy blow on the cheek. Black out.*)

Scene 15

(*Sigurd, Asta, Bodvar, Haddi, Gogo. The next day.*)

ASTA: (*To Haddi.*) Please go to the store for me.

HADDI: No, I don't feel like it.

GOGO: (*To Haddi.*) You go.

HADDI: I've already said I'm not going.

ASTA: Do you know what that's called? Laziness.

HADDI: Go out yourself and buy beer for that old monster.

ASTA: What kind of shitheads are you, all of you?

HADDI: Go to hell.

ASTA: I know I will in the end.

BODVAR: (*Lying on the floor under a blanket.*) Do you have to make so much damned noise?

ASTA: So sorry! Do you want anything from the store?

BODVAR: A cold coke.

ASTA: (*Puts on shoes and a parka.*) You're just like bedridden old people, smoking heavily and constantly pawing each other.

BODVAR: Do old people do that. What did you do when you were young?

ASTA: I had not started smoking at your age, God knows. (*Hesitates.*) Was I ever young? Not if that means having a sleeping partner while still a kid

. . .

BODVAR: Have you ever got anything out of making love? (*A long pause.*)

ASTA: Ah, I wish that Gugga and the boy were here. (*About to cry.*) Bodvar dear.

BODVAR: (*Angrily.*) Don't start that damned whimpering.

ASTA: (*Recovers.*) A big coke?

BODVAR: A big coke, yeah, and a chocolate bar.

ASTA: A chocolate bar?

BODVAR: (*Still sulky.*) Yeah, isn't that what I was brought up on, chocolate bars?

ASTA: Yes sir, you shall have your chocolate bar. Goodbye. (*No answer.*) Bye, do you hear? Bye!

BODVAR: (*Irritated.*) Yes, yes, bye, bye, bye!

HADDI: (*Calls.*) Mom! Bye!

(*Asta leaves. Sigurd enters in his long johns. He opens the refrigerator, searches, doesn't find what he's after, slams the refrigerator door, searches the kitchen cupboards, slams doors, leaves.*)

Scene 16

(*Haddi and Gogo. Haddi's room.*)

GOGO: Is he gonna stay here?

HADDI: Who?

GOGO: Your brother.

HADDI: How should I know that? (*Pause.*)

GOGO: Is there something wrong with him?

HADDI: Why do you think so?

GOGO: Why are they divorcing?

HADDI: (*Irritated.*) How should I know that?

GOGO: What's she like, his wife?

HADDI: Quite normal . . . just like most people.

GOGO: Sweet?

HADDI: I haven't tasted her.

GOGO: Are you ever going to divorce me?

HADDI: We are not married.

GOGO: We're going to marry.

HADDI: How should I know?

GOGO: Is she sweeter than me?

HADDI: She's different.

GOGO: How?

HADDI: Just different—older . . .

GOGO: Is she boring?

HADDI: (*More irritated.*) How the hell should I know?

GOGO: Am I boring?

HADDI: (*Sighing.*) Boring? Noooo. You're great fun.

GOGO: Is she elegant?

HADDI: Are you jealous?

GOGO: Because of her? Why should I be?

HADDI: She's got more brains than you.

GOGO: How do you know?

HADDI: Eh, it doesn't matter.

GOGO: Yes, it does matter.

HADDI: (*Rough.*) It damned well doesn't matter!

GOGO: Is he very intelligent?

HADDI: Is something wrong with you? Why this talk about brains all the time? Do you really feel that stupid?

GOGO: You think I am?

HADDI: So what? You're not the first stupid human being in the world.

GOGO: But you sleep with me.

HADDI: Screwing stupid women is the best.

GOGO: Oh, who says that?

HADDI: They get wetter than brainy females. Didn't you know?

GOGO: You are disgusting. (*Throws herself into his arms.*)

Scene 17

(*Sigurd, Asta, Bodvar, and Jona.*)

SIGURD: I didn't ask for anything.

ASTA: I'm offering you a beer.

SIGURD: I'm not used to being waited on.

ASTA: You're not. Do you want an aspirin?

SIGURD: I was not raised on aspirin. (*Asta goes to get some aspirin. Sigurd reaches for the beer and gulps.*)

ASTA: Here, take two of these. (*Pause.*) So you did want the beer?

SIGURD: You're maybe already regretting having waited on me? Why don't you pump it out of me? Go ahead.

ASTA: This is what you get from too much boozing. The filth you drink is not meant for human consumption. Some people have gone blind from drinking home brew.

SIGURD: They'd be just as blind if they'd had milk.

ASTA: Who's blind? I'm not blind.

SIGURD: I wouldn't know.

ASTA: If I am blind then you're definitely not a member of Friends of The Blind Club.

SIGURD: Why does he crouch on the floor like a dog? (*Points at Bodvar.*)

ASTA: He didn't want to go to bed.

SIGURD: He's just as damned stubborn as ever.

ASTA: Of course you can't eat anything today.

SIGURD: That's my business.

ASTA: Then I can just as well forget about roasting the rack of lamb.

SIGURD: Yeah, yeah, just throw it frozen on the table.

ASTA: You probably wouldn't know the difference.

SIGURD: Is there any more beer? (*Asta jumps up, but discovers that Jona is standing in the middle of the floor.*)

JONA: Oh, really, yes, I was right about your being back home, Bodvar!

ASTA: What would you like to borrow this time, dear Jona?

JONA: Oh, how nice it is seeing Bodvar again!

ASTA: Was it potatoes or sugar?

JONA: Sugar. Sugar, dear. One cup. Did you arrive yesterday evening, dear boy? I thought it was you. You still like chocolate layer cake, don't you? I have one downstairs that I baked last night.

BODVAR: Yum, yum! Who was that who said chocolate layer cake? (*He rises.*)

ASTA: He's divorced his wife, Jona dear, if that's what you want confirmed.

JONA: As a matter of fact, I heard it was your wife who divorced you.

BODVAR: That's a damned lie, Jona. She accused me of being a male chauvinist pig, who wasn't interested in doing the dishes, so I jumped her, beat her up. Bombed out of my mind, of course. But I'm not an evil person, Jona, deep inside I am a chocolate boy, you know.

JONA: And then she divorced you?

BODVAR: The choice was mine, Jona dear, either the dishes, wife, kids, and love or cold, death, and the devil. And what do you think was my choice?

JONA: You are always such a joker. The apple seldom falls far from the tree. And there are good reasons for keeping your sense of humor considering the way of this world.

BODVAR: Chocolate cakeless world of shit.

JONA: No, Bodvar dear, the world is beautiful. With me there's always plenty of chocolate cake.

ASTA: What a love affair!

BODVAR: Yes, it is a miserable life, Jona dear, can't even beat your wife up any more. Men are supposed to be soft and gentle, prepare dinner, do the laundry, and compensate in a few years for the oppression they have caused women for two thousand years.

JONA: Where's this going to end, dear Buddi?

BODVAR: And how's your nose, has it become flat like a pancake from pressing it against window panes, or has it perhaps taken the shape of a keyhole? (*Jona giggles and laughs.*)

JONA: There are endless complaints because people show no interest in their neighbors.

ASTA: Didn't you come for some sugar, Jona dear?

JONA: No, I don't need any sugar, honey. I just made that up.

ASTA: Now I'm really surprised, Jona dear!

JONA: I just couldn't wait to see my Buddi. And how big you've grown!

BODVAR: I've shrunk. Not my girth though. See my belly. It's the beer.

JONA: Have you been drinking a lot of beer?

BODVAR: Well, something had to replace coke and your chocolate cakes.

SIGURD: (*Enters in his long johns.*) No door sales, please!

JONA: Dear Sigurd, I was just saying . . .

SIGURD: Doesn't matter what charity you represent, I'm against door sales.

JONA: You're not in a good mood.

SIGURD: No, I never buy badges. Not even from the Red Cross. Out! Out!

JONA: Are you showing me the door?

SIGURD: It's no use pretending you're paralyzed down to your waist, you can't fool me.

JONA: Okay, Sigurd, if that's the way you want it.

BODVAR: Don't harrass the old girl like that.

SIGURD: I don't want any goddamn door sales in my house!

ASTA: Are you sure you don't need any sugar?

SIGURD: She's goddamned sweet enough as she is. And don't forget your pins.

JONA: You must be hallucinating, Sigurd dear, what pins?

SIGURD: You're cheating. She sells her badges without pins.

JONA: Well, thanks a lot for the coffee.

ASTA: I'll call you later for a cup of coffee Jona, don't feel hurt.

BODVAR: (*Shouts after Jona.*) I'm coming for a piece of chocolate cake later today, Jona!

Scene 18

(*Sigurd, Asta, Bodvar, Gogo, Haddi.*)

HADDI: Did you say that you had ice cream?

ASTA: Yes, I did. What flavor would you like?

HADDI: What flavors are there?

ASTA: Vanilla. That's the best.

HADDI: Too sweet. No orange?

SIGURD: You just eat what's on the table, young man.

HADDI: Ever heard that before?

SIGURD: Don't you want Russian dressing on your ice cream?

HADDI: Some people would like that.

BODVAR: Nothing's changed. Is that possible?

SIGURD: Have you ever seen anything change?

BODVAR: Perhaps there is something unchangeable somewhere.

SIGURD: Nothing ever changes.

BODVAR: It has been stated that the world's core is chaos, a continuous flow that goes forward but it has been said—now hold tight—that opinions of middle-aged people may change overnight.

SIGURD: Opinions? What goddamn opinions?

BODVAR: Don't you have any opinions? Aren't you a captain of your own boat who pisses on the concept of equality.

SIGURD: Equality? I have never seen any goddamned equality.

BODVAR: Then why bother cursing it.

HADDI: And he votes for the Commies. He doesn't make any sense.

SIGURD: I vote for no one and I have no opinions.

ASTA: You're at your best now, Sigurd.

SIGURD: Opinions are for idlers and idiots.

BODVAR: What about your opinion that a war is needed in order to make some money? Hire the damned boat out to the military and profit like hell. A good old fashioned war with landing barges and mountains of canned food.

HADDI: And lots of casualties to make space in the world.

ASTA: Don't listen to this kind of bullshit, you guys.

SIGURD: Fishing has never paid off, except during war and that's not an opinion, it's a fact.

HADDI: He also wants everyone over seventy exterminated. There's no reason for people to get older.

BODVAR: (*Laughing.*) And he pretends not to have any opinions.

ASTA: He likes being against everything.

HADDI: And we, fruits of love, are supposed to be for everything.

BODVAR: Otherwise he couldn't be against.

SIGURD: You two just try and behave like human beings.

HADDI: And stop talking for ten days like some do. (*Hints that it is Sigurd.*)

SIGURD: There's no shortage of bullshit discussions.

HADDI: Agreed.

SIGURD: What's agreed?

HADDI: Everything you say.

SIGURD: Everybody always blubbering all over the place. Never shut their mouths for a single moment. In parliament . . .

ALL THREE: . . . On the radio . . . On TV.

SIGURD: Ichthyologists really believe they know now what the cod is doing, what it thinks and what its needs are. They talk and talk until even the cod in the sea have had enough.

BODVAR: Is he trying to express himself on a special subject?

SIGURD: I know more about the cod than all those ichthyologist codheads.

HADDI: One hundred idiots can't beat one genius. (*To Bodvar.*) You haven't been following what's been going on here. He's against all con-servation.

SIGURD: Cod conserves itself.

BODVAR: See, there's a theory. How does the cod do that?

SIGURD: As soon as catching cod doesn't pay it will be left in peace.

BODVAR: And that will probably happen when the stock is dead and gone.

SIGURD: Fish stocks regulate themselves. Nobody needs to tell me that ichthyologists saved the herring. We simply quit catching herring because it did not pay. Then the stocks started to grow and multiply —it's as simple as that.

ASTA: I try to close my ears when you pretend to be dumber than you real-ly are.

SIGURD: That explains why you do not understand my points.

GOGO: Shouldn't we be going?

HADDI: We're going to the movies.

SIGURD: Make sure your hands don't grow together.

GOGO: Thanks for now.

ASTA: You're welcome, dear. Wear your warm jackets, kids.

SIGURD: No, you two just go about half naked, shirt open down to your navels and sleeves rolled up. Be sure to get a chill and catch a cold so medicine can be bought for you and you'll stay in bed for days, chain-smoking, and listening to the stereo blasting.

HADDI: Be careful you don't suffocate in your parka, old man.

SIGURD: I'm sure there would be a great deal of mourning.

HADDI: At least one would be able to borrow the car.

SIGURD: You wouldn't get a car, junior.

HADDI: Are you going to take it with you into the grave?

SIGURD: You can count on that.

HADDI: Imagine, the first funeral in history where the corpse is sitting under the steering wheel.

SIGURD: We finance buses for you. Make use of them?

HADDI: When was the last time you took a bus?

SIGURD: Buses are meant for old people, kids, and cripples. Not for strong, healthy working men.

BODVAR: He keeps improving.

HADDI: I know he's going to end up as an entertainer; for what is more beautiful in life than entertaining people. The top nagger, Sigurd Jonsson, is giving a show on Broadway tonight.

SIGURD: Go barefoot to keep in style. And don't forget your carton of cigarettes.

HADDI: Anyway, thanks for offering me the car. Who knows, you might even be chosen for ''The Father of the Century.''

SIGURD: Being your father is more than enough.

HADDI: I didn't ask for it, that's for sure. (*Gogo and Haddi leave.*)

BODVAR: Haddi has grown into quite a guy.

ASTA: He's a nice kid. A bit confused like all teenagers.

BODVAR: Is that girl any good?

ASTA: She's okay.

BODVAR: Is she really?

SIGURD: She's none of your damned business!

BODVAR: Was that the window shutting.

SIGURD: Mind your own business.

ASTA: Do you have any plans, Buddi?

BODVAR: Just to be.

ASTA: Just to be?

BODVAR: That's the situation: just to be, just to be.

ASTA: You'll have to find yourself some work.

BODVAR: To work or not to work, that is the question.

ASTA: Can you survive without work?

BODVAR: Living just to work is absurd.

ASTA: What do you want then?

BODVAR: What I want? Are you serious? (*Asta nods.*) I want to watch the sky, eat wild flowers, and watch the sky some more.

ASTA: Watching the sky is wonderful, Buddi, but it becomes boring in the long run.

BODVAR: The concept of "a long run" is on the retreat. Most people feel that time is far too short.

ASTA: But what about Gugga and the baby?

BODVAR: They're better off without me, mom.

SIGURD Dig a big hole, lie down in it and ask someone to fill it.

BODVAR: Is that a serious proposal?

SIGURD: Tie a stone to your leg and jump in the sea.

BODVAR: You're full of great ideas.

SIGURD: Or quit washing yourself like the hippies.

BODVAR: The world said goodbye to the last hippy many years ago. You have to bring your world view up to date.

SIGURD: (*Rises.*) When pigs are freezing they stick their snouts up the asshole of the nearest pig.

ASTA: Sigurd, this is gone enough! Thank you very much.

SIGURD: Not at all. (*He goes to the washroom. Pause.*)

BODVAR: I'm going to jail.

ASTA: (*Pause.*) That's it, is it? (*Pause.*) Then our family is in no need of further promotion. And for what are you to be honored?

BODVAR: Smuggling.

ASTA: Smuggling? What did you smuggle?

BODVAR: One of the squealers in Copenhagen must have thought I was a big dealer and called the police here. If I hadn't carried it someone else would have. I needed money.

ASTA: Drugs?

BODVAR: The world is full of junk. Daily they throw junk into the sea, enough to kill everything in huge areas. The fruits we eat are full of junk. (*Pause.*)

ASTA: Then you'll have time to read the Icelandic Sagas. (*Rises. Starts putting on her coat. Bodvar follows her.*)

BODVAR: Do I owe you anything?

ASTA: Yes, you do.

BODVAR: Why should I measure and plan everything I do from your point of view, mom! Listen to me, just this once: We do not live in the same world and I refuse to be accountable to you! (*Asta leaves.*) Mom, this isn't so serious, it's just bad luck! Perhaps I'll just get off with a fine!

SIGURD: (*Comes in.*) Your mother gone?

BODVAR: What does it look like.

SIGURD: Where did she go?

BODVAR: Out.

SIGURD: Why did she go out? (*Pause.*)

BODVAR: Dad.

SIGURD: What do you want?

BODVAR: Do you have a job for me on your boat?

SIGURD: Why?

BODVAR: Do I get it or not?

BODVAR: I have enough idiots on my hands.

BODVAR: Isn't there always room for one more in the galley?

SIGURD: (*A short pause.*) There's no future in it.

BODVAR: Is there any future in anything?

SIGURD: I don't know. Open a fashion shop. There's a future in that. A floating fashion shop which follows the fleet. That'd pay better than being a fool trying to catch fish.

BODVAR: Is there a chance I can get through to you?

SIGURD: I don't understand you.

BODVAR: Have you ever tried?

SIGURD: I've got sense enough to know it's useless.

BODVAR: Don't you have any interest in what I'm doing?

SIGURD: No.

BODVAR: That's it then. (*Pause.*)

SIGURD: It's a new thing if you want to tell me anything about yourself.

BODVAR: Okay, let's drop it, it's not worth the effort . . .

SIGURD: If you don't make the effort to speak up . . .

BODVAR: Crawl up your own asshole and stay in your stench.

Scene 19

(*Asta, Sigurd, Haddi, Gogo.*)

ASTA: (*Comes in wearing her coat.*) Where is Bodvar?

SIGURD: (*Sitting in the living room in the light from the television set.*) Are you asking me?

ASTA: What does it sound like?

SIGURD: He went out.

ASTA: Where? A long time ago?

SIGURD: I don't know. I was sleeping.

ASTA: Half an hour, one hour, two hours?

SIGURD: Do you think I count the minutes he's away?

ASTA: Sigurd . . .

SIGURD: Are you talking to me?

ASTA: Do you know what has happened? Did he tell you?

SIGURD: Tell me what?

ASTA: Did he tell you anything? (*Pause.*) Didn't he tell you anything? (*Pause.*) Didn't he tell you anything?

SIGURD: Didn't he tell me what, goddamnit? Do you have anything to eat?

ASTA: What's the matter with you guys?

SIGURD: Hunger.

ASTA: Hunger?

SIGURD: (*At the refrigerator.*) Yeah, I said hunger.

ASTA: I can't take any more, Sigurd. No more.

SIGURD: Really?

ASTA: There's a limit to everything.

SIGURD: Is there? (*Eating. They sit in silence for a while. Asta starts crying silently. Her head sinks to her chest. Finally.*) What's wrong with you?

ASTA: It doesn't matter.

SIGURD: Okay.

ASTA: (*Slumps at the table, hides her face in her hands.*)

SIGURD: (*Uneasy.*) Let's get to bed. It's late. (*Sound at the door.*) What the devil is that? Haddi and Gogo enter. One of Haddi's jacket sleeves is missing. He's obviously drunk.)

GOGO: (*Holding the sleeve in her hand.*) He didn't do nothing. Some guys tore it off.

SIGURD: (*Walks over to Haddi.*) There are some important parts missing in your head, boy.

GOGO: He didn't do anything. They attacked him.

SIGURD: Why not be consistent? (*Tears the other sleeve off the jacket.*)

HADDI: (*Looks in silence at his father.*) Thank you.

SIGURD: Thank you for what?

HADDI: You're a pretty good teacher when one looks at it objectively. (*Seizes Gogo by the arm and is going to guide her out. But Asta siezes his arm. Haddi frees himself from her.*)

ASTA: Haddi, dear Haddi.

HADDI: Do you think I'm a robot? I'm about to explode. I'm being blown to pieces! You make everything so ugly, boring, and hopeless! Leave me alone! (*They go. Asta lies on the floor.*)

SIGURD: (*After a long pause.*) Now come on woman.

ASTA: Why have we been doing all this?

SIGURD: Doing what?

ASTA: Don't act like a bigger fool than you are.

SIGURD: That's hard with such a big brain as you in the house.

ASTA: Is that all you have to say?

SIGURD: About what?

ASTA: I give up.

SIGURD: Does it matter what I say?

ASTA: Yes!

SIGURD: No!

ASTA: Sometimes I have the feeling that I'm always talking to myself.

SIGURD: Maybe you're going mad.

ASTA: Yeah, maybe I'm mad already.

SIGURD: Then you should see a doctor. (*A long pause.*) It can't get worse than it is. (*Pause.*)

ASTA: No, it can't get worse than it is.

END

The Glass Mountain

by

Tor Åge Bringsvaerd

Translated from the Norwegian by
Henry Beissel and Per K. Brask

Note: Everyone must play several parts

The actors in this piece have therefore been assigned letters (from A to H).

The letters do not identify the characters in the play, but the actor who speaks the line.

The letters A, B, G, and H represent male actors.

The letters C, D, E, and F represent female actors.

Act I

(Darkness. We hear pleading, muttering voices. Lights up slowly. C, D, and E are three witches. They sit in the background, center stage. They are stirring a large cauldron from which blue smoke rises. Colored dream-lights.)

D: *(Staring into the smoke.)* He is far away.

E: Can you see him?

D: He's still far away.

C: Is it anyone we know?

D: It's the one who's supposed to be coming.

C: Are you sure?

D: He doesn't know it himself.

E: But he's the one who's supposed to be coming?

D: He is the one. But he is still far away, and he does not understand his own dreams.

(Spot on the witches out. Spot up on H—he who may become the Prince. He stands downstage left, wearing large earphones.)

H: I've heard there is another world—just two weeks away from our own. And they say there is a girl there who is so beautiful that once you've seen her you can never take your eyes off her again. You cannot ever look at anything else again, but must follow her wherever she goes. Over a thousand men are already bewitched by her.

(H freezes. Spot up on C—maid—who is standing downstage right. She

faces the audience. H and C do not see each other. They are each in their own world.)

C: I speak on behalf of the Princess Irmelin. Is it her fault that she is so desirable? We live in a free country. Is it her fault that they all want her? Her father doesn't force them to pursue her. They come by themselves and of their own free will.

H: They've given up everything to follow her. They fight to be the one nearest her. They kill each other just to come a step closer to her. They're like migrating lemmings, like termites, like a swarm of grasshoppers. They have no thought for anything but her. They're an army that moves with its eyes closed. They don't hear anything other than her, they talk of nothing other than her. But she—she no longer sees them. She is like a statue of clouds in the daytime and a pillar of fire at night.

C: And I say: is it *her* fault?

(*Blackout. Sound: motorcycles. For a while we hear nothing but the sound of the motorcycles at full blast. The sound fades as a spot comes up on F—the corpse-robber's wife. The sound continues softly in the background while she is speaking. She is a grotesque figure.*)

F: I never ask him where he gets his money from. I never ask him anything. If he wants me to know he'll have to tell me of his own accord.

(*G—the corspe-robber—comes into a different spot. The two talk to the audience, not to each other.*)

G: I'm standing here right at the foot of the mountain.
F: But all the same—I know it has something to do with the bikes.
G: We know approximately where they're going to come crashing down.
F: They come here from all over the world. By the hundreds—by the thousands.
G: In the beginning there was no pattern. It was a matter of who got there first. Now we've divided the territory between us.
F: God knows what possesses them. And they're all so young. Mere boys!
G: Whatever comes down in my area belongs to me.
F: Very few of them survive the fall.
G: The higher the point from which they fall the harder the crash.
F: And those who survive end up as cripples or imbeciles. I don't know which is worse.
G: Sooner or later they come crashing down. All of them. They're bound to fall. The mountain is made that way.

F: And they're mere boys!

G: The only question is: are they going to fall where they're supposed to. And are they going to come down in my area. We're four or five of us who make a living in this way. Over the years we've reached a certain understanding with one another.

F: The mountain is as slippery as a mirror.

G: But things can get damn difficult if the guy survives. If he's knocked out, then there's no problem. But if he's conscious . . . He could recognize you later, right? . . . Well, you don't have a choice, do you . . .

F: And it's as steep as a cliff.

G: The first time is the worst. After that, like everything else, it becomes a habit.

F: I never ask him where he gets his money from.

G: She never asks me where I get my money from. But she knows.

F: I never ask him anything.

G: She knows. (*In self-defense.*) But is what I do any different from what everybody else is doing around here?

F: I know only that it has something to do with the bikes.

G: Don't we all live off the bikes? Each in his own way? Are the others any better? (*Waits for an answer. Turns to face F for the first time. Asks her directly.*) I said: Are the others any better?

F: I never ask him anything.

(*Slowly the light goes out. The sound of the motorcycles grows louder. The lights come up again and the sound of the motorcycles fades out. The stage is empty.*

The following scene should be played hectically and totally in revue style; the lines should overlap each other.

A—servant—enters with a record player with a large, old-fashioned trumpet. B—servant—brings in a small table. They put the record player on the small table.)

A: (*Plugging in the player.*) Have you found the records?

B: (*On his way out.*) Take it easy. I've got them outside.

A: Hurry up then. He'll be here any moment now. (*C—the maid— enters with an electric fan. Turns it on.*) A little less wind.

C: I only have it on three.

A: Turn it down to two.

B: (*Returns with a pile of records.*) Gallop . . . trot . . . or amble?

A: I said: turn it down to two.

B: I think we'll have an amble. Just for once. (*Puts on a record with sound effects: an amble.*)

(*D—maid—and E—maid—enter with green shrubs in their hands. Both yawn and rub their eyes as if they had just got out of bed.*)

C: Aren't we going to have any wind at all?

A: Do you want to blow his nightcap off? Dammit all, I have to attend to everything myself in this house. (*Turns the fan down to two.*)

B: An amble is probably not the right thing. Does anyone know where the slow trot is? (*D and E light up a smoke.*)

A: Where in hell have you been? Come on, line up! He'll be here any minute. (*D makes faces at A. D and E squat and hold the shrubs over their heads.*) And cut the smoking!

D: Are you afraid of a forest fire, maybe? (*But they do as he says and put out their cigarettes under their heels. E sneaks up on B and kisses him on the cheek.*)

C: Are you sure we don't need a little more wind? (*Turns the fan up to three again.*)

A: Help me bring in the horse. And turn the fan down to two! (*C shrugs his shoulders and turns the fan down to two again.*)

E: We should find the slow trot first. (*E helps B look through the records. During all this we still hear the amble.*)

A: You know as well as I how he likes to have things. Wind—

D: (*Flippantly.*) Not too strong.

A: (*Heatedly.*) That's right—not too strong.

D: Not too weak.

A: Not too weak.

D: It should ruffle his hair—

A: It should ruffle his hair but not blow off his nightcap!

D: Exactly.

B: (*From the wings.*) Shouldn't we push in the horse?

A: (*On his way out.*) And not this amble!

E: What do you think I'm standing here doing? Looking for a slow trot.

A: What in hell is wrong with you today? We do the same thing every Sunday.

B: (*Entering again.*) I can't push the horse in by myself.

C: But what would be wrong with changing things a little? (*B sees this opportunity to kiss E.*)

A: But he likes things exactly the way he likes them. He doesn't want them any different. (*B puts on a record with a slow trot. A rips the record off the player and pushes E across the floor.*) Sit down and be a shrub! Stick to your job!

E: I was just trying to be helpful.

C: (*To A.*) You think you can order everybody around.

A: Slow trot and slow amble? That's a downright insult. Find the record with the gallops. (*Scatters the records all over and exits into the wings.*)

E: I'm going to quit.

D: You're not going to quit.

E: I'm quitting as of now.

B: (*Puts his arms around E.*) He didn't mean it like that.

E: He meant every word of it.

A: (*Shouts from the wings.*) Do I have to stand here waiting all day?

(*B, C, and D run over to help him. E squats down and sulks, with the shrub high above her head. A, B, C, and D push in a stuffed horse— a real one!. As soon as it is on stage, B goes over to the records again. D picks up a broom and brushes off the horse so that the dust is flying all over.*)

C: Do you want it with its back to the door or—

B: (*Reading out loud.*) Gallop with headwind . . . Gallop with tailwind . . . Gallop with sidewind . . . Gallop in a moderate gale and in a violent storm.

A: It'll stand the way it always stands. We put it with its head pointing towards the window. It always stands with its head towards the window. (*They push.*)

B: (*Reads.*) Gallop through a pine forest and on a logging-road . . .

A: He likes to ride into the light.

B: (*Reads.*) Gallop on a race-track with crowds.

E: I'm not moving.

B: Gallop on a soft forest trail with bullfinch and lark.

A: Move over.

C: You're sitting in the exact spot where we have to put the horse.

E: I'm not moving. I'm a shrub in the forest and I'm not moving.

B: Shall we use the one with the bullfinch?

A: (*To E.*) Damn you, why can't you be more cooperative?

E: Have you ever heard of a shrub that's moved over because a horse was coming?

D: Don't be an idiot.

B: I said: Shall we use the one with the bullfinch?

E: Am I a shrub or am I not a shrub? I am a shrub and I don't move over for some stupid, moth-eaten, stuffed horse.

(*A and D carry her away. E howls. B puts on the record with the gallop on the soft forest trail with bullfinch and lark. He listens intently to the record without paying attention to the others. C turns up the fan full blast and aims it at them like a weapon—it sends their hair flying.*)

C: (*Theatrically.*) And the wind grew stronger and stronger. A violent storm blew up that day. And the poor moth-eaten horse stood there, swaying in the wind, its head pointing to the light, but not one damn shrub in the whole forest would move over.

(*F—a female herald—enters and bows to the audience. She carries a small gong.*)

F: The King is coming! (*Beats the gong. The chaos on the stage is instantly transformed into a world of order and respect. G—the old King—walks in. He is old and his face is full of wrinkles. He walks poorly and seems altogether feeble. He is dressed in pyjamas, slippers, and a nightcap with the royal crest.*)

A/B/C/D/E: (*In chorus.*) Hail thee, most noble King!
G: Hail thee.
A: I trust Your Majesty has enjoyed a restful night.
G: That we had, that we had. Except for those cursed motorcycles . . . (*He raises his old hand in a deprecating gesture.*) No, no, we know. We know there's nothing to be done about them. They represent progress, hope, the future. We know. Ah, yes. (*To the horse.*) And how are you, my faithful old steed? (*A stands parallel with the horse, throws back his head and whinnies.*) Now, now . . . (*B runs in with a chair. G climbs up on the chair and from there on to the back of the horse. B removes the chair, runs back to the record player and puts on the gallop record.*) Giddap, my spry steed! (*A throws back his head and whinnies.*) It's really blowing today. (*C turns on the fan. Without pausing, G says.*) Ah! Feel the wind! (*A whinnies. G pats the horse.*) Feel the wind which ruffles our hair. (*He throws off his nightcap. He is completely bald.*) A perfect day to go out for a ride. There's nothing like a brisk ride before breakfast. (*He bends down to break a twig from one of the shrubs D and E are holding. He almost falls off the horse. D has to get up and support him. G notices nothing of this.*) A ride before breakfast. In God's own nature! (*E breaks off a twig and gives it to him. He accepts it and pats her cheek.*) Giddap, my spry steed! (*A whinnies wild and long. The light is lowered and changes so that one has the illusion, almost, of being outside. What has been comical so far, should now take on a poetic quality. A neighs in the twilight.*) We've been out riding together for over fifty years, you and I. There'll never be another horse, not for me. And you'll never have another rider. We belong together, you and I. Man and horse.

(Sound: Romantic lute playing old English melody. G and his horse are the only things to be seen on stage now. G is riding and dreaming. A, B, and C exit in the darkness. Spot on F—the princess—who enters like a fairytale princess with three golden apples in her hands. The light on her shows that she is not real, but something he dreams, something he remembers.)

F: The king of this land had a daughter whom he allowed no one to marry who could not ride over the glass mountain—for it was a high, a very high mountain, bright and shiny as ice, close to the Royal Palace.

G: *(To the horse and the audience:)* Do you remember the glass mountain —bright and shiny as ice?

F: And high on top sat the King's daughter with the three golden apples in her lap.

G: Do you remember how beautiful she was?

(A and C have positioned themselves downstage left. A has a hand puppet on his right hand. C has two hand puppets, one on each hand.)

A: *(Without using the puppet and addressing the audience.)* While the King dreams and remembers, the country's leading men discuss the future.

C: *(Lifts up his left-hand puppet and uses a puppet-theatre voice.)* I am an architect. It is my responsibility to see to it that the mountain slopes are always slippery. That the curves are always sharp. And that the road is impassable.

A: *(Lifts up his puppet.)* I am the director of tourism. I disseminate information. I make arrangements. *(The light gradually narrows till one can only see the puppets, not the actor who holds them.)*

C: *(Lifts his right-hand puppet.)* I own a hotel. I receive guests. That's all I do.

F: And whoever succeeded in riding to the top and taking the three apples would have half of her kingdom.

G: Do you hear? The princess and half the kingdom!

F: And the king's daughter was so beautiful that everybody who saw her was spellbound by her, whether he wanted to or not . . .

A: *(Lifts his puppet.)* Is everything ready for Saturday? Are the slopes as slippery as they're supposed to be?

C: *(Left-hand puppet.)* Two hundred workers are polishing them right now.

A: *(Puppet.)* Are the curves sharp enough?

C: *(Left-hand puppet.)* We have everything under control.

F: And they came riding from all corners of the world.

G: Do you remember how many people there were!

C: (*Right-hand puppet.*) How many participants are there?

A: (*Puppet.*) Thirty. We're aiming for three heats. Ten in each.

F: Then came the day appointed by the king, and a great many knights and princes had gathered at the foot of the glass mountain, together with a large crowd of onlookers—for everybody who could walk or crawl wanted to be there to see who would win the princess . . .

G: Giddap, my spry steed.

C: (*Left-hand puppet.*) Is the hotel completely booked?

C: (*Right-hand puppet.*) Completely booked. As usual.

A: (*Puppet.*) We've never been short of onlookers. (*The spots on the puppets are turned off. A and C exit.*)

F: And they rode so hard that their horses foamed at the mouth, but to no avail. The moment the horses put their hooves on the mountain they slipped off again. For the mountain was as smooth as a glass window and as steep as a cliff. (*B—as the king's fool—rolls on stage in a wheelchair. He wears a helmet with fool's bells. He sits and listens to G and F, and makes faces to the audience.*) Will no one succeed? Will I have to sit here forever with my three golden apples?

G: Giddap, my spry steed!

B: (*Apes and mocks him in the wheelchair.*) Giddap, my spry steed!

F: Where is the one who can master the glass mountain?

G: Do you remember the knight in the copper armor?

F: My lord and my prince. (*Throws one apple to G who catches it in mid-air.*)

B: (*To the audience.*) Do you remember the one with the tiger on his back? A tiger of silk and velvet. (*Laughs a bitter fool's laughter.*)

G: Do you remember the knight in the silver armor?

F: My lord and my prince. (*Throws another apple to G.*)

B: Do you remember the roar in the twin exhaust pipes? Do you remember the sun glittering in the spokes of the wheels? (*Bitter laugh.*)

G: Do you remember the knight in the golden armor?

B: (*Shouts.*) My lord and my prince! (*Sound: motorcycles. B talks over them.*) Do you remember the third curve from the top, where the road narrows and the shoulder is loose, where the ground suddenly gives way and there is nothing to hold on to? Do you remember the wheels spinning? Do you remember the howl of the engine? Do you remember the screeching brakes? Do you remember how the handlebars looked? Do you remember the fall? The fear? The emptiness? The way down? Do you remember that you managed to look at yourself mirrored in the mountain slope?

G: Stop! (*Normal lights up on stage. F has exited. G is the feeble old king again, riding his stuffed horse. B laughs and laughs.*) Stop, I say! (*D and E drop their shrubs and run over to push B out of his wheelchair. B continues to laugh, writhing on the floor with laughter and tears.*)

B: Remember the fall? Remember the wind? Remember the shock? Remember the pain? Remember the darkness?

G: Get him out of here! (*D and E torment B, kicking him across the floor. As he creeps, crawls, and rolls on the floor he continues to laugh.*)

D: There was no one who forced you to it.

B: Do you remember the fall?

E: You did it of your own free will.

B: Do you remember the wind?

D: You knew it would be dangerous.

B: Do you remember the shock?

D: But you said you wanted to get ahead in the world.

B: Do you remember the pain?

D: You thought you could manage it.

B: Do you remember the darkness?

E: Do you remember how we laughed at you afterwards? (*B, D, and E exit. G sits on his horse, alone again. The sound of motorcycles stops.*)

A: (*Enters as a servant.*) Breakfast is served, Your Majesty.

G: (*Softly to himself.*) Do you remember the knight in the golden armor?

(*Blackout. F enters as a princess. Spot up on her—the rest of the stage is in darkness.*)

F: They say that I look like my mother. I don't know. She died when I was little . . . She sat up on the mountain the same way I did. With the three golden apples in her lap. And father won her . . . He managed to get all the way to the top. That's what he did. He's not evil. Many people think he's evil. But he's not. Just old-fashioned. And stubborn. Terribly stubborn. That's how he did it. Anyone who wants to get ahead in this world has to do it the same way. That's how it's always been and how it'll always be! Nobody asks me what I think of all of this. And it's easy enough for him. I'm the one who has to sit here! Day and night! Lately we've started to put a puppet here in my place at night—or on rainy days. Nobody notices the difference . . . (*G walks into the spot as the King. F continues without a break.*) Once I asked him if he liked my mother.

G: Liked?

F: Yes.

G: I married her, didn't I. I won her.

F: Yes, but did you like each other?

G: I won her and half the kingdom, didn't I. What in hell are you talking about?

F: But I think he liked her. Because one day he said—

G: (*Showing her how.*) You should hold the apples like this. Not like that. This is how you should hold them.

F: (*Tries.*) Like this?

G: Like that. That's much better. Your mother always held them like that. (*Moves over to the side.*)

F: (*To the audience.*) They say I look like her. (*C enters as a maid, carrying a mirror, a brush, and a comb. Gives F the mirror. Takes the crown off her head and begins to comb and brush her hair. F looks at herself in the mirror while they talk.*) Do you think I'm pretty? I mean, do you think I'm beautiful?

C: Princess Irmelin is both pretty and beautiful.

F: But am I the prettiest of all? Am I the most beautiful woman you've ever seen?

C: Nobody is more beautiful than Princess Irmelin.

F: It's not an easy business, I can tell you. It's not easy to have to be the most beautiful woman in the world. It's hard work!

(*Normal stage lighting. Music. C puts away the mirror, the comb, and the brush. E, D, and B enter. They perform for G, F, A, and C. B is, as usual, the king's fool. E and D have painted clown's mouths; they laugh continuously, but silently and with exaggerated grimaces, as clowns are wont to do. They use the large gestures and movements of pantomime. Everything should be exaggerated and baroque. There is background music throughout this scene. Every now and then a melody emerges.*)

E: (*Sings.*) I sing the sad song
   of Louise, oh Louise
   whose breasts were so small
   they could no man please,
   no man please.
   Oh Louise, what a plight,
   What pain, what distress!
   Not in the night, nor in daylight
   Could she find peace or happiness.

E/D: (*Sing.*) Rosebuds are pretty, but they're the pits,
   for men want only women who have big (*Honk—honk!—They have two old car horns which they honk.*)
   Louise, Louise . . .

D: (*Recites.*) She imagines she hears a ripple
   of laughter wherever she goes—
   Oh Louise, oh Louise—
   the question is simple:
   is what you've got a nipple
   or a pimple?
   Louise, Louise . . .

E/D: (*Sing.*) Rosebuds are pretty, but . . . (*Etc.*)

E: (*Sings.*) And then came your saviour,
   Oh Louise, right to your door,
   a fast talking saleslady
   who knew the score.
   Louise, Louise . . .

D: (*Sings.*) Your breasts are too little,
   but we're in the business
   for a small fee
   and without sweat or spittle
   to increase their size
   and transport you quickly to paradise.

E/D: (*Sing.*) Rosebuds are pretty, but . . . (*Etc.*)

B: (*Talks.*) Poor Louise. She was led to believe that it's important to have big breasts. She was led to believe that it's the most important thing in the world. This is called ''manipulation''—a fine word. One might also call it mind massage.

E/D: (*Sing.*) Rosebuds are pretty, but . . . (*Etc.*)

B: (*Talks.*) And Louise got started with her little electric massage machine. And she massaged and massaged . . .

E/D: (*Sing.*) Rosebuds are pretty, but . . . (*Etc.*)

B: And her breasts grew. Day by day they grew bigger and bigger.

D: She barely found time to eat. Oh Louise, Louise . . .

E: All she did was to rub and massage.

B: (*Sings.*) Rosebuds are pretty, but . . . (*Etc.*)

E: But Louise didn't stop when she should've.

D: Louise went on and on.

E: For now she had tasted blood.

D: And now she had a bosom like an Italian film star.

B: Now nobody made fun of her anymore.

D: On the contrary.

B: Now there was no lack of suitors anymore.

D: On the contrary.

E/D: (*Sing.*) Rosebuds are pretty, but . . . (*Etc.*)

E: But Louise didn't stop when she should've.

D: Could've.

E: Ought to.

B: Have stopped.

D: Louise was obsessed with the thought of big breasts.

E: She was convinced that the bigger your breasts the bigger your happiness.

D: Louise wanted to have the world's biggest breasts.

E: Louise wanted to be very happy.

B: So she forgot everything else. She forgot to go to work, she forgot about her friends, she forgot about her sick mother, she forgot to clean her apartment, she forgot to pay her bills, she forgot to feed her cat.

E: Meow, meow!

B: She forgot everything else.

D: She stopped going out altogether.

E: She just sat at home and massaged her breasts.

B: And one day.

E: A beautiful day.

D: One beautiful day she had breasts so big she couldn't get through the doorway from the livingroom to the kitchen.

E: She was imprisoned in her own livingroom.

D: Far away from her fridge.

E: Without food or drink.

D: She had even forgotten to bring her toothbrush.

E: There she sat.

D: (*Screams.*) Help!

B: Poor Louise, trapped on the seventh floor—with the world's biggest breasts.

E: They tried to cut her free.

D: It was hopeless.

B: They had to hoist food up to her with a pulley—three times a day.

E: And she had to take on work she could do at home.

D: People came from far and near to see her.

B: And Louise was hanging out the window.

E: Her breasts were hanging out the window.

D: And everybody was stunned to see how big they were.

B: In the beginning that made her just a touch proud.

E: Not just a touch.

D: Mighty proud.

B: Poor Louise.

E: Many years passed.

B: And one day she looked at the clock and discovered all of a sudden that she had grown old!

E: But her breasts were still growing and growing.

B: Eventually they burst the window frames and she cut herself on the glass.

E: And blood dripped into the street. From the seventh floor.

D: Her breasts grew.

E: And the blood ran.

B: Till Louise filled up the whole room. From wall to wall. From the ceiling to the floor.

E: And blood dripped into the street. From the seventh floor.

B: Her breasts filled up her whole living room. And there was not an inch left for the rest of her.

D: (*Screams.*) Can't someone call a doctor? (*The music stops abruptly. After a short pause it starts up again, but in a minor key.*) She died.

B: Squished between wall and ceiling.

E: (*Sings.*) I sing the sad song
of Louise, oh Louise.
All she ever wanted
were breasts to please,
but, alas, things went wrong
and she died in a very tight squeeze.

E/D: (*Sing.*) Rosebuds are pretty, but . . . (*Etc.*)

D: (*Recites.*) Louise set out to show
to be happy a woman must grow
big breasts, the biggest around—
but the burden of proof
forced her to the ground
when her towering tits hit the roof.

B: The burden of proof!

B/D/E: (*Sing.*) Rosebuds are pretty, but . . . (*Etc.*)

B: (*Without music.*) And now I ask you: do you think Louise was ever really happy?

(*The audience applauds. The performers take a bow. G makes a sign that they should leave the stage. Lights only on G and A. A has picked up the large hand puppet he used earlier.*)

A: (*With his own voice.*) The Director of Tourism seeks an audience, Your Majesty.

G: What does he want this time? (*Sighs in resignation.*) Show him in.

A: (*Lifts the puppet and speaks with a puppet-theatre voice.*) Your Majesty, you do me a great honor, a very great honor—

G: Cut it out. What is it you want?

A: (*Puppet.*) It's about the recruiting.

G: Recruiting?

A: (*With his own voice, addressing the puppet.*) What's the matter with the recruiting? (*Puppet.*) It's not as effective as it ought to be.

G: Then improve it. That's what you get paid for.

A: (*Puppet.*) With Your Majesty's most gracious permission—

G: You have it.

A: (*Puppet.*) With Your Majesty's most gracious permission I would like to remind you—

G: (*To A.*) You talk to him. (*Pulls a face that indicates that he considers the Director of Tourism an idiot. He exits.*)

A: (*His own voice.*) Come to the point. (*Puppet.*) It's about the support we get from the young. There isn't enough of it. They should be rallying around us. (*His own voice.*) Our young people are good people, aren't they? (*Puppet.*) Some are less good than others. (*His own voice.*) What do you mean by that? (*Puppet.*) They call it . . . (*Leans over and whispers in A's ear. A's own voice.*) Speak up! (*Puppet.*) The Social-Climbing-Society! (*His head in his hands; after a short while he looks up again. When the puppet begins to talk, the light focuses on it till A becomes invisible and the puppet he holds is the only thing we see.*) There are dangerous ideas. Da-a-angerous ideas in young heads! We must get them to pursue better thoughts. Make the whole thing more attractive for them. Maybe we could offer them a little bonus . . . or a couple of bonuses . . . even three. So that one wouldn't have to go all the way to the top before one could get any prize at all. This way no one could accuse us of caring only about those who reach the very top. And it would be a real incentive for the young . . . I was thinking of a whole steps-up-the-ladder approach: say a pledge for every three curves, and a cash payment for every fifth curve. Well, sooner or later they all fall off the mountain anyway and the bonuses come back to us, so why shouldn't we be a little generous. (*A's own voice.*) And at the same time we could raise the starting fees. (*Puppet.*) Yes, of course. At the same time we raise the starting fees. New incentives for everybody. (*Spot out on puppet. Spot up on C, D, and E who are the three witches again.*)

D: He has come closer.

E: Can you see him?

C: Soon he'll be here!

D: But he still doesn't understand his own dreams . . . (*Spot out on them. Spot up on H.*)

H: On the way I came across a woman sitting in a chair whose hands and feet were tied up—and who was blindfolded. I wanted to help her. (*Spot up on F, here not a princess but some unknown woman. She is sitting on a chair, tied hand and feet, and blindfolded.*)

F: Go away!

H: But I want to help you.

F: (*Sneers.*) Help.

H: (*To audience.*) She refused to allow me to untie her. She was convinced that she couldn't live without the ropes which tied her to the chair. She believed it was the ropes themselves that kept her alive and that her happiness was attached to every knot in it. (*To F.*) Don't you want to be free?

F: (*Laughs.*)

H: (*Leans over to her.*) Let me at least remove your blindfold. You can't see anything . . . (*F snarls and spits in his face. H walks away from her. Spot out on F. H hears a sound and turns around. Spot up on A. A is hanging from a wall, his feet off the ground, holding on to two pegs. His face is turned to the wall.*)

A: (*Talking to himself.*) This here is a fine wall. There are worse walls in the world. Ah well, it's hard work. But who said things would be easy? And this is a fine wall.

H: What are you doing up there?

A: Can't you see for yourself?

H: But why are you hanging on a wall?

A: Isn't that what everybody does?

H: I'm not hanging on a wall.

A: You're not hanging on a wall? But then, what are you doing with yourself?

H: I'm standing on the ground.

A: Ground? . . . I've never heard of it . . . Standing?

H: With my feet. Come down and try.

A: What good would that do?

H: You could rest your arms. You could walk about freely—wherever you wanted to go.

A: But first I would have to let go of the pegs.

H: Naturally.

A: That's easy enough for you to say. (*Pause.*) Let go of the pegs? What would I use my hands for?

H: For anything you want. It can't be much fun hanging on a wall all the time.

A: Who said it's supposed to be fun? But at least up here I know there is something to hold on to.

H: Except that this way you'll never go anywhere.

A: But I know what I've got. (*H walks a few steps away from A. Spot out on A.*)

H: (*To audience.*) Strange people in this country. Am I on the right road? Is this the road to the glass mountain? I'd imagined it to be different . . . (*Spot out on H. Spot up on C, D, and E as witches again.*)

C: But he still doesn't understand his own dreams.

D: Give him time. He has not yet become the man he is to be. He has not yet seen the mountain.

E: How long are we to wait?

D: Send him more dreams, sister, send him more dreams!

C: Is that all?

D: Dream must fight dream. Image must break image. That's the way it's always been.

(*Spot out on C, D, and E. Blue flashing lights of an ambulance. Perhaps the sound of a siren. H and B—the king's fool—are downstage on either side of the stage. B moves his wheelchair over to H and welcomes him.*)

B: Welcome! You're new here? I haven't seen you around here before. (*Grasps H's hand and shakes it. To the audience.*) He's new here.

H: I've just arrived.

(*C and D, dressed as medics in white coats, carry E, who is crying, on a stretcher past H and B. There is blood all over E. One of his hands is dangling from the stretcher clutching a helmet. H steps back a little.*)

B: (*Laughs.*) So you're thinking of trying your luck too?

H: (*Following the stretcher with his eyes.*) Yes.

B: (*To the audience.*) He wants to try his luck too. (To H.) But where is your bike?

H: (*Still preoccupied with the stretcher which now disappears in the wings on the other side of the stage.*) I don't have a bike.

B: (*To the audience.*) He doesn't have a bike. (*Smacks his lips.*)

H: I've thought of buying one.

B: (*Nods.*) Hmm.

H: I'm going to save up for a bike.

B: (*Nods.*) Hmm.

H: Everyone has the right to try.

B: Of course. (*Laughs and rings his bells.*) This is a free country.

H: I want to get to the top.

B: (*To the audience.*) He wants to get to the top.

H: (*Irritated and obstinate.*) This is a free country. Everybody has the same chances and opportunities. (*B rings his bells with a teasing laugh. Spot out on them. Spot up on group around the King's stuffed horse. G, the King, sits on his horse and talks with C, a minister, and A, a priest. G orders A and C to run on the spot so that it will appear as though he were riding.*)

A: (*Out of breath.*) Oh, I'm too old for this, Your Majesty. Can't I rest a little? Just a little?

G: Come along now! Keep going! It was your idea to have an audience with us this time. You know very well that this is the hour when we go riding.

A: But it was important. I thought it was a matter of great concern.

G: Alright, we have granted you an audience. Speak up then and tell us what's on your mind, pastor. (*Softly to C.*) What in hell kind of priests do we have these days?

C: He would like to talk to Your Majesty about the race on Saturday.

G: (*To C.*) Let him speak for himself. (*To A.*) Well? Come on, out with it!

A: I've been thinking about the possibility of holding a devotional service for the bikes.

G: (*To C.*) A devotional service for the bikes?

C: He would like to bless the bikes.

G: (*To C.*) Let him speak for himself!

A: There are going to be three heats, if I'm not mistaken. I was thinking of a short service before each.

G: (*Genuinely puzzled.*) Is that really necessary?

C: He would like to bless the bikes.

A: But not only the bikes that are in the race. Everybody who has a bike and wants to have it blessed can come. We won't refuse anyone. We won't turn anyone away.

G: (*Softly to C.*) Is the man mad?

C: On the contrary, Your Majesty, he is—

G: Let him speak for himself! (*To A.*) Come to the point! There ought to be a point here somewhere, right. What sense would there be in blessing all sorts of bikes just like that.

A: I find it hard to speak while I'm running.

G: (*To C.*) He has difficulties expressing himself.

A: Can't we take a short rest?

G: Come along! I want both of you to keep running!

(*D, as a maid, comes running in, mostly on the spot with knees raised high, carrying a rifle.*)

D: It'll soon be time for lunch, Your Majesty. (*Gives G the rifle.*) Good hunting, Your Majesty! (*Runs out with high-knee steps. G holds the rifle at the ready. Scouts around while A explains.*)

A: It would attract a big crowd. I'm sure it would attract a big crowd.

C: (*Makes notes on a pad while she runs.*) Do you think it would appeal to a different type of tourist? Is that what you have in mind? The kind of tourist we have neglected so far?

A: Absolutely. Exactly what I have in mind.

G: (*Fires a shot and screams.*) Where is the menu?

C: Can it be done—theologically speaking?

A: Well, we have St. Christopher, patron saint of all travelers. The blessing will of course be in his name.

(*E, as a maid, runs in, knees raised to the chest, with a turkey she holds high above her head. She cackles like a turkey. G follows her with the rifle.*)

C: Yes, I'm absolutely convinced that this will interest his Majesty. The blessing would not be free, I hope.

A: Of course not. (*G fires the rifle.*)

E: Did you hit it, Your Majesty. Was it a hit?

G: No, I missed.

E: I'm sorry. (*Runs offstage with the turkey. D runs in with a rabbit held high above her head. G follows the rabbit with his rifle.*)

A: You set the fee.

C: A sensible suggestion.

A: And the church gets half.

G: Is that a rabbit or a hare? Dammit, we can't even tell the difference between a rabbit and a hare any longer.

C: 20 percent.

D: A rabbit, Your Majesty.

A: But it's my idea. It's a church initiative.

C: Alright, let's make it 30 percent. That should be fair enough.

A: Okay. 30 percent. (*A and C shake hands on the deal at the precise moment at which G fires another shot.*)

G: You pushed us, you idiots. We could have you hanged for this!

D: Did you hit it, Your Majesty? Was it a hit?

G: Of course we didn't hit it. Those idiots messed up our aim.

D: Shall I have the turkey brought back once more? Or would Your Majesty prefer another shot at the rabbit?

G: Bring back the turkey! (*D runs offstage with the rabbit. E runs in with the turkey.*)

A: We could also sell medallions. Small medallions with a picture of St. Christopher on a motorcycle—and the glass mountain in the background.

C: And stamps.

A: And souvenir coins. (*G fires his rifle.*)

E: This time you've scored, Your Majesty. I have the definite feeling that you hit it, am I right?

G: Then drop the bird, you numbskull! A dead turkey can't stay aloft that long.

A: Turkeys can't fly at all, Your Majesty. With all due respect.

G: All the more reason to drop it then. (*To C.*) Fetch the game! Apporte! (*C at once plays the part of a growling hunting dog. Runs off to fetch the turkey which E puts in her mouth. Runs back to G who takes the turkey from her mouth and pats her on the head. G addresses the horse.*) Ho-o-o! (*He stops riding and raises the rifle and the turkey in the air. D, E, A, and C applaud enthusiastically. A wipes the sweat off his brow. D and E help G get off the horse by placing a chair next to it. F enters.*)

F: Did you have a good hunt, father?

G: (*Throws her the turkey.*) Give this to the kitchen, my pretty daughter!

(*Lights out on the whole scene. Sound: motorcycles. H is looking for a cheap room. He is at the house of an elderly gentleman who lives near the glass mountain. The landlord is played by B, looking completely different from the fool he played before.*)

H: (*Looking around.*) This is not a very big room.

B: For that price you can't expect anything bigger.

H: Is it always so noisy?

B: (*Closes the window so that the noise is less bothersome.*) What d'you expect with all those bikes around?

H: What about installing double windows?

B: You need more than double windows to shut out that racket.

H: But it would improve things a little, wouldn't it?

B: When I was your age I wanted a larger room too.

H: Did you get it?

B: (*Resigned.*) I live in the room next door.

H: With all this noise?

B: I thought you said you were going to get yourself a bike too.

H: There's no reason why I should like the noise they make.

B: The sound of bikes—there was a time when I found it exciting. I was young and ambitious. I wanted to get ahead, move up in the world . . . Later . . . Well, it just hurt to listen to them.

H: And today?

B: (*Shrugs his shoulders.*) One gets used to everything.

H: But they bother you.

B: No. I don't really hear them anymore. Not until you drew my attention to them. They're here all the time. No one takes any notice of the noise any longer. We notice it only when it stops.

H: Or unless somebody draws your attention to it.

B: (*Listens.*) Yes . . . or unless somebody draws our attention to it.

(*The sound of bikes increases and then fades out. Spot out on H and B. Spot up on F, the princess, who is standing by herself combing her long hair with a huge comb. She is wearing a long white night gown.*)

F: Have I prepared myself for nothing? Will he never come? . . . Is it my fault? Is there something I should do differently? (*Spot out on F. Spot up again on B and H.*)

H: I have such strange dreams.

B: The young always dream.

H: But lately I've had peculiar dreams . . . Last night, for instance . . . last night I dreamt I was following the tracks of an abandoned railway line.

B: What's so peculiar about that?

(*Spot up on F who lay down on the floor in the preceding darkness. Now she is lying as immobile as a corpse, with her hands folded and a wreath on her head.*)

H: Suddenly I saw a woman lying across the tracks. She was barefoot and dressed in a long white gown, her hands folded on her chest and a wreath of winter flowers on her head . . . (*While he talks he walks slowly out of his own spot into the circle of light around F. Spot on B fades out slowly. B stands frozen in the darkness. H continues without interruption.*) At first, I thought she was dead . . . I walked over to her. She just lay there, staring up into the blue sky. Then I realized she was breathing. But she didn't respond when I talked to her—(*He squats down by the side of her head.*)

G: (*In the darkness.*) Leave her alone! (*H turns in the direction of the voice. Spot up on G who is sitting on a folding chair with a weekly newspaper in his hands. He is a shriveled-up man now and wears an old-fashioned starched collar and a hand tied bow.*) Leave her alone. Mind your own business and leave decent people in peace.

H: (*To the audience.*) He was sitting on his folding chair reading the weekly paper. The woman was lying with the back of her head in the coal-gray sand, the hollow of her neck resting on the steel tracks.

G: Leave us in peace! We have enough trouble as it is.

H: Was she thinking of . . . But there are no trains on that line . . . (*Gets up.*) It's been abandoned. There won't be another train on those tracks ever.

G: (*Nods.*) I know.

H: (*Points to the woman.*) But she—does she know? (*G shrugs his shoulders.*) It must be at least twenty years since the last train passed this way.

G: I've tried to tell her. We used to talk about things. But not any longer. (*Runs his hand along the inside of his collar.*) She's been lying there for a long time. All summer and winter. I come out here and bring her something to eat three times a day. In the evening I put warm blankets over her. (*Sighs.*) The worst are the winters . . .

H: (*While he walks out of his spot and over to B, the light slowly comes up on B who is still standing there frozen. Behind him the lights slowly fade out on G and F.*) I looked up at the mountains. There was no haze over them as they outlined a sleeping crocodile against the horizon.

G: (*Behind him in the darkness.*) Her mother was exactly the same.

H: (*To B.*) Do you know what it all means?

B: Could you recognize who she was?

H: That's what was so strange. I think it was the Princess who was lying on the tracks.

B: Everybody dreams of her. That's the only kind of dream that flourishes around here. But what you dreamt—I've never heard anyone dream anything like that before. (*Spot on F who has gotten up, taken the wreath off her head and is now combing her hair again.*)

F: Have I prepared myself for nothing? Will he never come? . . . Is it my fauilt? Did I do anything wrong? Is there anything I should do differently? (*Spot out on F.*)

B: I was content with what I got.

H: But did you expect more?

B: I don't know what I expected.

H: Isn't that what you dreamt about?

B: When I was younger?

H: I thought you said everybody had the same dream.

B: When I was younger I had many different dreams.

H: But now you've given up.

B: You want me to get up on a bike again? I? At my age?

H: One should never give in. (*B laughs a bitter laugh.*) We live in a free country, don't we. Everybody has the right to try.

B: Everybody has the right to try.

H: Everybody can make it to the top if only they want to. There's equal opportunity for everybody.

B: First you have to own a bike. (*Spot out on H and B. Spot up on F. D now enters to help her get dressed. C stands a little to the side of them.*)

C: In the town around the glass mountain the walls have ears and where there are ears there's always a mouth . . . (*E enters and curtsies before F.*)

E: Your Highness.

F: Yes.

E: A stranger has come into town.

F: (*Ironically.*) Only one? (*D snickers goodheartedly.*)

E: Your Highness, he is not like the others.

F: Well? (*Whispers in D's ear; both snicker.*)

E: I've come to warn you, Your Highness.

F: To warn me? Really? Do I need to be warned? That's something new!

E: He has strange dreams.

F: The stranger.

E: He dreams about you, Your Highness.

F: (*To D.*) And she calls that "strange dreams."

E: He dreams that you are dead. Not that you're going to die, but that you are already dead. (*F reacts. Spot out on the group which freezes. Spot up on G and A, who plays the minister.*)

G: He dreams what?

A: He dreams that the world is governed by the dead, but that the living don't notice . . . Of course, it's perfectly laughable. Still, we have him under surveillance.

G: What's he doing now?

A: Looking for work. (*Spot out on them. B, as the king's fool, enters laughing in his wheelchair. E, C, D, and F gather around him.*)

B: And for whom does everything turn around and around? For whom does it all turn and turn?

D: For you.

E: It all turns around for you.

B: Wrong. For us!

D: For us?

B: Yes, for us. For you and me. It turns around for us. The whole thing is a wheel. Because, think—what is it all youngsters want?

E: A motorbike.

B: They save up to buy a bike. And where do they work to get enough money to be able to afford a bike?

C: At a motorcycle factory.

B: And after they've bought a bike, what happens to it?

D: They ride it till it's a wreck.

B: And what happens to the wreck?

E: It goes to a wrecking yard.

B: And the people take a piece from one and a part from another—and presto!—a whole bike—used of course—is ready to be driven away. And what happens to it? (*He communicates with a facial expression that things don't go well with it.*) And what about the people who don't work at a motorcycle factory or a wrecking yard or a bike repair shop, what do they do? What do you do, for instance? (*Points at C.*)

C: I sell motorcycle souvenirs.

B: To motorcycle tourists. (*Points at D.*)

D: I clean up around the foot of the mountain.

B: To remove the tire tracks. (*Points at E.*)

E: I attend to the injured.

B: So they can try again. (*Points at C.*)

C: I polish the sides of the mountain.

B: So that more riders can come crashing down. (*Points at D.*)

D: I sell postcards of the princess.

B: So that we can go on producing, producing. (*Points at E.*)

E: I send bills to the next of kin.

B: So for whom does it all keep turning around? For whom do things turn and turn? The whole thing is a wheel.

C: Oh, shut up! You're no better than the rest of us.

E: You're in on it too. (*B laughs. Spot out on this group and up on G and A.*)

G: What is he dreaming this time? Is he dreaming anything?

A: He's dreaming of a picture. A large, framed picture. Looks like a tourist poster. A crowd of people, on foot and on donkey carts, is coming down to the beach. A couple of fishing boats—they're dark silhouettes—are pulled up on the shore. There is a strange movement in the picture. As if the people wanted to stop at the beach but at the same time had to keep going, out into the sea—like lemmings. It's a color photo, taken at sundown. The colors in it are red, blue, brown, and yellow. (*Spot out on A and G, up on H who is sitting on the floor looking thoughtful.*)

E: (*Moves close to him.*) The princess likes to walk around town in disguise so that she won't be recognized. This time she's looking for someone in particular . . . (*Withdraws.*)

F: (*Comes close to H.*) You're new here aren't you?

H: Who are you?

F: What does it matter?

H: (*Misunderstands the situation.*) I have no money. Try somebody else.

F: I don't want your money.

H: What do you want?

F: (*Sits down next to him.*) You're the one with the dreams, aren't you?

H: Yes, I have dreams.

F: Tell me about them.

H: They are what they are. I can't do anything about it. Before, it was never like this.

F: What was it like then, before?

H: I used to have only one dream, the same dream everybody else had—the glass mountain, the princess with the three golden apples. I wanted to make it to the top. I wanted to get up there.

F: And now?

H: Now I don't know any longer. The closer I come to the mountain, the more unreal it seems. Sometimes I'm overcome by a particular fear . . . as though, if I'd stretch out my hands to touch the mountain it would disappear and my dreams would be the only thing left that was real.

F: But do you want the mountain to disappear?

H: (*Shakes his head.*) I've come a long way. I've given years of my life to get here where I am. From the time I was very little my goal was to come to the glass mountain. And now, at last, I've arrived, I'm standing at the foot of it. Why should I want it to disappear? Then everything I've done up to now would be meaningless.

F: But you're afraid.

H: Soon I'll have a bike. I'll start the engine, head straight for the mountain . . . I'll hear the crowds roar their approval . . . but I'm afraid. I'm afraid the mountain will move over, turn aside, or simply disappear . . . and that the wheels of my own bike will end up spinning in a void. I'm afraid that everything'll turn out to have been a dream chasing the wind. That it's *now* that I'm asleep. And I'm afraid to wake up.

F: Tell me what you dream.

H: I dream that I'm lying in bed asleep. I dream that I'm lying on my stomach with my face in a pillow and that the pillow is doubled up. Suddenly I notice that a feather is sticking out of the pillow. I pull on it. But it's not a feather. It's a human hair. It's a long, golden lock of hair. The whole pillow is filled with women's hair . . .

F: D'you know what it means?

H: No, but it must be a dream about the princess.

F: D'you look upon it as a good dream?

H: Well, now that I'm awake—if I am in fact awake right now—now I think of it as a nightmare.

(Spot out on them. Spot up on C, D, and E as witches.)

C: How much longer will he remain trapped?

D: It won't be much longer now.

E: Has he discovered that he's trapped?

D: He's in the process of discovering it right now.

C: So it won't take much longer.

D: It's a powerful dream that's trapped him. It's the oldest and most powerful dream of all. An air bubble full of evil mouths, greedy thoughts, and beasts in human skin. And he's still trapped in it—caught in a bubble.

E: Dream must fight dream.

C: Image must break image.

D: Send him more dreams, sister, send him more dreams.

E: Let us burst the hard-skinned, evil bubble in which he is trapped.

C: Because if one person can make a difference by breaking free . . .

(Spot out on them. Spot up on H. He is alone. He twinges as if in pain. Has he been struck by an arrow? He gets up slowly and as though in a dream. He wanders about. Sound: soft dream music.)

H: I'm looking for a door, but I can only find windows—small, large, round, oblong, square . . . windows with golden frames and baroque angels at the corners, windows with stained glass, leaded glass and thermopane . . . I have nothing against windows. I've always liked windows. But today I'm looking for a door. *(F enters stage left; she too is a dream figure. She stands with her back to the audience and seems to be looking in/out through a window. H continues without a break.)* For hours I've walked from window to window . . . They're all different. Each window presents a new picture, each window looks out upon—or, perhaps, out into—something else. *(Gesticulates wildly.)* That's all well and good. There's nothing wrong with it. I love windows. But today I'm looking for a door. *(Discovers F.)* Hey, do you know if there's a door anywhere around here? *(F doesn't reply and doesn't turn around. H gets closer to her.)* I said: do you know if there's a door anywhere around here? *(F slowly turns around. She holds a mask before her face. It's the mask of a skull.)*

F: Which window shall we talk about today? *(H doesn't answer. He turns around in resignation and slowly walks away from her. F calls after him.)* What's the matter? You've always been content with windows. Don't you like windows anymore? . . . *(H doesn't respond.)* I found a new window today. I'm sure it will interest you—it's brown and mauve, with little circles of orange and burgundy. It's a happy window. *(Spot on F. Normal light up on H. The dream is over.)*

H: (*To himself.*) I don't know if I'm looking out or in. I'm probably locked up . . . (*long pause*) or locked out. (*G enters as the corpse thief.*)

G: I hear you're looking for work.

H: (*Without expression.*) Yes.

G: Perhaps you too want to save up for a bike.

H: (*Without expression.*) Yes. I want to save up for a bike.

G: Come with me then. I have work for you. With me you'll have something to get your hands on. It's hard work, but I pay well. I'm sure we'll easily come to terms about your wages. (*G puts his arm around H's shoulders and leads him offstage. At the same time B, C, D, E, and F enter, wearing motorcylce suits and helmets that hide their faces. They come in from all directions and move slowly—like a ritual procession. The music underscores the sacred tone of the occasion. A, as the priest, walks in. The bikers kneel for him and make the sign of the cross. They get up. They remind us of Crusaders.*)

A: I greet you in the name of Jesus to this Saturday's first heat. The blessings of God and of holy St. Christopher on all of you. After the service you will have a chance to buy these small medallions. (*Shows them.*) One side has the picture of St. Christopher embossed on it—he's the patron saint and protector of all travelers. It's a nice piece and the edition is limited. For a small fee you can also have your bikes blessed—in the name of St. Christopher and the Holy Virgin . . . and holy water will be sprinkled over your gearbox and your breaks. (*Changes his voice.*) Today marks a turning point in the lives of everyone of you. It's a day you have looked forward to with great anticipation and happiness. And now it has arrived! And I want you to know that we are proud of you. All of us who belong to an older generation are proud of you. For you are the kind of young people a nation needs. (*The sound of the motorcycle engines starts. At first, softly, but it grows louder until it drowns out A. As the sound increases the light fades. A continues.*) Young people who have a goal. Young people who know what they want. Who want to get ahead in the world. Who are determined to move up and ahead. Who want to accept their share of the responsibility for society. Who want to forge ahead—(*The sound of the motorcycles drowns him out. The stage is now in darkness. For a while we continue to hear the loud and nerve-racking sound of the bikes.*)

Act II

(Darkness. Sound: roar of crowd in waves and breakers, as at a soccer match; noise of howling motorcycles and screaming brakes. Slowly light comes up to the level of dusk. The noise of crowd and race grows faint and distant. Instead, we hear the sound of wind, soft weeping and faraway screams. Two dark shadows—H and G—move across the stage. They each carry a gunny sack. Now and then they bend down and pick up the remnants of crashed motorcycles: a handlebar, a seat, a pedal, etc.)

G: *(The corpse robber.)* Junk, nothing but junk, But everything can be sold. You'll see, it's money easily earned.

H: But what about the people who sat on the bikes?

G: Blown to smithereens, most of them. If we're lucky we may find one of them.

H: Did you say "lucky"?

G: Hush! *(They listen—and hear someone moaning.)* Come again, my boy . . . He's lying in our territory. He can't be that far away either.

H: Is he badly hurt?

G: That's got nothing to do with us.

H: But shouldn't we help him?

G: Get on with your job.

(Spot up on B, a young, injured motorcyclist. He is lying on the ground, whimpering softly. G and H bend over him. G immediately begins to search through his pockets.)

H: (*To B.*) Are you in a lot of pain? (*To G.*) You can't do that sort of thing.

G: I can't?

H: It's theft. It's—

G: Look, I pay you to help me. Now take his wristwatch—if he's got one. Listen and make sure it's still running.

H: We must take him to a doctor. He's badly hurt.

G: (*Rifles through a wallet.*) What a niggardly wallet! $120. Small pickings.

B: Help me.

G: Shut up and don't move.

H: (*To B.*) Where does it hurt most?

B: Here . . . in the side . . . Am I bleeding?

G: Like a pig. (*To H.*) Has he got a wedding ring? If it's gold, take it off him. (*Begins to pull off B's boots; B moans and twists.*) Use the knife if you can't get it off any other way—(*He has pulled off one of B's boots.*)

H: Will you stop doing that!

B: Call a doctor, please.

G: (*To H.*) You're grown up now, my boy. This is not kid's play. This is hard work.

H: You didn't tell me it'd involve anything like this.

G: I thought you wanted a bike.

H: Not at any price, I don't.

G: What's wrong with this job? It's just as good as any other.

H: It's plain robbery!

G: (*Has succeeded in pulling off B's other boot and gets up to confront H defiantly.*) Okay, so it's robbery. I'm a corpse robber. So what?

H: I want nothing to do with it.

G: Oh, you've got a conscience, eh? You're one of those who can afford the luxury of a conscience, are you? (*Shakes H.*) You listen to me. Those up there—you hear them roar with approval? You think they're any better than us? Don't we all live off that mountain? Isn't it the same apples we harvest?

H: He has died.

G: (*Takes his hands off H.*) So much the better for us. (*Bends over B again. Spot out on G and H. Spot up on C, D, and E who are peering into the auditorium through binoculars as though they were watching a horse race. The sound of the bike is louder now.*)

E: Fascinating.

C: You see the blue one up there—on the yellow bike?

E: He won't make it through another two curves.

D: You want to bet?

C: I bet fifty dollars that he will.

E: The princess is pretty today. She's smiling all the time. How long has she been sitting there?

C: He's managed one curve!

D: That was very close—oh!

E: It must be strenuous to smile for such a long time. It can't always be easy to be royalty.

C: Come on—faster!

D: There he is—going into the next curve!

C: Watch out! It's all loose gravel!

D: He's too far over to make it.

C: Come on, come on!

E: And she holds those three golden apples as graciously as any ballerina.

C: Take it easy now! . . . Now give it all you've got and you'll clear the curve!

D: He'll never make it.

C: He made it!

E: It's an aesthetic thrill to watch her.

D: Dammit! I never thought he'd make it.

C: You owe me fifty dollars.

D: He's falling! Look—he's losing control of the bike.

C: But we agreed on two curves. You owe me fifty dollars.

D: His mouth is wide open. He's probably screaming like hell.

C: We're too far away to get the benefit of that.

E: I hear they're thinking of installing microphones by the side of the road.

D: Now he's falling! Hell's bells! Couldn't he have crashed twenty yards further down?

C: (*Consoles her.*) Next time you'll win!

E: How many are left?

D: That was the last man in the first heat. There'll be a short inter-mission. They've got to clean up and spread sawdust.

E: It's well organized.

C: Let's go in and get a drink. It's cold standing around out here.

E: Yes, we don't want to catch our death out here. (*Spot out on them. Spot up on G and H.*)

H: You killed him.

G: He died all by himself.

H: We could've helped him.

G: It was those up there who killed him.

H: But you're as much to blame.

G: Look, we're down here . . . All we do is pick up the crumbs from the cream cakes of the rich. (*He laughs loudly.*) Dammit, you could at least smile a little. (*They hear moaning close by.*)

G: Another one! This is our lucky day. (*A lies in a blue suit, twisted beyond recognition on the ground.*)

H: Lucky?

(*Spot out on them. Spot up on C, D, and E downstage. E has a hand puppet in his right hand. C has two hand puppets, one in each hand. They are the same puppets which were used in the first act.*)

D: Intermission time between the first and second heat! While the bikes are being blessed and the workmen are washing the blood off the slopes and spreading sawdust on the red gravel, the leaders of the nation talk. (*She withdraws.*)

C: (*Lifts up the puppet in her left hand.*) I am the architect.

E: (*Lifts up her puppet.*) I'm the director of tourism.

C: (*Lifts up the puppet in her right hand.*) I'm the owner of the hotel.

E: (*Puppet.*) My compliments to the architect. The mountain is really in excellent slippery condition today.

C: (*Right hand.*) And my compliments to the director of tourism. The organization is splendid. Really outstanding.

E: (*Puppet.*) Thank you, thank you. One does one's best.

C: (*Right hand.*) The hotel is completely booked up. And the credit for that belongs to you. Yes, to you alone!

E: (*Puppet.*) But friends, dear friends—

(*Spot out on them. Spot up on H and G who are bent over the twisted figure of A. B enters, dressed as a grotesque corpse robber.*)

B: I saw him first.

G: What are you talking about? He's lying in my territory, isn't he?

B: No, in mine.

G: Since when is this your territory?

A: Help me, please. (*H kneels by his side and puts his head in his lap.*)

B: We can share him.

G: So you admit that this is my territory.

B: I offer to share.

G: You'd never share with me if he were lying in your territory.

B: You take what's below the belt, I take what's above.

G: (*To H.*) Check his teeth! Does he have good fillings?

B: It's a fair offer.

G: (*Suddenly swings a club.*) Go to hell! (*B withdraws, snarling like an animal.*)

H: (*Partly to himself.*) Whenever I dream of the princess I see a shadow behind her. A dark, ominous shadow.

G: What the hell are you blathering about?

H: She's never alone. There's always a shadow close to her.

G: Shut up!

H: I've never told anyone about this.

G: Get on with your job. We don't have all eternity. (*H gets up.*) What d'you think you're doing?

H: (*Tired.*) I'm not going on with this.

G: Oh, you're not going on with this, are you? Well, I'll teach you to go on. (*He puts down his club and pulls out a knife to cut A's throat.*) But first we'll cut short this poor fellow's pain.

H: No!

G: He's as good as dead already. If you find a wounded animal it's your duty to kill it.

H: He's not an animal.

G: (*Sneering.*) I hope you can bear to see a little blood. (*H hits G over the head with the club just as G is about to cut A's throat. He drops the club and stands there completely helpless.*)

F: (*Comes storming in as the wife of the corpse robber.*) You killed him! I saw you kill him! You killed him in cold blood. (*Screams.*) Murderer! (*Attacks H with hands raised.*) Murderer! (*H avoids her and runs off. Black out. Spot up on D and E, two maids in the palace.*)

D: There's no doubt that it was murder.

E: In cold blood.

D: And the poor man's wife stood there and saw it happen!

E: Right before her very eyes!

D: Do they have any children?

E: We knew all along that there was something wrong with that boy.

D: We knew it all along.

C: (*Joins them.*) How many died today?

D: Thirty, I think. (*To E.*) Wasn't it thirty in the race?

C: It was a fine race.

E: Yes, it's fun when everything goes according to plan.

D: But isn't that awful about—

C: Have they caught him?

D: Not yet. But they will. For sure.

E: There's no place for him to hide.

D: No one'll hide a murderer.

(*Spot out on them. Spot up on F and H. F is sitting on a bed; H is hiding under it. F gets up abruptly as the spot comes on.*)

F: Oh my! A man under my bed! There's a man under my bed.

H: (*Stays under the bed.*) Hush!

F: How did you get in here? Do you know who I am?

H: You are Princess Irmelin. I was once in love with you.

F: You were? And now?

H: I was in love with your picture. I never knew you.

F: But you haven't given up yet, I see. That's why you're under my bed.

H: Perhaps it wasn't even your picture—

F: (*No longer afraid, she's enjoying the situation.*) Not even my picture? What was it then?

H: I fell in love with my own dream of power and pride. You were just a symbol for it.

F: Thanks. Do I look like a symbol?

H: You're just as beautiful as they say you are.

F: But you don't love me any longer?

H: No.

F: Do you know . . . you're the oddest young man I've ever had under my bed.

H: I've come to warn you.

F: (*Laughs.*) So that's why you're here. I was wondering about that, but I thought it might be considered impolite of me to ask. So you've come to warn me. What's your name?

H: There's always a shadow behind you. Whenever I dream of you . . . And in your pictures.

F: For a moment I was hopeful that you'd come to seduce me . . .

H: I don't know what the shadow represents. I don't know who it is.

F: It gets quite boring here sometimes.

H: All I know is that it's always very close to you. That's why I came here. To see if it's just something in my dreams.

F: Do you often have dreams like that?

H: It's not a dream.

F: You mean the shadow is here now.

H: Gray and fuzzy. Difficult to make out. Without a definite shape. But he's here. I know that he's here. (*F laughs. Spot out on F and H. Spot up on E, D, and C, dressed as maids. B comes rolling in as the king's fool.*)

D: Have they caught him?

B: Not yet. But they will, they will.

E: Everybody is talking about him. What does he look like? Is he dashing?

B: He looks like most fools

D: Has he had any more dreams?

B: He dreams all the time. And he throws them to the winds. Tells them to anyone who'll listen.

C: Tell us about them!

B: They're his dreams, not mine.

C: Tell us anyway.

B: They say he calls on people to break into stores.

E: Is that true?

B: They say he incites them to rob as many stores as they can.

D: You're lying.

B: I'm just saying what people say that he says.

E: (*To D.*) Hush!

B: Apparently he tells people to steal only superfluous goods and luxury items, like mink coats, jewels, and electric toothbrushes. Carry all this junk into a small park, he says, and hang the jewels in the trees, wrap the mink and sealskin coats around the tree trunks and plant the flower beds with electric toothbrushes. Spread Persian carpets on the grass. And then put up signs: Do Not Climb Up The Fur Coats! Do Not Pick The Electric Toothbrushes! Do Not Walk On The Persian Carpets!

D: Are you just making this up?

B: He says that in this way a lot of so-called "valuables" which are really worthless can give people a little happiness and thus acquire at least some "value." (*A enters. He was listening.*)

A: (*As a minister.*) It certainly looks as if you had a competitor, my dear fool. (*B laughs suddenly and stupidly, ringing his bells.*) He is more brazen than you. The question is: is he too brazen for a fool? (*Looks B coldly in the eye.*) And . . . will he be content to play the fool? And . . . is there room for two fools? (*B lowers his eyes, he can no longer endure A's stare.*) With you we know where we're at. (*Spot out on them. Spot up on F and H. H is still under the bed.*)

F: (*Laughs.*) You are a fool. Don't misunderstand me. I like fools.

H: You shouldn't laugh about a fool.

F: Should I cry about you?

H: A fool tells the truth.

F: But isn't a fool someone you're supposed to laugh about?

H: He is the alibi society needs.

F: I don't understand.

H: You've eradicated all opposition. Eliminated it—except for one opponent. And him you've put on a regular salary. (*Mimics.*) In this country everybody can say what he likes—we have a fool to prove it! We live in a free country—we have a fool to prove it!

F: And the fool? Why does he play the part?

H: At first he doesn't. At first he's genuine. He means what he says.

He fights to convince others . . . But step by step . . .

F: Step by step he realizes that he's mistaken.

H: He bangs his head against the wall and hopes his head is the stronger of the two . . . but usually it's the wall . . .

F: And so he gives up. (*Tries to kiss him.*) Hmm. You're a sweet fool!

H: (*Draws away; stares frightened in front of himself.*) It's not that he wants to struggle all by himself. But he can't get anyone to follow him . . . Everybody laughs at everything he says . . . When a dream is looked upon as a joke for long enough it becomes a joke, even for the dreamer . . . That's the fate of the fool.

F: And he gets well paid for it. Don't forget that. He gets well paid. (*Spot out on H and F. Spot up on G, sitting on his horse, and A, the minister, who stands next to him.*)

G: What on earth is all this prattle about a shadow? Has he begun to see ghosts now as well?

A: The man is unpredictable, Your Majesty. He knows not what he does nor what he says.

G: Get a hold of him. Put him behind bars and lock him up.

A: We're doing our best, Your Majesty.

G: Dammit all, the man is positively dangerous.

A: He has already killed once, Your Majesty.

G: We know that. We were informed.

A: But I'm not concerned about the lies he's spreading everywhere.

G: Yes, exactly. That's our primary concern too.

A: My main concern is the effect he might have on young, impressionable minds.

G: Dammit, that's exactly what worries us. (*Pause.*) In the old days . . . in the old days something like this would never have happened.

A: It would have been unthinkable, Your Majesty. (*Spot out on A and G. Spot up on H and F.*)

H: It wasn't my fault.

F: They call you a murderer.

H: I had no choice.

F: Then there's only one way out.

H: What is that?

F: Reach the top of the glass mountain.

H: I can't.

F: If you reach the top you have nothing to fear. You can do what you like. No one can touch you.

H: I don't have a bike.

F: I'll give you one.

H: I don't want to reach the top.

F: You don't want to? (*Spot out on H and F. Spot up on A and G.*)

G: We've never heard of anyone who didn't want to. Isn't that what they all want?

A: He tries to talk people out of wanting it.

G: But how are we supposed to function? What'll happen to society if no one wants to try anymore? (*Pause.*) We don't understand any of this.

A: I think people are more sensible than that, Your Majesty.

G: Let's hope so!

A: But the ideas he's spreading could poison the system.

G: Personally we've never been able to understand economics . . .

A: Your Majesty has been an outstanding king. (*Bows. Spot out on A and G. Spot up on H and F.*)

F: And you're determined not to.

H: I'm neither able to nor do I want to. Not any longer.

F: Not even if I promise to help you? (*H is silent.*) I have connections. People who can direct you all around the corners and up all the steep slopes, provide you with studded tires and winged feet if you need them. (*H is silent.*) Give you elbows as sharp as knives . . . (*With a different, colder voice.*) You know they're looking for you.

H: I know.

F: You know that I cannot hide you here forever.

H: I know.

F: And still you're saying "No" to my offer? (*H nods.*) Many men have asked for my hand. You're the first one I've encouraged. And you say "No"? (*H doesn't reply, looks down; F claps her hands and calls.*) Take him away! (*D and E, as guards, enter from both sides of the stage. Spot out. Spot up on G who is still sitting on his horse; he is alone.*)

G: If only I could understand what this is all about . . . Isn't everything just fine? Aren't we all happy? Don't we live in a society where everybody can create a future for himself, all according to his wishes and his efforts? (*B rolls in, ringing his bells and laughing idiotically.*) Isn't that true? Isn't that true, fool? (*B just laughs louder.*) I've never been able to get a sensible word out of you.

B: You're troubled, brother.

G: You're damned right I'm troubled. And it's your job to cheer me up. Come on, play the fool and make me laugh.

B: Dear brother.

G: Don't call me brother.

B: But aren't we brothers?

G: That was a long time ago.

B: My poor dear little brother—you're afraid someone'll smash your splendid glass mountain . . .

G: I'm not thinking of myself.

B: (*Smacks his lips in sympathy.*) Of course not. You've never done that, little brother, you've never done that.

G: Everything we are . . . everything we have we owe to the glass mountain.

B: (*Mocking.*) Give us today our daily bread, oh mountain. Let the young and hopeful come unto you, oh mighty mountain. Lead them into temptation, for thine is the kingdom, the power and the glory—

G: No one mocks the mountain!

B: I am not mocking the mountain. (*Bitter.*) But I'm part of all this, am I not?

G: (*Evil and content.*) You're part of it. But you've lost.

B: I lost.

G: It's made you bitter and envious.

B: It's made me bitter and envious. (*Suddenly laughs idiotically again, ringing his bells like a madman. Just as suddenly and abruptly he is normal again, observing in an ice-cold voice.*) I lost, I'm a loser. You won, you're a winner. There are many losers, we're numerous. There are few winners, you are rare. (*Pause.*) I am a fool. (*Abruptly turns to G.*) Take it easy, brother.

G: And stop calling me "brother" all the time.

B: As you like—brother. (*Rings his bells. Spot out on B and G. Spot up on C, D, and E as witches.*)

E: Where is he now?

D: He's in jail. This is his last night in jail.

C: Is he afraid?

D: No, he's not afraid . . . And a priest is visiting him. (*Spot out on C, D, and E. Spot up on A, as a priest, and H, now a prisoner.*)

H: I don't need a priest.

A: You need peace.

H: I'm not looking for peace, I'm looking for answers.

A: You've killed another human being.

H: That's my responsibility and my burden.

A: God'll lift the burden from you.

H: Is there forgiveness for everything?

A: For everything.

H: Go away.

A: You're still plagued by evil dreams, I hear.

H: Who says they're evil?

A: God can take them away from you.

H: Can God also take away shadows?

A: That depends what kind of shadows they are. The devil and those who've sold themselves to him are supposed to have no shadow.

H: I'm not talking about that kind of shadow.

A: What kind of shadow d'you mean then?

H: In the beginning it was hazy, obscure and vague. But now I see it clearly—all the time.

A: There's something wrong with your eyes.

H: And I ask you, Father—can God take away that shadow?

A: He can heal your eyes.

H: So that I don't see it any longer. No, thank you.

A: I don't see these shadows.

H: But I do.

A: There's something the matter with your eyes.

H: What if there's something the matter with your eyes?

A: I see what everybody else sees. And everybody else—we don't see these shadows you talk about. I tell you they exist only in your head.

H: They're not shadows—it's the same shadow all the time. The same shadow behind everybody.

A: God can give you peace.

H: By putting a screen over my eyes.

A: If that's best for you.

H: Leave me alone!

A: I'll be just outside—praying for you. (*He withdraws. At the same time B rolls in. He stops right behind H. H turns around slowly. B is serious.*)

H: What d'you want? Have you come to pester me too?

B: I've come to say goodbye. (*Spot out on them. Spot up on C, D, and E as witches.*)

E: Has he come to say goodbye?

D: That's what he says.

C: But does he mean it?

E: Or is this another temptation?

C: Is it another easy way out?

E: Another excuse?

D: He's taking off his foolscap . . . and he puts it on the young man's head. (*Spot out on them. Spot up on B and H. B has taken off his foolscap with the bells. He now puts it on H's head as though he were crowning him king.*)

H: Why are you doing this? (*B is quiet and serious.*) It's you who's the fool.

B: Not any longer.

H: I've never asked to wear a foolscap. (*Spot out on B and H. Spot up on C, D and E as witches.*)

C: And what is he answering?

D: He's just laughing.

E: He's laughing?

D: He says: Now you're the king's brother.

E: (*A soft chant.*) Now you're the king's brother.

D: He says: Now you're a drop of rain.

C: (*A soft chant.*) The drop of rain that'll someday pierce the mountain. (*Spot out on them. Spot up on B and H.*)

H: And you?

B: I'll change my clothes.

H: But tomorrow . . . tomorrow I may be condemned to death.

B: That's the luck of the draw. But listen to me now. Here is the message we fools pass on to each other. We take care of it and spread it like a fable to all who have the courage to listen: no one has ever climbed to the top of the mountain.

H: No one?

B: They see to that.

H: And the king?

B: He's no Cinderella. His crown is inherited. He's never made it from the bottom up.

H: But Cinderella—

B: Belongs in a fairy-tale . . . a fairy-tale the rich tell the poor to keep them happy and encourage them to go on.

H: And the princess?

B: She's a puppet. Without life. A machine. A rented whore. Forget about her.

H: But everyone believes—

B: Because they want us to believe.

H: But they believe it themselves! The king believes it!

B: Those in power always believe in their own myths. That's how they justify themselves and their actions, and buy themselves sleep and rest at night.

H: But the glass mountain . . . I've seen it with my own eyes.

B: The glass mountain is the only thing that's real. Smash it to pieces! (*Spot out on B and H. Spot up on G and his horse. D and E are shrubs. C works the wind machine. A ''runs'' alongside the horse. Sound: gallop on soft forest trail with bullfinch and lark.*)

G: Where the hell is dinner? (*Waves his rifle about.*) What do we have to choose from? Come on, come on! What's on the menu? Let's at least have the menu! (*To A.*) There's no order in anything anymore.

(*C comes running in, knees up the to the chin; she carries a sheep's head on a pole.*)

C: Sheep, Your Majesty. For God's sake: sheep!

G: Is there no choice?

C: (*Shakes her head and imitates a sheep.*) Ba-a-a-a . . .

G: (*To A.*) We hate shooting sheep. (*Aims and fires.*)

C: Did Your Majesty hit it? Was it a hit?

G: We didn't have any choice, did we. (*To A.*) We didn't have any choice.

(*F, the princess, comes running in normally.*)

F: (*To G.*) You'll have to talk to your fool. He's gone completely wild and crazy. You should see in what clothes he goes about now.

(*B rolls in. He is dressed in ordinary clothes, without any of the insignia of a fool.*)

B: In what clothes he drives about, Your Majesty. Not "goes." Drives.

G: Dammit, we're in the middle of our dinner hunt.

B: I've had a dream.

G: (*To A.*) He too? Dammit all, is this contagious? (*To B.*) It's years since you've had anything at all.

A: (*To B.*) You mean: you've heard about a dream.

B: (*Smiles.*) I *had* a dream.

F: Just as I told you.

G: (*To F.*) This has nothing to do with you.

F: Then listen to what he says.

B: The world is full of good stories.

G: The stories you tell, dammit, are rarely any good.

B: For instance, have you heard the story of the scoundrel who wanted to forge an old treasure-hunting map?

A: (*Vehemently.*) Have you come here only to—

B: (*Raises his hands defensively.*) I've told you many a story. But listen to this one now, because it may well be the last one I'll ever tell you.

A: We paid you well for your stories.

G: And what did we get in return? Nothing but nonsense!

B: (*Nods.*) I've come to the same conclusion.

F: You've been a most ungrateful fool.

B: No, no . . . it's no good flattering me any longer!

G: What would you have done without us?

A: You're so clever at attacking society, but it's our money that keeps you alive.

G: Without us you wouldn't have got as far as you have. And what have you given us in return?

F: Nothing but ingratitude!

B: It's no use.

A: And prejudices.

B: It's no use flattering me. This is the last story I'm going to tell. A dream, but I'll tell it as if it were a story.

A: (*To G.*) Let him finish it. Let him get it out of his system. (*The light narrows. A, C, D, and E exit in darkness as B continues his story. F and G are listening.*)

B: There was this certain scoundrel—I won't mention any name— who planned to forge an old treasure-hunting map. He was a wily devil, you can be sure of that. He got himself parchment, ink and a quill, and away he went. Now I can't remember if he drew a map that purported to show the way to El Dorado or to some ordinary pirate's treasure. Be that as it may, this scoundrel worked at his map day and night for weeks because he wanted it to be first class. He wanted it to be impossible for anyone to tell the difference between the map he drew and a genuine treasure-hunting map. So he really applied himself. It turned out to be a superb map. It was impossible to tell the difference between it and the genuine article. He himself couldn't tell the difference . . . And he admired his excellent map. It was as accurate and precise as any treasure-hunting map could be. So this character decided he wouldn't take a chance of letting it fall into other people's hands. And he went out to look for the treasure himself . . . That's the end of the story.

G: What the hell kind of stupid story is that?

B: That was a story about you, brother.

G: About me?

B: And now comes the moral.

G: I've heard enough!

B: You're allowed to run around and take care of your damned treasure.

G: Will you be quiet!

B: And, dear brother—

G: Quiet, I say! (*Raises his rifle.*)

B: You're also allowed to hoodwink anyone you can.

G: Shut up! (*Aims at B.*) We command you to shut up!

B: But if you think—

G: I'm going to shoot!

B: But if you think I'm going to go on walking around carrying your spade—

G: I'm counting to three. One!

B: —then—

G: Two!

B: You're sadly mistaken. (*G shoots. B is thrown backward. He gets up from his wheelchair and stands on his own two legs. He is fatally wounded.*) This is meant as a resignation from my job. (*He collapses.*)

(*Black out. Drums. B and the wheelchair are removed in the dark. The prompter also leaves her place in the dark. She has been sitting in plain view of the audience throughout the play. So that she was practically part of the set. Now C takes her place. The prompter was dressed like a fragile, little old woman. C wears the same costume. The audience is not to notice the exchange. The light slowly comes up again. F and G, as the princess and the king, are on thrones. A and B, completely unrecognizable, and D and E enter as ragged, down and out, angry invalids, as if after motorcycle accidents. They are bandaged and walk oncrutches. Now H also enters slowly. He is serious and quiet. He is wearing the foolscap on his head.*)

A/B/D/E: Hang him!

A: Wring his neck!

G: Now, now . . .

D/E: (*Spit on H.*) Phooey!

D: (*Moving closer to H.*) You think you're so much better than the rest of us.

E: You think you know everything better than us.

A: But we haven't asked for your help.

E: If you didn't like our mountain, you could've gone somewhere else.

B: We didn't ask you to come here.

E: You could've gone to the prairies.

B: We could've seen how you'd like it there!

G: Now, now . . .

A/B/D/E: Let him swing!

G: (*Quiets them with his hands.*) We all know what the mountain means— —for society as a whole—for each of us individually.

F: If there's anyone who wants to bring charges against this man, let us hear them now.

(*This is what happens in the following scene: The actors must appear to need the help of the prompter. She raises her voice more and more. This creates the sense of an echo. It looks as if the actors need more and more help. But slowly the audience realizes that the prompter is not so much helping as directing and dominating them. They say what she wants them to say. This should also be built up visually. The gray, little old prompter literally grows. She casts a larger and larger shadow. At the end she towers over them like a giant. While she is growing larger, the actors look as if they were growing smaller and smaller. At the end they're without a will of their own, like marionettes. A steps forward.*)

C: (*Whispers.*) My whole life.
A: My whole life I've tried to be a good citizen.
C: I tried.
A: I tried to do my duty.
C: But now comes this . . . this . . .
C: Agitator.
A: Agitator . . . and mocks everything I've stood for.
C: Everything.
A: Everything I've believed in.
C: Hang him.
A: Hang him.

(*D steps forward.*)

C: Nothing is good enough.
D: Nothing is good enough for him.
C: It seems.
D: It seems.
C: It's not good enough.
D: It's not good enough for him—what we have.
C: What we stand for.
D: What we stand for.
C: Hang him.
D: Hang him.

(*B steps forward.*)

C: He wants to turn.
B: He wants to turn everything upside down.
C: Twist.
B: Twist and turn everything.
C: But we're proud.
B: But we're proud of our mountain.
C: And we won't.
B: And we won't bloody well tolerate.
C: That a malcontent and agitator.
B: That a malcontent and agitator.
C: Throws shit.
B: Throws shit at what we enjoy.

C: Hang him.

B: Hang him.

H: But it's for your sake.

C: Quiet!

G: Quiet!

H: It's entirely for your sake.

C: Will you be quiet this instant!

F: Will you be quiet this instant!

H: But look at yourselves! Just look at yourselves! What good has the mountain done you? What has it ever given you? Who profits from your unhappiness?

C: He must wait.

G: (*Roars.*) He must wait till it's his turn.

C: Here we like things.

G: Here we like things to proceed in a more or less orderly fashion.

(*E steps forward.*)

C: He says.

E: He says it's for your own sake.

C: But how can we.

E: But how can we know that he's telling the truth?

C: Isn't it rather.

E: Isn't it rather that.

C: He has his own.

E: He has his own nest to feather.

C: Isn't he merely.

E: Isn't he merely out to find a shortcut to the top?

C: Just for himself.

E: Just for himself!

H: That's not true.

C: Don't listen to him!

H: I just want to help you.

A: Help us?

C: Have we.

A: Have we asked for your help?

C: No.

A: No.

C: So dammit all.

A: So dammit all.

C: We'll make it.

B: We'll make it on our own.

C: Without you interfering.

D: Without you interfering.

F: You're a fool!

C: Hang him.

A/B/D/E: Hang him!

F: You're a fool. And you didn't mean a word you said. It was all for fun, isn't that right? It was all to amuse us. (*H is silent.*) You didn't mean what you said. Isn't that right?

G: Did you mean what you said? (*H is silent.*) Wasn't it just a lot of crazy dreams. (*H is silent.*)

C: We'll give you.

G: We'll give you a chance.

F: It was just for fun, wasn't it? Say that you didn't mean it.

(*A, B, D, and E now have two hand puppets each. They hold them high in the air. The light is adjusted so that we see only the hand puppets and not those who hold them.*)

C: Hang him.

A/B/D/E: (*As hand puppets.*) Hang him!

F: It was just something you made up. (*To G.*) You see he's wearing a foolscap. He's a fool, isn't he. (*To H.*) You want to be the new fool? We need a new fool . . .

C: And we always.

F: And we always make an exception for a fool.

(*A, B, D, and E point at H and laugh. Silence. H looks around. Then he slowly takes the foolscap off his head and places it carefully on the ground. Without a word.*)

C: (*Suddenly and sharply.*) Hang him!

A/B/D/E: Hang him!

H: I am not a fool.

F: Are you sure?

H: I have made my decision.

F: You know what that means, don't you?

C: You must be held.

G: You must be held responsible for all you've said and done.

C: Hang him.

A/B/D/E: Hang him!

C: Hold it.

F: Hold it!

C: He still has.

F: He still has a chance.

G: What chance?

C: If he manages to ride to the top of the glass mountain.

C: And fetch.

F: And fetch the three golden apples.

C: Then he is free.

F: Then he is free.

C: And nobody.

F: And nobody will harm him.

H: I don't want to.

F: You could try, couldn't you.

C: He doesn't want to.

A: He doesn't want to.

B: But it was good enough for us.

C: But he doesn't want to.

D: But he doesn't want to.

C: But he shall.

B: But he shall!

G: It's only fair and just.

C: You have no.

G: You have no choice. (*D and E roll in on a motorcycle.*)

C: Sit on it.

G: Sit on it. (*A and B force H to sit on the motorcycle.*)

C: Look at us.

A: Look at us.

C: We've tried.

D: We've tried our best.

C: We've done.

A: We've done our best. And that's all we ask of you.

C: Tie him to the handlebars.

G: Tie him to the handlebars. (*B ties H hands to the handlebars.*)

C: Push.

G: Push.

C: Him.

G: Him.

C: To the start.

G: To the start.

C: (*Points.*)

G: (*Points.*)

C: Have you anything.

G: Have you anything else to say to us? (*H is silent. A and D push the motorcycle with H on it offstage. The others follow them. C stays behind alone. She has risen and now towers like a dark and ominous shadow of war over the stage. The light fades out on everything except her. Sound: motorcycle engine starts up. Engine noise. The noise moves away. While C stands there without moving, a threatening figure, we hear the voices of C, D, and E over the loudspeaker. They are the three "witches" talking to each other again.*)

E: Is he the one who was supposed to come?

D: He's the one who was supposed to come.

C: But nothing has changed. He didn't change anything. (*The light goes out on C, the prompter. A spot comes up that is focused solely on the foolscap lying on the ground. The rest of the stage is black.*)

D: (*Without a break.*) You just think so.

C: I just think so?

D: You just think so.

END

And The Birds Are Singing Again

a radio drama for human voices and music
in 10 pictures

by

Ulla Ryum

Translated from the Danish by Per K. Brask

CHARACTERS:

1st Soldier—an elderly woman
2nd Soldier—a young woman
3rd Soldier—a young man
Martha
Dora
Kaj Hugo
Werner

TIME: The play is set in a future which is probably not too distant.

PLACE: An amusement park in the woods not far from a big city.

1st. Picture: Arrival as planned
2nd Picture: The search for the white box and its retrieval
3rd Picture: The playback of the tape begins at 4:00 p.m. that afternoon
4th Picture: The evening is warm
5th Picture: Expectations
6th Picture: Recognition
7th Picture: Confirmation
8th Picture: The dew will soon fall
9th Picture: Birds in the night
10th Picture: The earth emits fragrances

1st Picture: Arrival as planned

(*We hear a driving truck. It shifts gears, slows down, speeds up.*)

3rd SOLDIER: Are we there already—I thought it'd take longer.

2nd SOLDIER: Longer! Why didn't we fly all the way instead of being holed up in this damned truck?

1st SOLDIER: It's not far from here. We're about halfway there, I think. We must be going up a hill. (*The truck shifts from a lower to a higher gear.*) We need the best possible protective equipment, that's why we're going by truck.

3rd SOLDIER: I've never been on an assignment like this—we're going up a hill?

2nd SOLDIER: Why aren't we allowed to look out the windows till we reach our destination?

1st SOLDIER: For security reasons.

3rd SOLDIER: I'd like to take a look. I can't wait to see what it looks like.

2nd SOLDIER: You'll have to. Our assignment calls for "closed envelope" —code telex.

1st SOLDIER: We'll be the first ones out there.

3rd SOLDIER: I'm sorry. It's just that I came directly from the catering corps and I'm not used to your methods of work. I wonder what the landscape is like.

2nd SOLDIER: Nothing special. Nothing to see. Not even the drivers can know the territory inside a security zone. They use radar and equipment like that.

1st SOLDIER: Human vision is fallable.

2nd SOLDIER: Don't talk so much, eh!

3rd SOLDIER: I'm sorry.

1st SOLDIER: No need to apologize, we've all been carefully chosen for this assignment.

3rd SOLDIER: I'm very proud to have been chosen as 3rd soldier.

2nd SOLDIER: You needn't be. We're all simply doing our duty.

1st SOLDIER: We're here. Notation: May 4, 2006 at 1500 hours. We will arrive as planned in three and a half minutes. (*The truck is heard clearly. It slows down, stops.*)

2nd SOLDIER: The lights on! (*The cabin door is closed with a heavy thud— the sound of a heavy and well-insulated door.*)

3rd SOLDIER: Is it still dangerous? I mean, how long ago was it?

1st SOLDIER: This area was cleaned out ten years ago. There may be some residual radiation.

3rd SOLDIER: You must have been on an assignment like this before.

1st SOLDIER: I have—several times. And I've never experienced any erroneous reports about the level of radiation in an area. There are sometimes problems with accuracy in large cities because of forgotten pockets of poison for example. But this area isn't a city as far as I know.

3rd SOLDIER: What is it?

1st SOLDIER: I don't know.

3rd SOLDIER: Of course not. I'm sorry. It's incredible, isn't it?

1st SOLDIER: Incredible!? How?

3rd SOLDIER: Everything here has remained untouched, ready for use. When you take their level of technology into consideration . . .

1st SOLDIER: We have a signal from Number Two. We can move about without safety gear.

3rd SOLDIER: I'm really anxious to see it.

1st SOLDIER: Please remember to check your alarm watch regularly.

3rd SOLDIER: Is that necessary?

1st SOLDIER: I trust you've learned to use an alarm watch even though you're from catering.

3rd SOLDIER: I have . . . I attended a safety course—aren't you at all excited?

1st SOLDIER: About what? (*Sound of a door opening.*)

3rd SOLDIER: About the forest . . . What . . . used to be a forest!

1st SOLDIER: Move about with care. The clean-up detail has reported the possibility of mud slides as a result of rain. Apart from that everything is ready.

3rd SOLDIER: A large forest.

1st SOLDIER: Are you ready to receive your orders.

2nd & 3rd SOLDIERS: We're ready. (*An inaudible message on the radio is interrupted by 1st Soldier.*)

1st SOLDIER: Roger.

3rd SOLDIER: Now I've seen a real forest.

2nd SOLDIER: This isn't a tourist excursion! How long are we staying here?

1st SOLDIER: As long as it takes.

3rd SOLDIER: Does it really contain voices and sounds—sounds from their life? I mean, the white box.

2nd SOLDIER: Please calm down already.

1st SOLDIER: It contains a recording of life at this place during the last twelve hours of its existence.

2nd SOLDIER: Before the area was subjected to a total clean-up job.

3rd SOLDIER: What's my job here? I'm not in the humanities corps.

1st SOLDIER: Your task is to collect information about their food culture —about their general and their specific eating habits.

3rd SOLDIER: But I won't be able to understand what they're saying— on the tape, I mean.

2nd SOLDIER: Cool it now, number three. They speak Danish. That's why we were selected.

3rd SOLDIER: Incredible! Where are we! My parents have clear recollections of that country.

1st SOLDIER: We're at an amusement park outside what used to be the capital.

3rd SOLDIER: The capital! Incredible!

2nd SOLDIER: This area is going to be colonized and resettled.

1st SOLDIER: We know nothing about that. Number 2, you collect plant and earth samples. You will also take measurements of the least destroyed tree trunks so we can get an idea of the size and kind of the forest.

2nd SOLDIER: Yes, Ma'am.

3rd SOLDIER: Are they going to reconstruct the forest?

1st SOLDIER: I don't know. Do you have your equipment?

3rd SOLDIER: Yes. Amusement? In what way?

2nd SOLDIER: A kind of amusement which, as we have learned, morally undermined people and which broke down their ability to work.

1st SOLDIER: We don't know what. We are here to map out the area and to describe its usefulness. Firstly, we will find the white box. Secondly, we will research the whole area, draw a map of its present condition and form our own impression of the essence of the place before we listen to its last report.

2nd SOLDIER: Is it necessary for us to form our own impression of the place? I mean, the level of uncertainty . . . I just want to point out that it is an unscientific procedure, in particular where Number 3 is concerned.

1st SOLDIER: We are expected to report on our own impressions of the essence of this place. Your particular task concerns the forest.

2nd SOLDIER: Yes, ma'am!

3rd SOLDIER: I don't understand what you mean by "essence." No one has survived here.

2nd SOLDIER: See! Number 3's a mistake.

1st SOLDIER: Number 2, you've received your orders.

2nd SOLDIER: Yes, ma'am.

1st SOLDIER: Experience has shown that certain places—that is, certain smaller areas have proven to be unsuitable for their intended purpose because of the appearance of unidentifiable—that is of disturbances of undefinable character, either atmospheric or electronic in origin—or maybe something completely different.

3rd SOLDIER: Something unknown?

1st SOLDIER: Yes . . . a lot of scientific effort is being applied to discover and explain what it is.

2nd SOLDIER: Radiophonic influences . . .

1st SOLDIER: Perhaps. Maybe part of the explanation can be found in the way in which people have made use of the place in the course of time.

2nd SOLDIER: Nonsense!

3rd SOLDIER: But what are the symptoms? Cramps? Pain? Vomiting? Or a process of decay? Is everyone affected by the essence of a place?

2nd SOLDIER: Let us find the white box. Only humans are affected.

3rd SOLDIER: Is it related to eating habits?

1st SOLDIER: It's very hard to explain.

2nd SOLDIER: Then don't!

3rd SOLDIER: I have to ask.

2nd SOLDIER: Am I grateful to be in the biological and chemical sciences!

1st SOLDIER: It affects a person's mind.

3rd SOLDIER: That sounds horrible. Can you protect yourself against it? How about wearing a complete safety unit?

1st SOLDIER: That's why we enforce such a long strategic quarantine after being in areas where we suspect that social intercourse and emotions were more important to the people than material goods and scientifically quantifiable items were.

2nd SOLDIER: That's why we need the white box.

1st SOLDIER: Our selection gives us a great responsibility. We have been entrusted the task of listening to the recordings of life in this area and we shall prove ourselves worthy of that trust.

3rd SOLDIER: What do I do if my alarm watch registers changes?

2nd SOLDIER: Leave the spot you're in.

3rd SOLDIER: Do we have to work separately? Wouldn't we be safer if we worked together? I mean . . .

2nd SOLDIER: Let's get started.

1st SOLDIER: This way.

3rd SOLDIER: The forest must have been huge back then.

2nd SOLDIER: Calm down. Our own forest back home is just fine. The leaves never turn. They stay the same all the time.

3rd SOLDIER: Yes, but there's a different feeling to everything here— even the brush and the bushes seem alive in a different way.

2nd SOLDIER: What do you mean? Just look at it! It may have been alive once, but so what? It had no resistance.

3rd SOLDIER: Some of the plants have new shoots. (*Sound of a shovel digging into the earth.*)

2nd SOLDIER: It's that time of the year. The soil seems to be good.

1st SOLDIER: At the bottom of this hill lies the area which was originally constructed to look like a small town. (*Music. Distant noises as if from the amusement park Dyrehavsbakken.*)

2nd Picture: The search for the white box and its retrieval

3rd SOLDIER: A whole town filled with amusements!

1st SOLDIER: They sold food and little mementos—that is little items which made you remember the place when you looked at them later on. Little items like monkeys, trolls, flags, pictures of the wheel of fortune, the rollercoaster and women called singers. Items we have difficulty understanding the value of today.

2nd SOLDIER: All of it entirely without purpose. The well-functioning part of the population had many years previously declared the establishment a place of pure entertainment. Attendance was declining. It couldn't last.

3rd SOLDIER: Why?

2nd SOLDIER: The memory didn't last. All the many items you could buy to help you remember the joy or the experience the place was supposed to have given you, they didn't work.

3rd SOLDIER: I've read about the place. I believe my mother was here once as a child, but I'm not quite sure.

2nd SOLDIER: I'm glad it's all gone. It's such an unpleasant reminder of unrestrained consumption. I've never been able to comprehend it even when I read about it. It's hard to believe that this place was purged only ten years ago.

1st SOLDIER: Some places achieve historical status faster than others.

2nd SOLDIER: Everything eventually reaches a point of saturation after which the organism can't absorb any more.

1st SOLDIER: I don't think it's that simple.

3rd SOLDIER: Is it because you've had more training than us that you understand these things better.

1st SOLDIER: Maybe.

2nd SOLDIER: Of course it's because of her training. Number 1 has the best and most developed education possible in the humanities, that's why I listen to her. But I always double check the data and I'd advise you to do the same. Keep in mind that we represent the elite of the future!

3rd SOLDIER: That's always on my mind.

1st SOLDIER: This isn't an easy task. We'll help you, Number 3.

3rd SOLDIER: I'd appreciate that. Does that mean we'll stay close to one another?

2nd SOLDIER: I think that'd be best.

3rd SOLDIER: In an hour we'll take our energy allotment. We only received a triple combo when we left this morning. We will have used that up in an hour.

1st SOLDIER: Fine. Let's begin working right here.

3rd SOLDIER: What was here? It must have been a watch tower.

1st SOLDIER: On the map it is identified as a newspaper stand, used for the production and sale of ice cream cones.

2nd SOLDIER: Apparently sales were conducted on the east side.

1st SOLDIER: That's correct.

2nd SOLDIER: The street we seem to be following now is identified as the main street. What does that mean?

1st SOLDIER: It is known that many people considered this street as a kind of primary approach route.

2nd SOLDIER: A white box is usually located fairly centrally. Let's move toward the center.

3rd SOLDIER: There isn't much left. The houses and shacks must have been very small. They're completely useless.

2nd SOLDIER: This place should be torn down. Let's find that damned box.

1st SOLDIER: Watch out! The floor boards are rotten. (*They move into an empty, vaulted hall.*)

2nd SOLDIER: A space used for dancing. There are the remains of a platform here for the orchestra. I've seen this type of establishment in photos. Here's the exit to the kitchen.

3rd SOLDIER: Let me see. Electrical units. This is a perfect example of how impractically arranged everything was back then. And this wasn't even a place for the preparation of the very complicated meals we've studied in the history of cooking. This seems very primitive!

2nd SOLDIER: Look out! Those may be left over fragments from grenades.

3rd SOLDIER: No, those are pots and those are pans.

2nd SOLDIER: Pans? Are you sure? I think we'd better make certain that they aren't left over from a military operation.

3rd SOLDIER: This is my field of expertise. I know those are pans. They were used to heat up the meat from edible animals, birds, or fish.

1st SOLDIER: It does sound very cumbersome. However, I can prove the accuracy of Number 3's statement. The procedure was finally prohibited definitively everywhere because of the waste of resources it entailed . . . not to mention that fact that the animals by then were extinct.

2nd SOLDIER: I see! I prefer our system.

3rd SOLDIER: So do I. But it is fascinating to find out that everything was so different back then.

1st SOLDIER: They paid a great deal of attention to taste.

3rd SOLDIER: Yes, I know. Taste is always mentioned when you read books about the nutrients of the time.

2nd SOLDIER: Just imagine. Up until ten years ago people lived here in such a pointless and irresponsible manner. What is taste, actually?

3rd SOLDIER: I don't know. I don't understand its connection with food and nutrition.

2nd SOLDIER: There are signs about food and drink everywhere!!

3rd SOLDIER: It's horrible to imagine to what extent their notion of entertainment bordered on the suicidal. (*We hear the sounds of digging and of equipment being moved back and forth.*)

2nd SOLDIER: I found it. Come and help me, please . . .

3rd SOLDIER: I'd rather not. I'll wait here.

1st SOLDIER: Don't be afraid. Number 2 can't do it on her own.

3rd Picture: 4:00 p.m. that afternoon

1st SOLDIER: Let's put that box here. Does the playback mechanism work as it's supposed to?

2nd SOLDIER: Everything works. I have just forwarded the tape. The recording starts at 4:00 p.m. and it finishes at 4:00 a.m.

1st SOLDIER: I suggest that we begin. Whenever anyone of us is in doubt as to the meaning of something, or, we have problems understanding, or, if there are obscure technical references on the tape we'll stop it.

3rd SOLDIER: I feel restless. Will we hear their voices?

2nd SOLDIER: The tape contains a complete soundscape, though it focuses on the area in which the box was placed. Our security forces back then must have considered that the—for posterity—most useful utterances concerning this place, its use, its cultural habits and traditions and the kinds of expectations associated with it, would be expressed in relative proximity to where they placed the white box.

1st SOLDIER: Write this down.

3rd SOLDIER: Just a minute. I'm not sitting very comfortably.

1st SOLDIER: Are you ready?

2nd SOLDIER: What are you afraid of?

3rd SOLDIER: Nothing.

1st SOLDIER: Place: The white box was placed under the counter of the barbecue and draft beer establishment called "Small Pleasures" . . . Responsible for the find were specially selected troops from units with training in the humanities.

(*The tape recorder is started. After some scratches we hear a clear atmospheric recording, as if we were descending through a sea of distant bird noises which grow in volume. Then we hear the distant sounds of people and music—they come nearer—the sounds of Dyrehavsbakken. These sounds retreat into the background as individual voices come through more clearly.*)

MARTHA: Pass me a beer. A warm one please.

DORA: Is he giving you a hard time again?

MARTHA: He wants a raise.

DORA: Isn't he on commission?

MARTHA: He gets ten kroner per fall, but I can barely afford that nowadays.

DORA: You'll have to sit up on the bar yourself then. Then you could keep your ten kroner. He's your son, for crying out loud. Isn't he entitled to a decent life?

MARTHA: Who kicked him out?

DORA: Don't start on that again. A big strong sailor like him wasn't meant to sit on a bar in a cage and let every Tom, Dick and Harry knock him off it if they can hit the target. "One shot for ten . . . three for twenty" . . . His muscles are shrinking.

MARTHA: His muscles . . . He could have gotten a different kind of job so he could provide for his old mother. I don't know how we'll make ends meet. This summer isn't looking that good. It's too cold.

DORA: Oh come on. Drink up. You could chain him to the bar. (*They both laugh.*)

MARTHA: You're always so crude, Dora.

DORA: You have to learn to take life as it comes.

MARTHA: Have you planted flowers in your yard? I've put in sweet peas, marigolds, and dahlias. My nasturtiums I've planted in two hanging pots.

DORA: I'm going to try roses again this year. Roses and asters.

MARTHA: Roses need so much care and I get so depressed when they die. But I really don't like that they take up so much space.

3rd SOLDIER: What are they talking about?

1st SOLDIER: Flowers.

DORA: Roses are real plants. The others are just flowers. A rose is a rose. It is always something special.

2nd SOLDIER: How could they afford flowers. They sound like perfectly ordinary people.

1st SOLDIER: Flowers were common.

MARTHA: I don't agree at all.

3rd SOLDIER: They must have liked them because of the colors.

1st SOLDIER: Some roses had a scent as well.

DORA: What does he want to do instead of sitting on the bar.

MARTHA: If I only knew. After all, he hasn't quite been himself since he fell into that cargo hold.

DORA: There is nothing wrong with him. He wants to sail again, that's all. Didn't you know that that was all a lie?

MARTHA: What are you suggesting? He was in the hospital for three months. He came home just as pale and sick as when he was a kid and had smoked and thrown up in the chicken coop.

DORA: He had to tell you something. He had smuggled whiskey and cigarettes. He was in for three months.

MARTHA: Is that true. Oh, I'm so happy to hear that. I've been so worried every time he fell down from the bar. Every time I thought "Thank God you didn't fall all the way down into that cargo hold again!"

DORA: Your son's a dink if you want my opinion. Want another beer?

2nd SOLDIER: They drank a lot.

1st SOLDIER: They were cold.

MARTHA: Maybe just another warm one.

DORA: When Kaj Hugo takes a break tell him I have a hot bottle for him.

MARTHA: I like you Dora. I've always wished you were my daughter.

DORA: Then things would have been really crazy. What do you think Kaj Hugo would have said to that?

MARTHA: He wouldn't have noticed. (*Both women laugh. Their voices retreat. Soundscape from Dyrehavsbakken. Then, we hear the spinning of a wheel of fortune.*)

WERNER: Try your luck! There's a first time for everything. Try your luck.

MARTHA: I'll give it a try.

WERNER: We don't give comps. Try your luck!

MARTHA: I was just over at Dora's having a beer. What are you wearing on your feet?

WERNER: Straw shoes and thick socks. I can't keep warm any other way.

MARTHA: I'm just wearing fur lined boots. I wish summer would arrive quickly.

WERNER: Me too. My feet and fingers get really cold and I can't stand here spinning the wheel of fortune wearing huge mitts—people will just start believing that they'll win. Try your luck over here! Prizes almost every time. But I love this time of year even if it's cold.

3rd SOLDIER: Luck—Try your luck?!

WERNER: I love the light. In a month that kind of light will be gone.

2nd SOLDIER: The wheel of fortune was a kind of game. You'd choose a number and you'd win if the wheel stopped by it.

MARTHA: Yes, by midsummer it starts to fade away. The birds sing less then.

3rd SOLDIER: He just said "Try your luck," but you don't know what you're going to win.

1st SOLDIER: That's what's meant by luck.

WERNER: People are starting to arrive. I understand that Kaj Hugo isn't too pleased with your arrangement. He's welcome to come down and relieve me once in a while.

MARTHA: You're a good body, Werner. Dora just told me that fortunately nothing happened when he . . . you know nothing happened to his head.

WERNER: That's good news.

MARTHA: It was all a lie.

WERNER: That's not unsusal. Try your luck over here! That's two cards for twenty kroner. You look like you've brought lady luck. (*The wheel spins—comes to a standstill.*) What did I tell you. We got red and here's a little jumping jack to hang in the rear window of your car. Try your luck over here. Prizes every time.

MARTHA: You're exaggerating. Why do you think Kaj Hugo didn't dare tell me that he'd been in jail. Lots of people have. I've never been angry with him. Never.

WERNER: Maybe he was embarrassed.

MARTHA: Embarrassed. . . ? I would have gotten used to it.

WERNER: Dora is not a good influence on him.

MARTHA: Stop that. We talked about that a long time ago. I won't listen to anything bad about Dora.

WERNER: Well, you'll have to if you want to hear my opinion.

MARTHA: Let's say no more about her then. You've got customers and I have to get back. (*Sound of the wheel of fortune slowly replaced by background sounds from the amusement park.*)

WERNER: (*Distant.*) Try your luck! Two spins for twenty kroner.

MARTHA: The weather seems to stay nice today. We should be getting lots of customers. How is it going?

KAJ HUGO: I had two customers but it's too much work when I have to get down to take their money . . . and then get back up on the bar. You'll just have to stay put if you want me to sit up here.

MARTHA: Are you cold, Kaj Hugo? Dora's keeping a warm beer for you. We could close for a moment.

KAJ HUGO: Yeah, great idea, just when people are arriving. Either we're running a business or we aren't.

MARTHA: Don't be so moody, Kaj Hugo. I just suggested it to make you happy.

KAJ HUGO: Just sit down and mind the shop.

MARTHA: You're getting to be more and more like your dad; stubborn till the end.

WERNER: Shut up, already!

MARTHA: I wish you'd break your neck. Why did you lie to me? You were in the pen for three months for smuggling whiskey and tobacco. How stupid can you get?! No one in our family has ever had dealings with the police and then you get caught with five bottles of booze and a couple of cigarettes! What do you think your dad would have said if he'd found out his son's such a twit. You're a stupid, ungrateful louse. You are! Even Dora says so.

KAJ HUGO: Shut up! I'm not going to sit here waiting for another ball to hit if you don't shut your face right this minute. Do you have to yell like that. Louse. Dora has never called me that. She calls me a dink which is completely different. You don't have the guts it takes to cope with life. I didn't tell you because I didn't want to hurt you.

MARTHA: If you get down off that bar now you won't get a penny.

KAJ HUGO: I'll do as I please. I'm finished with this kind of life. You're supposed to be my mother but you're like a leech. You drain all my strength with your nonsense. And then you put me up here—three balls for twenty kroner—that's no life for a sailor, you know. You can sit up here yourself. That'd attract the customers. I'm through.

MARTHA: You don't mean that. I've taken care of you all winter. Even the lettuce for the bird you ate. You did nothing but sleep and flop about on my sofa all day. I couldn't have people over because you didn't feel like getting up. Now, let's get to the truth about you. No, Kaj Hugo stay up there, please don't come down. I've just sold three balls. Please stay there.

KAJ HUGO: Okay, I will. I'm ready to try for a bull's eye. Come on, now. (*Sounds of balls hitting a back cloth.*) Alright! Good try.

MARTHA: Let's make up. I'm sorry I got angry with you. Go down and have your beer at Dora's. I'll take care of things here.

KAJ HUGO: I didn't mean it like that. (*Sounds from the amusement park.*)

3rd SOLDIER: Why didn't he have a job?

1st SOLDIER: It was difficult to get one.

3rd SOLDIER: I see. I don't like it. They always seem to be talking about something different from what they're saying.

2nd SOLDIER: They lie to each other.

1st SOLDIER: I think we should reserve our judgment. There's much we don't know yet.

3rd SOLDIER: I know enough to know I don't like what I'm hearing. His mother made do as well as she could.

2nd SOLDIER: Number 1's right, we don't know enough yet. I don't like it either.

1st SOLDIER: Should we start the tape again?

3rd SOLDIER: Let me just give you your energy allotment. A triple combo red, green, and yellow. There you are. That should give us some stamina.

1st SOLDIER: Okay, let's continue. We have to get to the end. (*The tape is started. We hear the sounds of "The Bear Hunt" and from "War Ships and Planes." Games which involve the shooting of guns accompanied with loud explosions.*)

2nd SOLDIER: What's happening? Shots. Explosions! It's war! . . . There are no references to this in the historical documents.

1st SOLDIER: It was a popular entertainment to shoot bears—well, not real bears. They were mechanical models which emitted a cry when you hit them and scored. Sometimes these models were of ships or planes or space vehicles. You'd shoot them down and they'd explode. That's probably what we're hearing.

2nd SOLDIER: Didn't they have respect for anything?

1st SOLDIER: They had fun. The point of the game was to hit the target . . . It might be difficult to understand now . . . but as you can hear there's someone laughing.

3rd SOLDIER: Someone's laughing. Why? It's not funny. Where's the will will to be future oriented. The ideals? Was that why the place was purged?

2nd SOLDIER: All purges are a logical result of the need of the elite societies for ever-increasing expansion in elite activities.

1st SOLDIER: We don't know enough to make conclusive statements like that.

2nd SOLDIER: People are laughing and having fun at the expense of their most advanced technical know-how. I don't understand Number 1's point.

3rd SOLDIER: Number 1 knows more about historical conditions than I do and I'd like to know if they also did target practice on their food items. After all, we know that food was a form of entertainment for them as well. Did they, for instance, shoot at sausages?

1st SOLDIER: There used to be a place where you could throw balls at stacks of plates and glasses. It was considered greatly entertaining to hit them and smash as many as possible using as few balls as possible.

3rd SOLDIER: You mean, they enjoyed destroying things?

1st SOLDIER: They paid for their enjoyment at every stand. People came out here to meet friends.

2nd SOLDIER: Was it always this noisy? Was there always that much music?

1st SOLDIER: Many establishments were built for dancing. (*We hear dance music and the sounds of joy.*)

2nd SOLDIER: Dancing! How? There's a chapter in *The Biological Conditions for the Development of Muscle Tissue* which recommends certain dance exercises to train the suppleness of the body in order to achieve the highest possible control over your movements. Did they practice out here in that noise?

1st SOLDIER: They enjoyed it . . .

2nd SOLDIER: Who enjoyed it? Those who were already trained?

1st SOLDIER: They enjoyed dancing with one another . . . moving to the music . . . to be together with another person while moving . . .

3rd SOLDIER: Weird . . . They moved together to the music???

2nd SOLDIER: We can't use this for anything.

3rd SOLDIER: I'm beginning to understand. They knew that by doing so they could produce a specific emotion which they liked, right?

1st SOLDIER: That's right. Let's start the tape again. (*The sounds of laughing, talking people. The clinking of bottles and glasses.*)

DORA: Please sit over there Kaj Hugo then you're not in my way.

KAJ HUGO: Why do you always talk to me like that. I know very well that I'm a fool but there was a time when you did see something in me.

DORA: You've changed. We all have. Everything's changed.

KAJ HUGO: Don't be sad. We can start over. I'll buy myself a new flannel suit. One of those gray ones you like. And a couple of new shirts.

Then you'll like me again. Just wait and see.

DORA: It'll take more than that this time. You're sweet, Kaj Hugo, but you're so predictable.

KAJ HUGO: So what? A little peace and quiet never hurt.

DORA: Would you like to build a wall of geraniums around us?

KAJ HUGO: Don't make fun of me. You've been alone all winter and spring, Dora. Mind you it doesn't show. But that kind of thing isn't healthy for anybody in the long run. And at the moment I'm not tied down either. It'd be nice, Dora.

DORA: And what about your mother?

KAJ HUGO: I could move in with you.

DORA: I've planted roses everywhere. There's really no room for you, Kaj Hugo. You take up too much space.

KAJ HUGO: My mother doesn't want me at her place either. What kind of life is this anyway? Both you and my mother used to be fairly reasonable, now you're both so cold. It's just because I don't have a regular job with a pension. It's really sad. If my mother comes over tell her I've gone for a walk.

DORA: She's almost seventy years old. You can't just let her sit up there on that bar. She could have an accident.

KAJ HUGO: She's tough. People would pay double to see her fall off. (*Sounds of balls hitting the back cloth.*)

MARTHA: Ooops! You got me . . . (*She breathes heavily.*) I'm not quite as good at taking this as I used to be. (*Sounds from the spinning wheel of fortune. It stops.*)

WERNER: Green! Does anyone have green? Okay, my game then. That's right—try a different board—black, red, white, and green—try your luck . . . Oh, it's you, Kaj Hugo!

KAJ HUGO: I'll try white. (*The wheel spins. Stops.*)

WERNER: Red. Red wins a lovely, large stuffed dog. Here you are. You can wash it in your washing machine but don't use the spin cycle.

KAJ HUGO: I'll try again.

WERNER: I'll give you a comp on red.

KAJ HUGO: Okay. (*The wheel spins.*)

WERNER: If it lands on red, what's your wish?

KAJ HUGO: I'm not going to say.

WERNER: I'll make a wish for you then.

KAJ HUGO: Okay. I wish that all of Dora's roses would die.

WERNER: Won't you ever learn? I don't understand you. You could move in with me. We'd have a good time . . . Peace and quiet. I've got a T.V. and everything.

KAJ HUGO: Werner, you know very well how I feel about that. I'd love to be your roommate but that just makes you so sad, so why do it when we can avoid that. My mother's angry because I won't sit on the bar any longer.

WERNER: You're all she's got and she wants to make you happy.

KAJ HUGO: Happy?! She yells at me all the time. She thinks I've let her down because I haven't become a somebody. So, I'm not going to let myself get knocked off that bar at ten kroner a fall. And Dora despises me. At least you understand me, Werner.

WERNER: To be honest, I don't understand you but I'd like to help you. And since you won't move in with me I can only listen to you whenever you come over here complaining. You haven't even noticed that red came out twice.

KAJ HUGO: You don't say. Amazing. I'd better go tell Dora. It's good to have a friend like you, Werner. I'm off. (*The wheel of fortune spins.*)

3rd SOLDIER: It sounds like there are more people there now. I guess it's about 6 p.m.

2nd SOLDIER: The singing girls will perform in their tent soon and acts will perform on stage. According to the historical information we've obtained regarding the functioning of the place on this particular evening the famous cycling pigs from Holland were to perform at 7:30 and at 9:00. The singing girls would perform in their tent every hour from 8 o'clock on.

1st SOLDIER: As a child I heard the singing girls.

3rd SOLDIER: What kinds of emotions were associated with listening to them?

2nd SOLDIER: Singing girls and cycling pigs!

1st SOLDIER: They were remnants of an old, popular tradition. You'd throw money up onto the stage and request songs you'd like to hear.

3rd SOLDIER: Were the songs well known.

1st SOLDIER: Yes.

3rd SOLDIER: If you knew the songs yourself you could just go ahead and sing them.

1st SOLDIER: I guess you had to be there . . .

2nd SOLDIER: This kind of talk lies well beyond our concerns here. I object to this kind of discussion!

3rd SOLDIER: I don't understand.

1st SOLDIER: They drank beer and enjoyed themselves. They applauded the singing girls, met with old friends which was why people went there to begin with.

3rd SOLDIER Were they good singers?

1st SOLDIER: Not many could sing like them.
3rd SOLDIER: I see . . .
2nd SOLDIER: They deserved what they got.

4th Picture: The evening is warm

MARTHA: He'd better come back soon. He can't just leave me here. I'm almost seventy years old, but does he care? If I dropped down dead he wouldn't notice—not until they started to clean up at the end of summer when they'd find my decomposed body. No, no, I think Werner would miss me. And Dora would ask for me—but not Kaj Hugo, my own son. Sometimes I think he hates me. When he sees me he's reminded of himself and all the things he can't pull himself together to get done. He should have been a businessman or worked in a bank. I know that his dad's deepest wish was to see him employed at some respectable bank or insurance company—or even better in a computer firm. He had the aptitude and he was good at math . . . Yes, sir, don't be shy—three balls for twenty kroner . . . You're a good shot, I can see that—Kaj Hugo was always one of the best students in school. Suddenly everything went wrong. He'd only a year left as a trainee at the bank. His dad always said that there's nothing more international than the banks. "Get yourself a decent job, my son. That's how you will get acknowledged. And there is nothing more important in this world but to receive acknowledgment." But he didn't care. Suddenly one day he'd signed aboard a tanker, and when we received a postcard from him he was on his way to the Persian Gulf. He was a deck hand, and in Nice he'd bought a little box decorated with snail shells for me as a beautiful reminder of him. His dad got furious and if it hadn't been because the season had just started out here and he himself had to sit on the bar, he'd have gone out to pick him up and drag him home by the hair on his head. (*A tune comes faintly through.*) Now they are playing that song again. It always makes me think sad thoughts. He was always good about writing to us. He ought to come and relieve me now. It will be a nice evening. Maybe summer is on the way after all. (*Increasing noise from the amusement park.*) Step right up! Three balls for twenty kroner. If you've got exact change then just put it on the counter. If you hit the target I'll fall down. Give it a shot. (*Sound of ball hitting back cloth.*) Too bad. One more time . . . Missed . . . Try again. I've gotten too old for this. When I was young I could manage the whole of the hot water section during the winter. But I'm not a young girl any longer. Cleaning twenty cabins after closing was nothing back then. It's different now. Now I spend all winter sitting sewing handkerchiefs, looking forward to getting out of here in the woods to be among people who're having a good time. Kaj Hugo's dad was a real entertainer, but he realized that it wasn't a life for Kaj Hugo. For him life was meant to be full of options—and there are many of those provided you can find them. Oh, there he is. He looks happy. Kaj Hugo, where have you been?—I'll get down now. (*Sounds from the amusement park.*)

KAJ HUGO: I just dropped in on Dora. I'll go up on the bar.

MARTHA: You look happy.

KAJ HUGO: Werner's wheel stopped twice at red. And Dora will think it over—as long as I don't mess up her roses.

MARTHA: That's good, dear. I'll sit here and take the money. You should take off your shoes. You don't need them.

KAJ HUGO: Okay, mummy, I'll put them here. How about painting a new back cloth. You know, with a church and houses and some trees. Wouldn't that be pretty.

MARTHA: It's a good idea. Your dad thought we should paint a tower, a tower of Babel I think he said. So it'd look like he was jumping out of the tower when people hit the bar.

KAJ HUGO: A tower of Babel! What on earth is that? Aren't a church and some houses just as good?

MARTHA: I don't know. Your dad had read about it somewhere. Some people down south once built a tower like that. It was supposed to reach up through the clouds.

KAJ HUGO: Jesus Christ! I've never seen nor heard of such a tower anywhere I've ever been. It's probably a lie—an old lie. Why do you always say "your dad" or "the old man." His name was Ove, wasn't it?— You're a little weird sometimes, you know?

MARTHA: Never you mind. I called your father my old man because . . . well, he liked it. (*Kaj Hugo laughs.*) Don't laugh. Everything was different when he was alive. You had respect for him, I can tell you. (*Kaj Hugo laughs louder.*) Just you be careful he doesn't hear you all the way up in heaven.

KAJ HUGO: His name was Ove Simonsen.

MARTHA: Why are you doing this? Now you've made me sad. I was very happy before sitting thinking about how well the two of us used to be getting along and how nice you used to be towards me. I was sitting up there saying to myself that there aren't many who can be as proud of their child as I can. Now you've ruined everything.

KAJ HUGO: I didn't mean to. But you talk about him as if you were fond of him and as if you were a real widow. But the last few years he was alive you left him sitting on a chair outside in the back whether it was raining or it was cold. He just sat there without being able to move under a piece of tarpaulin which he could barely pull up around himself because his hands were so weak.

MARTHA: I didn't want your father to sit among strangers when he belonged here. He wanted it that way himself.

KAJ HUGO: Whatever happened to that waiter you used to go out with?

MARTHA: He moved out of town. It's none of your business. I don't meddle in your life. Only when I have to provide for you—something your dad would have done as well. He was always so caring. So, don't attack me like that.

KAJ HUGO: I just asked . . .

MARTHA: And please tell me where he was supposed to live, anyway. There's no space for anyone else when you're in a room. So just stay up there on your bar, Kaj Hugo, and shut up. If it hadn't been for me you'd have reached the bottom a long time ago. And your dad would have done the same if I hadn't put some order into his life. So, let's not talk any more about that.

KAJ HUGO: I'm going to end up killing you one day.

MARTHA: Kaj Hugo!

(Sounds from Dyrehavsbakken. A tune—the same one Martha heard earlier.)

DORA: Don't the two of you look cozy. I just dropped by to ask if either of you have seen Werner.

KAJ HUGO: He was down by his stand a moment ago. Maybe he went for a walk.

DORA: He has customers. They were lined up but he didn't show up.

KAJ HUGO: Strange.

DORA: I just thought I'd mention it to you.

MARTHA: Maybe some old friends came by?

DORA: Werner'd never leave his shop. He must be unwell.

KAJ HUGO: I'll come down. Let's go and take a look. Did you check in the back?

DORA: There was no one there.

KAJ HUGO: You smell nice, Dora.

DORA: It's just some old perfume.

MARTHA: I'll come along. I'll ask some of the boys to look after things here.

DORA: I don't like it, Martha . . . What do you think is the matter? He's been so calm all season.

MARTHA: He can probably tell that . . . things aren't over between you and Kaj Hugo.

DORA: Well, we've only just begun to pick things up a little again.

MARTHA: When you're fond of somebody you notice subtle changes like that long before they become obvious.

DORA: Do you think that's why he's left his stand?

MARTHA: How should I know? I think so. Kaj Hugo was so happy and he said some really harsh things to me. When he's happy it's as if he wants to take revenge for something or other I've done to him ages ago.

DORA: What did he say.

MARTHA: He talks about how I let his dad sit out back the last few years of his life. As if he could have done anymore than I did. He didn't want to be sent to a home. So, he might as well've sat back there where everyone knew him. They'd drop by and visit him for a little while. Don't believe for a moment that I enjoyed it. But you're probably on Kaj Hugo's side, right?

DORA: Oh, shut up. We all thought it was great that you had your old man out here. So, don't listen to Kaj Hugo. He's just a big baby.

MARTHA: Is that why you're fond of him and want him to come back to you?

DORA: I don't know. I just know him. I don't think I'd have the energy to start anything new, you know . . . in high heeled shoes, bright-eyed and bushy-tailed. And, after all, Kaj Hugo is your son.

MARTHA: Where do you think Werner's gone to. Kaj Hugo can take care of the wheel while we look around out back. Such a beautiful evening. A little on the cool side but nice and there are so many people.

DORA: Let's go over to my place and see if he's there.

5th Picture: Expectations

(*The sounds from Dyrehavsbakken become distant.*)

3rd SOLDIER: What's that sound? We've heard it several times now.

1st SOLDIER: Birds. I think.

3rd SOLDIER: Birds!

1st SOLDIER: Sounds like a blackbird.

2nd SOLDIER: Let's check to make sure.

(*Sounds of the wind moving through bushes and twigs. In the distance we hear a blackbird.*)

1st SOLDIER: It is a lovely evening—warm and gentle. It's a blackbird.

3rd SOLDIER: What does it look like.

2nd SOLDIER: You must have seen a picture of one in your manual. It belongs to the group of birds who sometimes move through a purged area and cause plants to start growing again. It is black and has a yellow beak.

3rd SOLDIER: Are birds part of the essence of a place. Its sound makes me feel quite peculiar.

1st SOLDIER: It sings beautifully. It's been so many years since I last heard a live blackbird. It must be somewhere over there.

2nd SOLDIER: Do we really have time for this. Shouldn't we rather keep listening to the tape.

3rd SOLDIER: I want to see the blackbird.

2nd SOLDIER: Fine . . .

1st SOLDIER: It might help us to get closer to an understanding of the essence of this place and the people who used to live here if we spend some time listening to the blackbird and the wind.

3rd SOLDIER: I've never felt like this before.

2nd SOLDIER: That's not part of our assignment.

1st SOLDIER: If the blackbird is part of the essence of this place then it is important.

3rd SOLDIER: I think Number 1 is right. I'm terribly happy I was selected for this assignment.

2nd SOLDIER: ''Terribly happy!'' What kind of an expression is that? It's dangerous to give in. We've seen too many examples of that. A sudden weakening sets in due to unexplainable influences from unknown sources.

3rd SOLDIER: You scare me Number 2.

1st SOLDIER: I should like to point out that it is a known fact that even the best and most capable elite soldiers experience moments of weakness. There's no need to become frightened by the experience of a sudden weakness. It is important to know how to get past it and return to a state of natural capability. No one will hold it against us that we experienced a few moments of weakness. That's expected to happen. But it is also expected that we will be able to return to a level of optimum service with our private—because they are private—with our private experiences intact so that the report we have to hand in can be deemed trustworthy.

3rd SOLDIER: I didn't know it was possible to feel this way.

2nd SOLDIER: How?

1st SOLDIER: I'll go back to get a couple of micro-recorders so we can make some notes.

2nd SOLDIER: We'll wait here.

3rd SOLDIER: We should take off our helmets. I have a real desire to feel the wind in my hair.

2nd SOLDIER: I wouldn't advise it even if the area was declared safe a long time ago. Tell me how it feels.

3rd SOLDIER: Everything sounds different—so close by—try it! It feels like being back at the base, but everything sounds much better. It's as if the air is filled with little songs.

2nd SOLDIER: "Little songs!" You'd better put your helmet back on.

3rd SOLDIER: Try to take yours off. We can always put them right back on if anything happens. Let me help you with yours.

2nd SOLDIER: No, that won't be necessary, thanks. You're right, it does sound strange . . . very strange.

3rd SOLDIER: Your hair is brown. I've never thought about that before.

2nd SOLDIER: We don't normally pay attention to each other's hair back at the base.

3rd SOLDIER: Of course! But right now your hair looks prettier than anything I've ever seen at the base.

2nd SOLDIER: Thank you! I know it is thick and healthy. At medical check-ups I've always been told that my hair is thick and healthy. They say that about my nails too—fingers and toes.

3rd SOLDIER: I'd like to see them some time—both kinds. If I may. May I?

2nd SOLDIER: Of course. I'm very proud of them. I have some good qualities to pass on to the next generation.

3rd SOLDIER: You do. Do you hear the bird? I think there are more of them farther away. I think I can hear them. Isn't it true what I said, it sounds like the air is filled with little songs?

2nd SOLDIER: I don't know about this—

3rd SOLDIER: Listen! There are insects as well.

2nd SOLDIER: These areas of wilderness in the security zones are no doubt of great interest to science. You talk as if you'd rather live here than back home.

3rd SOLDIER: Don't joke about things like that.

2nd SOLDIER: I'm sorry if I hurt your feelings but you really irritate me. You seem so excited.

3rd SOLDIER: No one loves the base as deeply as I do. But back then . . . I mean before the efficiency of human nature was radically improved there were people who were poets . . . Of course, you've heard about that . . . Right now I feel like I'm about to say some peculiar words because I can't contain my experience in our usual language.

2nd SOLDIER: . . . because of a couple of birds producing sounds in their throats.

3rd SOLDIER: I'm sorry but I suddenly feel so happy. To move on from your hair, your eyes have the same color as your hair. Perhaps your eyes are just as healthy as your . . .

2nd SOLDIER: I think we'd better put our helmets back on and collect the the last few samples. When Number 1 arrives we can explore the immediate environment. Your working method makes me uneasy.

1st SOLDIER: Did you observe anything relevant to our assignment?

2nd SOLDIER: Just various sounds produced by birds, a few insects and a faint rattle produced when the wind moves through the bushes.

1st SOLDIER: Let's record those sounds and attach them to our report.

3rd SOLDIER: Without wearing helmets!

1st SOLDIER: Excellent suggestion.

2nd SOLDIER: I must warn you! Number 3 and I have listened to the indigenous sounds of this place and I've observed that these sounds have an unfortunate effect on Number 3's ability to register actual conditions here . . .

3rd SOLDIER: I'll keep on my helmet. I feel affected by the sound those birds make with their throats.

1st SOLDIER: I suggest that we all take off our helmets. Not doing so would be unscientific on our part given the nature of our assignment. We should also take off our gloves and maybe even our boots in order to be able to add our personal experiences of the essence of this place.

3rd SOLDIER: That's incredible. I was just thinking we ought to make use of our sensory abilities in hands and feet.

2nd SOLDIER: I'd like to be excused from baring my hands and feet. The measurements and tests expected from me I can conduct in proper attire. I'll refuse to bare my hands and feet.

1st SOLDIER: I would on the other hand find it reasonable if Number 2 would participate fully and add her experiences to ours.

2nd SOLDIER: I would not refuse an order but I should always doubt its measure of reason.

1st SOLDIER: It's an order.

2nd SOLDIER: Yes, ma'am.

3rd SOLDIER: In the old days people in certain cultures would eat larks.

1st SOLDIER: We have not observed any larks. What we hear are blackbirds.

3rd SOLDIER: It just occurred to me, that's all.

2nd SOLDIER: As it is my duty to inquire about things I don't understand, I'll ask you this, Number 1. Did they eat its voice because of its taste?

1st SOLDIER: You can't eat a voice. But their knowledge of the timbre of the voice undoubtedly enhanced their impression of the taste of the meat.

2nd SOLDIER: That sounds sick—

1st SOLDIER: Okay! Our schedule is as follows. We continue to listen to the tape at 6:30 p.m. base time which will correspond to the time on the tape. We will then stop the tape at 8:00 p.m. sharp to take five minutes for individual experiences of that hour and the atmosphere surrounding dusk. Then we'll continue to listen to the tape and like before we will skip some of the longer continuous passages which we can analyze back at the base.

2nd & 3rd SOLDIERS: Yes, ma'am.

6th Picture: Recognition

(*The sounds of Dryehavsbakken. There are a lot of people there now. The wheel of fortune is spinning.*)

DORA: You scared us, Werner. Where've you been?

WERNER: I just went for a walk. I suddenly felt really weird. Like I had a premonition that it'll all be over soon, that we'll all die soon. I've never experienced anything like it. I got frightened. Then black came out three times in a row and I thought to myself ''you'd better take a little walk to cool down, Werner.'' It was nice of Kaj Hugo to come and look after things. He's gone home now.

MARTHA: Did you come back long ago? We've been all the way down to the old bridge and over on the island looking for you. Dora said you like to go there sometimes.

WERNER: Too bad you missed me. That's where I was.

DORA: I don't think those kinds of feelings have to mean anything.

WERNER: In any case, it's not a good sign that black came out three times.

DORA: That's just superstition, Werner.

WERNER: History shows several examples of how people's premonitions come true.

MARTHA: Depending on who has them. Premonitions can be completely wrong. My premonitions almost always are. Maybe that's because they're really my wishes.

DORA: Werner isn't wishing for us all to die.

MARTHA: I didn't suggest that. I just said that my premonitions are my wishes which is why they never come true.

WERNER: I have no wishes—I don't have the courage to wish for anything. That's why I work on the wheel of fortune—a wheel of fortune is organized chance. When I was young I worked as a white clown and I always prepared my acts in accordance with a wheel of fortune. It was a good system.

MARTHA: Don't be sad, Werner. We know you're thinking about Kaj

Hugo.

WERNER: I don't feel bad about that. What really unsettles me is that I seem to recognize so many things this evening.

MARTHA: Recognize!? You mean, like people you've seen before—suddenly they're all of them out here at the same time? The weather's good . . . Recognize?

DORA: I'm going back to my stand. Come on over later. Werner, please don't be angry with me for taking an interest in Kaj Hugo again. It makes everything so complicated.

WERNER: We won't talk any further about it.

MARTHA: There's nobody left anymore . . . It's as if I haven't lived . . . I haven't left any tracks.

WERNER: Are you sitting more comfortably now? You can sit in my chair over in the corner.

MARTHA: Splendid . . . Thank you! I'd like to recognize someone . . .

WERNER: It's not people I recognize. It's situations, actions. Something happens right in front of my eyes and it brings me back in time.

MARTHA: It's age. I feel that sometimes. It's mainly Kaj Hugo who makes me go back in time. Looking at him I'm reminded of this and that.

WERNER: Some days are worse than others. I don't like being alone, Martha. I can't stand it any longer . . .

MARTHA: Werner!

WERNER: I apologize for being so direct. I don't want to be alone. I want to live together with someone. Someone I love or someone who'll allow me to live for him. I don't expect to be loved back. It would, of course, be wonderful if that were to happen. I'd really just like to be with someone who I could love and take care of. Do you understand that, Martha?

MARTHA: Of course, I do. But it could be a tough time for the other person who might not love you or be fond of you . . .

WERNER: But I'd do anything—anything.

MARTHA: Maybe this other person would feel that there wasn't enough space because of your enormous love. I don't know how to put it. But I do understand what you're saying.

WERNER: There must be somebody who could use my feelings.

MARTHA: Probably. But why do you have to use them up all at once on one particular person. Couldn't you share them around a little so that several people could get the sense that there'd still be room left over for them and their regular emotions. I have more trust in small, regular emotions shared with many. I'd be terrified if someone loved me as enormously as you want to love somebody. But, then, I don't think about things as much as you do, Werner—so, maybe you're right after all.

WERNER: Did you love Simonsen a lot?

MARTHA: My old man?!

WERNER: Well, you did a lot for him, even after he was completely gone and just sat in his chair staring.

MARTHA: It's strange you should bring him up. Kaj Hugo mentioned him only a couple of hours ago. No, I didn't love Simonsen like that. Not like you describe. Our relationship was different.

7th Picture: Confirmation

2nd SOLDIER: I'm not feeling well. I feel this heavy pressure in my chest (*Her line is heard on top of a passage of indecipherable talk from Martha.*)

1st SOLDIER: Let's stop here for a moment. It is not unusual to feel unwell when confronted with historical data. Please keep in mind, both of you, that we are dealing with a recording of human beings of a kind which no longer exists.

3rd SOLDIER: I feel like Number 2. Why didn't they do something about their condition? Several times I felt like they were alive and could come towards us at any time.

2nd SOLDIER: I suggest that we interrupt our assignment. I no longer have any sense of what I feel or know.

1st SOLDIER: We've stayed in the same spot for almost four hours and we can conclude that all of us have been influenced by the essence of the place and by listening to the tape.

3rd SOLDIER: Are we infected?

1st SOLDIER: Yes, but in order to understand the message of the white box it is necessary to allow oneself to become infected. That's one of the reasons why we were given so much time for this examination.

2nd SOLDIER: I'm less worried now that I know my symptoms are related to the essence of this place.

3rd SOLDIER: We have learned that the worst we can do is begin doubting ourselves. I.e., doubting what we are; i.e., doubting what we have learned; i.e., doubting that we are the human elite.

2nd SOLDIER: The worst we can do is begin doubting ourselves. I.e., doubting what we are; i.e., doubting what we have learned; i.e., doubting that we are the human elite.

1st SOLDIER: Are you ready to continue the tape?

2nd & 3rd SOLDIERS: Yes, ma'am. (*The tape is turned on. We hear the sounds from the amusement park and a melancholy country-and-western song.*)

3rd SOLDIER: Why did they feel the need to love someone.

1st SOLDIER: It was the greatest emotion they were capable of.

2nd SOLDIER: I've read somewhere that hate was seen as an equally great emotion.

3rd SOLDIER: Was it difficult for humanity to get beyond these feelings?

1st SOLDIER: Well, now we are in control of everything—nothing surprises us. It wasn't the emotions which we deemed useless but rather that they were uncontrollable.

2nd SOLDIER: I still don't feel well. Is it known when this pressure will disappear?

1st SOLDIER: We can't do anything about it out here and back at the base it would never have occurred.

3rd SOLDIER: Do you think it would be of any help to take off our gloves?

2nd SOLDIER: I don't know about that.

3rd SOLDIER: If both of us took off our gloves then I could hold your hands. Your hands would sense mine. I feel fine now.

1st SOLDIER: That's a good suggestion, Number 3.

2nd SOLDIER: Does Number 3 have to hold my hands? Couldn't we just hold on to our own hands?

1st SOLDIER: As it is not contrary to the special character of this assignment to hold one's own hands or somebody else's because the essence of this place requires untraditional working methods, I suggest that we all take off our gloves and continue to listen to the tape without wearing them. (*The sounds from the amusement park fade up—the song finishes.*)

KAJ HUGO: (*Yelling from up on the bar.*) I just arranged to have the little bald fellow take over for me for half an hour. How about you and I take a little trip round back? Wouldn't that be nice, Dora?

DORA: Doesn't it bother you to leave the customers and everything? We've barely found Werner and you want to go in the back.

KAJ HUGO: Come on Dora. You're your own boss. You could easily do it. You just tell someone "I don't feel well. Cover for me for a while. I'll have a rest in the back." They'd understand, Dora. You work so hard.

DORA: Isn't this a little too fast, though? Two hours ago I couldn't stand the sight of you and now you want me to "take a break" with you. You're the biggest dink I know.

KAJ HUGO: Your own little dink. Why don't you try to shoot me down? I'll be down in a minute. As soon as the bald fellow is here . . . Do we have a deal, then?

DORA: You're a tricky guy, Kaj Hugo. I'll go down and check it out. But you can forget it if the place is crawling with customers. Who do you think you are . . . Sitting up there yelling at one of the leading ladies around here.

KAJ HUGO: I love you, Dora.

DORA: Dont yell so loud. People will hear . . .

KAJ HUGO: Look at the ass she's got. I'm the luckiest man ever on this bar. I wish someone would come and shoot me down. It looks so unprofessional when I use the ladder to get down. And the bald guy never hits. Try your luck over here. You look like a lucky person. You're sure to hit. Come on! Just pay over there. Correct change. Great! Let's go. Oops! Bull's eye on the first shot . . . Okay, here I am again . . . You've got two more turns . . . Okay . . . I'm waiting . . . Missed. Try again . . . There's baldy! The sharp shooter here is going to shoot me down and the bar'll be yours . . . Come on! Oops! Going down in style. I'll be back in about half an hour. I'll just get myself back in shape here.

3rd SOLDIER: How are you feeling?

2nd SOLDIER: I feel a little better, I think. But I find it incredibly unscientific that none of these experiences can be tested, neither chemically nor mathematically.

3rd SOLDIER: Have you noticed how beautiful and healthy Number 2's nails are?

1st SOLDIER: Yes, they are remarkable.

3rd SOLDIER: May I touch your nail to check their degree of hardness.

2nd SOLDIER: I don't see the relevance of that to our assignment.

3rd SOLDIER: Not many are so well-equipped . . . Look at mine.

2nd SOLDIER: No, not many are . . . Do yours break easily.

3rd SOLDIER: Yes . . . I mean no. I don't know . . . Maybe.

2nd SOLDIER: You should know. It could be a symptom of . . . of . . .

3rd SOLDIER: Of what?!

1st SOLDIER: You're both so well-trained and of such high elite status that I'll leave you to the tape. I'll go and outline a map of the area before it gets dark.

2nd SOLDIER: We could help you.

1st SOLDIER: That won't be necessary. We've already gotten so far that we can continue our work without further delays. I'll take a little communicator along. You'll be able to reach me at all times, and I'll be able to reach you.

3rd SOLDIER: You can trust us with the tape.

2nd SOLDIER: Is that an order?

1st SOLDIER: Yes.

3rd SOLDIER: We will continue according to plan one in order to finish our assignment.

2nd SOLDIER: Very well. I'll start the tape then. (*The tape continues. At first with interruptions.*)

8th Picture: The dew will soon fall

(*Distant noise from the amusement park.*)

KAJ HUGO: Here I am. I'm crazy about you, Dora.

DORA: If you trample my roses . . .

KAJ HUGO: I'll sit very quietly. Where's the long bench, Dora? Why the hell do you need all those roses . . . especially when you're engaged and everything.

DORA: Fooled you, eh? I got myself a fold-out bed. I didn't think you were going to come back. But I can tell, you couldn't function on a fold-out.

KAJ HUGO: You've always been rude to me, Dora, but this is ridiculous. Here I am with a small bottle of Akvavit in my pocket and I can barely fit in here because of roses! Don't you love me anymore, Dora?

DORA: You're the greatest love of my life, Kaj Hugo. Just imagine the smell and the colors when all these roses bloom. Then we'll sit right in here surrounded by them like in a secret house where no one can find us and where everything is transformed.

KAJ HUGO: Do you want a sip? Dora, I really am looking forward to when the roses are in bloom. I was just surprised to see so many.

DORA: I've got a drumstick for each of us.

KAJ HUGO: Okay! You're so thoughtful

DORA: I don't think that we need plates, do we? If you move the table a little then we'll both be able to sit down. I left enough space for two people and the table.

KAJ HUGO: How cosy. Dora pass the salt please and I'll have a piece of bread if you have.

DORA: I'll be right back. I have some white bread downstairs.

KAJ HUGO: I've always said that Dora can arrange anything.

3rd SOLDIER: That's what they called chicken legs.

2nd SOLDIER: Did they always eat?

3rd SOLDIER: They slept, worked, and ate.

2nd SOLDIER: What a waste of resources.

3rd SOLDIER: I'd like to taste a piece of chicken.

2nd SOLDIER: I wouldn't.

DORA: Here's the salt and the bread.

KAJ HUGO: Cheers.

DORA: When did I last sit in your lap? What's that smell? I don't recognize that smell.

KAJ HUGO: Lilac soap.

DORA: I've missed you. But I fought it. I wanted to prove to myself that I could live and be happy without you—and I could.

KAJ HUGO: But you're happier now, right?

DORA: I'm happy now but it is because I know I can manage without you.

KAJ HUGO: You really know how to be encouraging. I know that I can't be without you. When you don't love me my world is without meaning, as they say. Nothing works for me then. Everything falls apart . . . I promise that I'll behave. I promise . . . It's really a shame about the long bench.

DORA: Watch out! You'll knock over the glasses . . . You want some more bread? . . . You've lost so much weight since I saw you last. What's that scar on your shoulder? You're totally white and soft like a marzipan baby. You need some sunshine, honeybun!

KAJ HUGO: We haven't had any. You have to take me like I am.

DORA: And I will. We'd better go inside, the dew could fall on you, my dear . . .

KAJ HUGO: God, you're wonderful, Dora.

DORA: Not here . . . Inside, please . . . The roses . . .

KAJ HUGO: The roses . . . Will you look at my planting stick. I'll give you roses . . .

DORA: You haven't changed, Kaj Hugo . . . I've missed you.

KAJ HUGO: Here I come . . . (*Music from the amusement park. Squeals from the roller coaster.*)

2nd SOLDIER: What is that noise. We've heard it several times before.

3rd SOLDIER: It sounds like people eating. But I'm not sure.

2nd SOLDIER: It must be another of the amusements.

3rd SOLDIER: Yes! It's not a noise I recognize as related to my field. At least the voices are human. Maybe it's a form of laughter?

2nd SOLDIER: Connected with eating?

3rd SOLDIER: If I hold your hands I might be able to solve the problem.

2nd SOLDIER: Maybe you should contact Number 1 and ask her.

3rd SOLDIER: Doesn't it feel strange to hold hands like this?

2nd SOLDIER: I don't know. There's nothing normal about this assignment. I don't feel well. Let's contact Number 1. The sooner we're done here the sooner we can return to base. I'm not a very good soldier out here. I want to do entirely unscientific things here.

3rd SOLDIER: So what? Number 1 will assume responsibility. It's part of the essence of this place.

2nd SOLDIER: You could talk about my hair.

3rd SOLDIER: Let me help you with your helmet.

2nd SOLDIER: Do you think they're eating? The man and woman in the rose bushes.

3rd SOLDIER: All you can hear is music and lots of people, and that un-identified sound. But everyone seems happy. I'm not certain they're still eating.

2nd SOLDIER: What are they doing, then? Shouldn't we call Number 1?

3rd SOLDIER: Your hands are warm! . . . They mentioned "taking a break." I don't know how wide a term that is.

2nd SOLDIER: Words upset me.

3rd SOLDIER: Someone's talking now. (*Martha's and Werner's voices come closer.*) Don't be afraid Number 2.

WERNER: You're right, Martha. Kaj Hugo is not interested in me. It would be better if he and Dora could get something going.

MARTHA: You're a good person, Werner. That's your problem. To live with someone you have to be a not-so-good person sometimes.

WERNER: I'm not as good as you think. If I did what I feel right now I'd go and set fire to Dora's rose garden so both of them would get trapped.

MARTHA: It's hard to believe that you have room for such thoughts in your head, Werner. Fire? What good would that do? I respect you and I always take your advice. Why don't the two of us spend a little more time together, eh? When things were bad before my old man died I used to get up in front of him and tell him everything. I'd talk a blue streak, and when I needed an answer from him I went over to him and moved his head as if he were saying "Yes, you're right" or "Everything will work out alright." Or, I'd move it to say "That's awful. Are they really like that." That'd help. I felt I'd had a conversation. I felt so lonesome when he finally died.

WERNER: Did he understand anything at the end?

MARTHA: I don't know. In the beginning I could tell from his eyes that he understood. But later on I don't think he did. I was mean to him, Werner. I hope he didn't understand. I forced him to say yes to things I know he'd have said no to. That was my revenge, Werner. He raped me three times on the floor in the back one night. He was drunk and insisted that I'd smiled to one of his enemies. Quite a few people didn't like him; but you know about that. I was so scared of him when he was like that. The swine!

WERNER: He despised people like me. And he let me know whenever he saw me.

MARTHA: The night I just mentioned he got me pregnant with Kaj Hugo. I think about that when I look at Kaj Hugo. I can't help it. I could hardly walk for days after.

WERNER: I see . . . Do you have any family left?

MARTHA: I had a brother but he's dead. So are my parents. I believe I have some cousins but I've never seen them. I've only got Kaj Hugo and the people out here . . . And you? Tell me everything about you if you like.

WERNER: Thanks. Two of my brothers and a sister were chosen for elite training and my parents moved away with them. I had to fend for myself as best I could. I haven't seen any of them since they were chosen. I tried to write to them to tell them about my life and that they shouldn't worry about me . . . that I was happy. Then I started to travel with a fair together with Leif. He was a daredevil racer. I was a white clown . . . Later I took over the wheel of fortune from his mother. And I traveled with that after Leif was killed in an accident. Then, I got hold of this tent. And that's all about me . . . and the wheel . . .

MARTHA: The dew has begun to fall. Do you feel it? Doesn't it smell wonderful. Where did you learn your skills, Werner?

WERNER: . . . I don't know. I'll be good to Kaj Hugo and Dora; I promise you. I feel better now. You were right. It helps talking to somebody. Can I come and visit you sometime, Martha? You're alone now too.

MARTHA: I'd be so happy, Werner, you can't imagine how happy I'd be if you visited me and if I can be of help. All I can do is listen.

WERNER: That's a deal, Martha. We have to support each other—we for whom the party is almost over.

9th Picture: Birds in the night

(*Sound of the evening song of blackbirds and the twitter of other birds.*)

1st SOLDIER: It was true. I've just found the remains of his name plate. Tent No. 76, Werner Juhl K . . . There was something familiar about the voice. Werner! He was the youngest. He didn't want to come along with us—maybe that's true. The wheel of fortune! When he was a boy I remember that he always wanted to be different. He followed his own impulses. Now the grass is growing here and the birds are singing again. Number 2 and Number 3 have called on me several times now. They have difficulties understanding "unidentifiable sounds of human and mechanical origin." The most terrible thing humans can do to one another is to deny their humanity. And how is that to be rediscovered if the next generation of seekers don't know what to listen for; don't know what to look for. They can no longer trace the tracks and follow the sign posts which lead to the life of true humanity.

2nd SOLDIER: Station U calling Number 1. Calling Number 1.

3rd SOLDIER: Repeat: Station U calling Number 1.

1st SOLDIER: This is Number 1. I'm on my way. (*Birds are singing.*) I wonder if the birds upset them? Or the evening? Or the smell from the earth and the grass as the dew falls? This is Number 1. I'm just finishing off the last bit of surveying making use of the last few minutes of natural light. Leave Station U and explore the grass. That's an order!

2nd & 3rd SOLDIERS: Yes, ma'am! Leaving Station U. (*The sound of footsteps, muffled laughter.*)

3rd SOLDIER: Did you laugh Number 2?

2nd SOLDIER: I think so. How about we take our boots off?

3rd SOLDIER: Sure. Are you feeling light inside as well? Do you think it's dangerous? Do you think we've been poisoned?

2nd SOLDIER: Maybe we have oxygen poisoning? That's possible. I feel the grass between my toes. It's cold.

3rd SOLDIER: That's because of the dew. The nails on your toes light up like flowers in the grass.

2nd SOLDIER: Your nails look healthy, too. But your hair . . . Would you allow me to pull out a couple of hairs and check them under my microscope? I'd really like to know your hair.

3rd SOLDIER: You would? I'm proud of it. We could examine each other's hair. I could check yours and you mine . . .

2nd SOLDIER: Here's the microscope—Come on Number 3!

3rd SOLDIER: May I have a look? Does it look alright?

2nd SOLDIER: The composition is fine but you're lacking in calcium.

3rd SOLDIER: I think I can get to know your hair better if I touch it. Now I touch it with my right cheek. It's all warm and dry and it smells of the lining in your helmet.

2nd SOLDIER: You say many strange things, Number 3. Your hair smells of . . . No, I don't know. It's all so strange Number 3, I think I'm going to cry. You have to look the other way because nobody's ever seen me cry. I think I'm sick . . . No, turn around Number 3.

3rd SOLDIER: I want to see you. It helps if I'm looking at you. Don't you feel it? Your cheeks are wet and cool . . .

2nd SOLDIER: What are you doing Number 3 . . . The grass . . . we were to explore the grass. (*Pause. Silence.*) Was that a kiss? Did you kiss me?

3rd SOLDIER: Yes.

2nd SOLDIER: How do you know? Who taught you?

3rd SOLDIER: Nobody has. I read about it. Didn't you?

2nd SOLDIER: It's dangerous. It undermines our elite conditioning.

3rd SOLDIER: Yes.

2nd SOLDIER: We'll have to record the event and take it into consideration in our report . . .

3rd SOLDIER: No.

2nd SOLDIER: Why not? You sound so self-assured. Are you operating from a scientific basis right now?

3rd SOLDIER: Yes.

2nd SOLDIER: Where does it fit into the report? What are you doing, Number 3?

3rd SOLDIER: We're kissing again. Don't you feel it? It's an effect of the essence of this place.

2nd SOLDIER: It's dark now. Number 1 is on her way . . . What is that strange smell?

3rd SOLDIER: It's from the grass and the earth. It's a wet smell. It must be because of the dew . . . Listen, if you put an ear to the ground you hear Number 1's footsteps. The sound moves through the grass.

2nd SOLDIER: It's Number 1. I find it strange to think of her as a woman.

3rd SOLDIER: She is—just an older one.

2nd SOLDIER: I've never really thought about the fact that we're . . . different.

3rd SOLDIER: It's not that important. What is important is . . . inside . . . our essence.

2nd SOLDIER: What do you mean? Now you're impossible to understand again . . .

1st SOLDIER: Did everything go according to plan? Have you completed your assignment? Good!

2nd SOLDIER: Yes, we've recorded all essentials and collected samples.

1st SOLDIER: Good. We're making good time. Let's rest a little. I'm tired. In three months my tour of duty will be over. I've been active in the elite for fifteen years. That's a long time when you started as late as I did. There are not many of us left. The transition to the techno-cerebral age was more difficult than anticipated . . . We know that now . . .

2nd SOLDIER: More difficult . . . Let's turn on a few search lights.

1st SOLDIER: No, wait a while . . . We don't experience darkness that often.

3rd SOLDIER: Are you alright? Your voice sounds different Number 1. Are you affected by the essence of this place? Why don't you take off your helmet? You'll feel lighter without your helmet . . . We've taken ours off . . .

1st SOLDIER: I can see that.

2nd SOLDIER: Do you see . . . it all?

1st SOLDIER: Not all.

3rd SOLDIER: She means can you see our hair . . . our faces . . .

1st SOLDIER: Yes. It's nice.

2nd SOLDIER: Your hair is old, Number 1. You don't look as I imagined.

1st SOLDIER: I'm old. People expend themselves.

3rd SOLDIER: It's beautiful . . . You were here as a child, right? . . . Back then—before . . .

1st SOLDIER: Yes, I've been here before. I don't remember it well any longer. But it's probably not as difficult for me to understand the tape.

3rd SOLDIER: It's become easier for us as well.

2nd SOLDIER: Let's rewind to the unidentifiable sound. It's starting to get cold . . . Is it the darkness that's cold?

1st SOLDIER: You can feel the night. (*The tape is being rewound.*)

2nd SOLDIER: This is it. (*The sound of the roller coaster with squeals and loud happy laughter.*)

3rd SOLDIER: It's there often.

1st SOLDIER: It must be the roller coaster . . .

2nd SOLDIER: Were they afraid? . . . It was screams of fear like I said.

3rd SOLDIER: They're laughing as well . . .

1st SOLDIER: The roller coaster was lots of fun. I've tried it. With my brothers and sisters . . . With Werner, my youngest brother.

3rd SOLDIER: Werner is your brother? You know that now?!

1st SOLDIER: Yes.

2nd SOLDIER: You're certain.

1st SOLDIER: Yes.

2nd SOLDIER: What are those screams?!

1st SOLDIER: They were part of the fun. You drove up really fast up and down through dark tunnels and suddenly you'd be up so high you felt like you'd fly out of the car of the roller coaster—out through the trees and into the forest. I can't explain it any other way. Is there anything else you didn't understand?

3rd SOLDIER: No, we're ready to continue. (*The tape is started. Sounds from the amusement park fade up.*)

10th Picture: The earth emits fragrances

WERNER: You've been standing there a long time. There's a lot of people out here tonight.

KAJ HUGO: I'm sorry Werner. I feel sorry for you. I'm so damned happy myself. Do you think you can learn to accept that? I'm fond of you too, you know, as a friend or whatever.

WERNER: It's alright. Let's not talk about it any further. Everything is fine. I was just being weak. When you've been alone as long as I have you get this sudden desperation sometimes. I've been alone since Leif died and I've kept to myself. But there are so many other pleasures in life as long as you're not completely alone. At least out here we've got each other. I mean, those of us who work here. It's just that everything seems so much better and so much more beautiful—larger, even—you know, like . . . yes, larger—when you share your life with someone. And I guess in a certain way we do do that for each other out here. And as long as you and Dora are . . . It must be the poplars I can smell. It's amazing that they can seep all the way here through the smell of french fries and onions. I just love the confusion of things out here.

KAJ HUGO: I don't know. It's a different kind of job. It doesn't seem suf-ficient to me to sit on a bar now that Dora wants me back. Even though she hasn't said anything I can tell that she's expecting me to do something about it. She'd like me to apply to become a bus driver. You know, get a permanent job on a permanent route—from terminal to ter-minal.

WERNER: That sounds good . . . You get to travel a little and see people . . . What would Martha think?

KAJ HUGO: Little Baldy—you know the little guy from the hot dog stand —he said that he'd like my job here. I've already talked to him about it. He's smaller than me so we'll have to take the costume in somewhat.

WERNER: You could come out here to visit me once in a while. You'd look great in a uniform with a cap and everything.

KAJ HUGO: Dora would be pleased, I know that.

WERNER: There she is.

KAJ HUGO: Werner and I were just talking about you.

DORA: I must have sensed that. Let's try our luck, Kaj Hugo. (*The wheel spins.*)

KAJ HUGO: Holy smokes, we won. The prize, please, Werner.

WERNER: Let me check . . . a coffee pot . . . Boy, are you lucky.

DORA: You'll be the first to taste a cup of coffee made in it, Werner. We'll have a garden party when the roses are in bloom.

KAJ HUGO: We'll have to move some of them. People can't move their legs at your place for thorns.

WERNER: It's a deal. I'll bring some booze. We'll have a great time . . . I'll look forward to it. (*The tape is turned off abruptly.*)

1st SOLDIER: Why did you turn it off Number 3.

3rd SOLDIER: It's . . . It's late . . . Maybe we should stop here . . . We know how it's going to end.

1st SOLDIER: You don't have to stop on my account.

3rd SOLDIER: How can you be so . . . I mean . . . Here we are.

2nd SOLDIER: Imagine if we could have warned them.

1st SOLDIER: They are dead.

3rd SOLDIER: How much time is left on the tape?

1st SOLDIER: About six hours, I think.

2nd SOLDIER: Shouldn't we listen to the whole tape?

1st SOLDIER: We could just forward it.

3rd SOLDIER: I don't dare to think anymore. I refuse . . .

2nd SOLDIER: What about me?!

1st SOLDIER: It's now you really begin to think.

2nd SOLDIER: Number 1 knows what she's talking about. She's tried this before. We'll fast forward the tape. (*Sound of a tape being fast forwarded. Then the sound of footsteps and laughter moving away. Shutters and doors are being closed.*)

MARTHA: You can leave now Kaj Hugo. I'll do the rest myself. Tell Dora that I'm very happy for the two of you . . . It's been a good day . . . Good night . . . Look at the animals! They are already here. The last customers have barely left and here they are. How many of them are there?

KAJ HUGO: (*At a distance.*) Three stags and several deer.

MARTHA: It's amazing that they dare come this close . . . Don't frighten them . . .

KAJ HUGO: (*Further away.*) They aren't afraid of us . . . They can tell we mean them no harm! (*The sound of animals eating, chewing on their grass.*)

2nd SOLDIER: The animals?!

3rd SOLDIER: Don't stop the tape . . . Don't stop it!!

2nd SOLDIER: People are going to bed . . . We can only hear the animals . . .

3rd SOLDIER: I have to speak to them. Before it's too late.

1st SOLDIER: They are dead, Number 3 . . . all of them . . .

3rd SOLDIER: We must be able to warn them before it's too late.

2nd SOLDIER: Don't cry, Number 3 . . . Let's take a little walk. Their presence can still be felt. (*Distant sound of birds.*)

3rd SOLDIER: Hold on to me with your hands . . .

2nd SOLDIER: I'm here . . . Can you feel me now? There we are . . . The darkness . . . They are all here . . .

1st SOLDIER: We are not alone. There are others who know what we know.

(*Sounds from Dyrehavsbakken segue into bird song and then silence.*)

END

For Julia

by

Margareta Garpe

Translated from the Swedish by Harry G. Carlson

CHARACTERS:

Julia, 18 years old
Gloria, 40 plus
Charlie, definitely past 40

SETTING:

An old, crowded three-room apartment in Sweden, with high ceilings and plaster walls. The walls were once white and are studded with holes where paintings used to hang. The living room is center stage. The furnishings have been chosen in a free and capricious way. A bookcase is overloaded with piles of newspapers, yellowing play manuscripts, books. A clothesline stretches right across the room, with Julia's wash drying on one side and Gloria's on the other. To the left a combination bedroom and study with a double bed. Full length mirrors cover the insides of a closet's doors. To the right a smaller room, presently in turmoil, with a single bed. Posters have been taken down. Gaps between the door frame and surrounding plaster show that the door has slammed a lot.

Prologue

JULIA: At night I'm an astronaut, walking on the moon. I hold my breath as I put one foot down and raise the other. For a long moment, I hover in the air. The air is dark and weightless. And I'm afraid with every step I take on this strange planet that I'll never set foot on solid ground again. My heart is pounding. I'm an astronaut and I'm walking on the moon. I'm in a hurry. I have just a few minutes to collect enough samples to answer all mankind's questions . . . And I have this great fear that I can never return to earth. It hangs there in the distance, far away, bluish white and shining. Around it, stars are twinkling. It's so terribly fragile. Suddenly I hear the beating of a giant heart. The sound fills the whole universe.

Act I

(*The living room in late afternoon. Dusk. A pair of high heel shoes are scattered in the middle of the floor. A handbag lies open on a table, its contents spilled: make-up, tampons, cigarettes, a prescription bottle filled with white pills. Julia enters. She is wet with rain and carries a large, wrapped bouquet of flowers, a pack of sheet music, and a roll of black plastic trash bags. Without thinking, she picks up Gloria's shoes and carries them into the hall. Returning to the living room, she kicks off her own shoes mechanically. She puts the sheet music and the flowers on the table and catches sight of the pills. She picks up the bottle and reads the label.*)

JULIA: Gloria . . . (*She crosses to the door and opens it brusquely. She sees Gloria lying on her back, motionless, her arms and legs outspread, as if she were dead. Gloria's face is covered with a white towel. Julia's voice is filled with urgency.*) Momma . . . (*Pause.*) Gloria . . . (*Julia crosses quickly to her mother, drops to her knees, and starts shaking her. Gloria sits up with a start. Her face is covered with a white cosmetic mask. She pulls away tape recorder earphones. Julia's fear changes into mirth. Gloria puts her hand over Julia's mouth to prevent her from laughing. She holds up six fingers. Julia rises and returns to the living room. Gloria, dressed in tights and sweater, follows.*) Yeah, yeah, I know. Six minutes to go. And no laughing or crying, or your mask will crack. The oxygen will get in and the pores won't close—it'll all be wasted. (*Gloria automatically picks up the shoes that Julia kicked off and puts them out in the hall. Julia gets a vase in which she places the bouquet, still wrapped.*) So your skin gets tighter for a couple of hours. Then Cinderella has to rush home. But by then she's managed to conquer the prince. Everytime you have to see a director you put on that mask. What role is it this time? (*Gloria holds up four fingers to indicate the time left. Julia crowds her provocatively.*) Don't worry, I won't break it. You can wear all the masks you like. You know, as it dries, all the wrinkles show . . . It's like reading a map. Here around the eyes I can see smiles. Did you ever think about that—smiles leave marks, while tears . . . never show afterwards? And this is Grandma up here in your forehead. She had sharp creases just like that. She always looked as if she was trying to solve a humongous problem. I think it's neat. And this is from smoking . . . (*Gloria suddenly tears herself free, crosses to the table and defiantly takes a cigarette. She realizes she can't smoke now. She looks at the clock and feels the mask.*) It's all beautiful . . . except for the smoking. Naturally a disgusting habit like that leaves ugly traces. "What smells do you remember from your childhood? Clean sheets? Fresh bread? Sirloin steak? Roses?" No—smoke. Stale smoke, fresh smoke. My mother always smoked. So did her boyfriends. Even the cat smelled like French cigarettes. It's a miracle my singing voice survived . . . "Was it hard leaving home?" "No, I just got smoked out." (*Julia forces a laugh. Gloria lies down on the floor and begins pedaling furiously with her legs. Julia watches and decides that the time is ripe.*) . . . It's all set. I was up at my new landlord's today. You know, from my window I'll be able to see your chimney. And from the kitchen, the radio tower out by Poppa's. I'm on the seventh floor. That's high when you've grown up on the second. Guess what the landlord said: "Don't kid yourself you can grab the apartment. This is just a sublet. When Emma Andersson dies, the apartment goes back to me." But Emma says that when she and Gustav are dead I can have their apartment because I'm the nicest nurse in the whole home. Emma doesn't know that Gustav is dead . . . No one has the heart to tell her. (*Quickly, almost timidly.*) I have to pack. It'll take a couple of hours. (*Pause.*) I got a hold of Poppa. He's coming to pick up me and my things tonight. The bed too. (*Gloria's legs stop pedaling, involuntarily. She starts again, then rises quickly and exits into the bathroom. She locks the door. Julia goes into her room and gets a few packing cartons.*) Some night has to be the first. (*Julia goes to her room. Things to be thrown away she heaves into the black plastic bags; the few things to be saved are placed carefully in the cartons.*) I'm making room for Henrik's things in my closets. (*To herself.*) Just taking what I really need. Like *The Little Prince* . . . The Five Books series are shit . . . (*Throws them away.*) Where the hell is *Pippi Longstocking in the South Seas?* (*Loudly, to the closed door.*) Where the hell is *Pippi in the South Seas* . . . the one I got from Charlie? Have you seen it?

(*Gloria enters from the bathroom, dressed in a bathrobe and wiping the last of the mask from her face with a towel. She takes a cigarette out of her handbag but finds that her lighter won't work. She hunts for matches.*)

GLORIA: It's Strindberg's *Miss Julie.*
JULIA: Which part . . .?
GLORIA: (*Sarcastically.*) The butler . . . (*Frustrated over not finding matches.*) Dammit!
JULIA: (*Crossing to the bookcase.*) No matches here either . . . I know I didn't throw *Pippi* away. Did you?
GLORIA: . . . or Kristine, the cook. What did you think it would be?
JULIA: Miss Julie . . .
GLORIA: Then why did you ask? You know damned well I want to play Julie.
JULIA: Sorry. (*Gloria finds a matchbox, shakes it, and opens it.*)
GLORIA: Why do I save used matches? (*She continues searching in Julia's room.*)
JULIA: I don't smoke!
GLORIA: Unbelievable. Not a match in the whole house! (*With rising panic.*) I can't very well go out like this and buy some . . . (*She lifts up the telephone receiver and checks to make sure she hears a dial tone. Julia rises, hops up on a chair, and finds a box of matches resting on the top of a picture frame. She waves it triumphantly.*)
JULIA: Your old hiding place . . .
GLORIA: Fantastic . . . I'll never forget the morning . . .
JULIA: As a kid I couldn't reach this high.
GLORIA: . . . I woke up smelling something strange . . . Smoke . . . (*Looking in the matchbox.*) Two left. (*She lights a cigarette. Julia hands her a candle, which she lights.*) I leaped out of bed and found you sitting on the sofa. You were only three but you'd made sandwiches and something approaching coffee . . . And you'd put candles in all the candlesticks and lit them. It looked like high mass on Christmas Eve. And you sat there so devoutly, staring at the candles. By the time I got up they had almost

burned down. A couple of them were flickering close to the curtains . . .
They're all still there. All the memories. Like rolls of undeveloped film.
All of a sudden a picture plops down in the developer . . .

JULIA: I just remembered you used to keep them up there . . . (*Gloria inspects her face in the mirror. Julia continues to inspect books. She collects a pile of Heidi books, which she throws away, one after the other.*)

GLORIA: That was a welcome memory. Then there are other pictures
that should be left to yellow in some locked drawer . . . But even if you
lock up the copies, the negatives remain . . . (*Gloria is suddenly conscious of what Julia is doing.*) Julia! You can't throw those away!

JULIA: Why, do you want them?

GLORIA: They were gifts. From your grandmother.

JULIA: But I read them. And Grandma's dead . . . Or maybe you think
she's sitting up there now, looking down on us? Watching little Julia
throw out all her old birthday presents.

GLORIA: (*After a pause.*) No. I don't believe that . . .

JULIA: How do you know?

GLORIA: Because the dead are dead. Stone cold dead.

JULIA: How do you know the dead don't go on living?

GLORIA: They're only immortal as long as we remember them. They
can haunt us only as long as we let them . . . You're right. Throw them
away . . . Now that I think about it, I threw mine away too. With a feeling of guilt, I guess. For Grandma who was dead and would grieve to see
Gloria throw away the presents she paid for out of her meager pocketbook. And for the starving children of Africa . . . Think how happy
they'd be to get fourteen volumes of Heidi in Swedish . . .

(*Julia, browsing through her books, opens one.*)

JULIA: (*Reads.*) "To Julia, on her tenth birthday, from grandmother." This was the last one. And she didn't even give it to me
herself. It was just sitting there on the table, beautifully wrapped. With a
cake that had ten burned-down candles. I'd been lying in bed waiting for
congratulations. Finally, I got up to get ready for school. You were sitting alone on the sofa, with your coat on. Staring at the candles. "Grandma died last night," you said. You were so calm. Not a tear. "Grandma
wanted to die," you said. And you gave me this book from her. And
neither of us cried? Wasn't that strange? (*Julia tosses all but the last of
the books in a black trash bag.*)

GLORIA: She couldn't stand solitude, but she couldn't break out of it.

JULIA: But if she bought me a present, she must have planned to bring it
herself, as usual . . .

GLORIA: (*Evasively.*) Unhappy people don't act logically.

JULIA: Oh, I know that—only too well. (*Pause.*) I'm just going to pack up my things quickly. I'm only taking what I really need. (*Julia puts her grandmother's present in the carton. Gloria waves her hands aimlessly, trying to get her nail polish to dry.*)

GLORIA: Do you have to leave tonight. . . ? Why tonight? What's the hurry? Henrik was going to drive your things . . .

JULIA: I got the key and I don't want to take a chance . . .

GLORIA: I'm not trying to stand in your way.

JULIA: . . . that the landlord will change his mind and say I can't live in Emma's apartment . . .

GLORIA: I haven't even seen it. You're moving someplace I haven't even seen . . .

JULIA: You'll have to come and visit. I'll invite you to dinner . . . (*Gloria takes the bouquet out of the vase.*)

GLORIA: So it's going to be "So long, Gloria. Thanks for everything. Take care . . ." (*She tears the paper off the bouquet.*) Daisies and cornflowers . . . daisies and cornflowers . . . Just like Midsummer Eve. You were five, and we were picking flowers to make garlands. Up in the house they were getting ready for the big party. And we were waiting. Your dress was still spotless . . . I braided two garlands.

JULIA: Three . . . You always forget Charlie . . .

GLORIA: . . . and I thought . . . freeze this moment. Let her remember it. Julia and Gloria together on a meadow on Midsummer Eve . . .

(*Julia grabs the bouquet brusquely from Gloria and carefully rewraps it.*)

JULIA: These are to Emma from Gustav.

GLORIA: I even ironed your dress. (*Pause.*) Gustav? Isn't he dead?

JULIA: You should see Emma when she gets flowers . . .

GLORIA: How the hell can Gustav send flowers to Emma when he's dead?

JULIA: She blushes . . . And smells every flower . . .

GLORIA: Julia!

JULIA: You just don't want me to move away from home.

GLORIA: Crap!

JULIA: We all take turns buying flowers for Emma, from Gustav.

GLORIA: You're letting poor Emma live a lie. Just to get her apartment.

JULIA: I'm keeping a human being alive . . . and getting my own life . . .

GLORIA: And you haven't had one here. . . ?

JULIA: Yeah . . .

GLORIA: Have I stood in your way?

JULIA: . . . no . . .

GLORIA: What are you *really* saying?

JULIA: Just what I said . . . that you never stood in my way . . .

GLORIA: You don't sound especially convincing . . . (*She crosses to Julia, who pulls away and goes out into the hall.*)

JULIA: Poppa said he'd come as soon as he could get away.

GLORIA: Well, then there's no hurry. (*Pause; suddenly shouting.*) My God, *I'm* in a hurry! Put on my clothes, try to look halfway decent . . . (*Gloria dashes into her room. Pokes about in her closet. Puts a dress out on the bed. Takes off her bathrobe. Looks at herself in the mirror. Puts on underthings. Julia drags a pile of clothes into the living room. Pulls out a trash bag and begins to sort things.*) They could call any minute. He's up there right now, making his decision—the great guest director. The producer wants me to play Julie. He promised he'd fix it . . . (*Gloria stops looking at herself in the mirror. Julia tears off a new trash bag, drags a carton over, and begins to sort her old clothes. She holds up some discarded pieces to see how they would look on her.*) . . . I have to be ready . . . to make an entrance . . . We should pack your things in peace and quiet . . . not like this . . . Have dinner together, with candles . . . Just the two of us . . . Dear God, let me get the part . . . give me a part I can really bite into . . . It's my turn to play Miss Julie. (*Gloria is in front of the mirrored doors. She begins reciting lines from Strindberg's play.*) "For that matter, everything is strange. Life, people, everything. Like floating scum, drifting on and on across the water, until it sinks down and down! That reminds me of a dream I have now and then. I've climbed up on top of a pillar. I sit there and see no way of getting down. I get dizzy when I look down, and I must get down, but I don't have the courage to jump. I can't hold on firmly, and I long to be able to fall, but I don't fall. And yet I'll have no peace until I get down, no rest unless I get down, down on the ground! And if I did get down to the ground, I'd want to be under the earth . . . Have you ever felt anything like that?" (*Julia interrupts with a whistle.*) Usually I forget lines as soon as I finish playing a part. But not these, because I never got to play it . . . A week before the premiere the producer comes in to watch a rehearsal . . . I barely managed to say my opening line before he bellows: "My God, you're pregnant, Gloria!" "But I'm only in my fourth . . . and I can hold my stomach in . . . I can lace myself up." "But it's so damned obvious, even now . . . That's a bun that's only going to keep rising . . . We can't have a pregnant Miss Julie . . . Not before Jean even screws her. Miss Julie can be plump . . . nearsighted . . . hunchbacked . . . walk with a limp . . . but she goddamned well can't have a bun in the oven! It would violate everything the playwright intended, don't you see. . . ?

Gloria! This was so damned unnecessary!'' (*Pause.*) So I was thrown out
. . .

JULIA: You could have gotten rid of . . . the bun.

GLORIA: Some people thought I should . . .

JULIA: And you. . . ?

GLORIA: You know the answer to that.

JULIA: I want to hear it again.

GLORIA: It never crossed my mind . . .

JULIA: Because it was too late . . .

GLORIA: It was too late because I really wanted a child. I never wanted
to be alone again. (*Gloria embraces the sitting Julia from behind.*) You
always ask the same question . . . and get the same answer. But if there's
any justice in this world, I'll get the role now. And the bottom line will
be that I'll have both you and the role.

JULIA: Of course you'll get it . . . (*Takes off her jacket.*)

GLORIA: You're planning to get rid of your whole childhood in a couple
of hours? Seems a little unrealistic . . .

JULIA: Poppa's borrowed a van, so I might as well take advantage of it.

GLORIA: How wonderful that Rollie finally wants to do something for you.
For a change.

JULIA: (*Sharply.*) Roland.

GLORIA: To me he'll always be Rollie . . .

JULIA: No one else calls him that . . .

GLORIA: He was Rollie when we met and Rollie when we broke up . . .

JULIA: At least you got rid of the name Gloria Svensson.

(*Gloria crosses to the bathroom and pokes around on the shelves. She
returns quickly.*)

GLORIA: Julia . . . Have you seen my new Tabu perfume?

JULIA: Nope.

GLORIA: It couldn't have walked off on its own . . .

JULIA: I don't have it! (*Gloria crosses determinedly into Julia's room
and picks up her daughter's handbag.*) Stop digging in my bag . . .

GLORIA: I'm just looking . . . ever so carefully.

JULIA: . . . I just straightened it out.

GLORIA: . . . I'm just looking for . . . this! (*Fishing out a perfume bottle.*)
Which I got as a Christmas present from Henrik.

JULIA: But you don't like it . . .

GLORIA: It's still mine.

JULIA: You said I could take it.

GLORIA: Fat chance! I know exactly what's mine and what's yours. God

. . . it'll be so wonderful . . . not to have someone taking my stockings, which I later find filthy under the sofa . . . not to have someone sneaking into my room at seven in the morning to take my last pair of clean panties . . . While all the others are lying soaked in bleach in the washbasin, and I'm supposed to start rehearsing at ten. So there I am, scrounging in the clothes hamper for the least shitty pair. (*She exits into the bathroom.*) It'll be wonderful not having anyone borrowing my expensive new suede boots to go horseback riding in. (*Returning from the bathroom with a lathered toothbrush.*) No one taking money from my wallet. No one pouring water in the sherry bottle. No one using my script as a notepad by the telephone . . . All my things lying exactly where I've put them. (*Exits again.*)

JULIA: Thrown them.

GLORIA: For the first time in my life what's mine will be mine. It takes my breath away just to think about it. Mine . . . mine . . . mine alone.

JULIA: And that's *my* toothbrush . . . (*Gloria stops brushing, toothpaste around her mouth.*)

GLORIA: It's yellow . . .

JULIA: Yes. (*Gloria calmly continues brushing.*) . . . *I'm* yellow and *you're* green . . .

GLORIA: Isn't it the other way around. . . ?

JULIA: . . . and Charlie and the others were blue . . .

GLORIA: We're quarreling over trifles . . . are you sure about that? (*Gloria goes to the bathroom to change the toothbrush.*)

JULIA: I detest finding my toothbrush wet. I hate getting other people's bacteria in my mouth.

GLORIA: (*Returning.*) Don't you think we have the same little bacteria . . .

JULIA: You're gonna make me throw up.

(*The telephone rings. Gloria picks up the receiver anxiously. She says her name in a soft voice, then says "Just a minute!" Holds the receiver out to Julia.*)

GLORIA: Anna. Make it short.

JULIA: (*Taking the receiver.*) I'm packing like mad . . . of course you'll sleep over. (*Pause; she laughs.*) No, I'm not afraid of the dark—it's to celebrate. Because it's cool, that's all. I got a bottle of wine and some shrimp . . .

GLORIA: Short . . . Julia. (*Gloria goes back into her room and puts on a slinky black dress with a zipper up the back.*)

JULIA: You hear? . . . she's hysterical. Yeah, hopeless. Poppa's coming to get me . . . Call me in a couple of hours. Promise? Do you have the new number? (*She slams the phone down and goes to the hall to get more clothes.*) I'm taking my winter clothes too, to give Henrik more room. (*When Julia returns with her arms full of clothes, she finds Gloria, her back turned, waiting expectantly for help with her zipper.*)

GLORIA: (*Pleading.*) Sweetheart . . . A dress like this is not made for someone living alone. (*Julia begins tugging at the recalcitrant zipper.*)

JULIA: Henrik will have to help you.

GLORIA: Who said he was moving in?

JULIA: He was going to move in when I moved out.

GLORIA: It's probably too late now . . .

JULIA: I never stood in your way . . .

GLORIA: People should move in together when they first fall in love. Pang. Bam.

JULIA: I could have moved to Poppa's.

GLORIA: Sure. Sure. But it didn't happen.

JULIA: And you know why.

GLORIA: Well. . . ? How do I look? (*Julia looks past Gloria as if she were thinking about something else.*) Is someone standing over there?

JULIA: No.

GLORIA: Then what are you looking at?

JULIA: I'm looking at you.

GLORIA: You're looking at some point behind me.

JULIA: (*Indifferently.*) It's nice . . .

GLORIA: Are you sure?

JULIA: (*Realizing.*) My sheet music! The most important things of all. (*She runs into her room and fetches a pile of sheet music from under her bed.*) Even if I can't sing late at night, I can lie in bed and read them . . . I think I'm the only person in the world who reads sheet music to fall asleep. I can't understand what happened to *Pippi in the South Seas* . . . the one I got from Charlie . . .

GLORIA: I sweated helping you try things on in stores . . . buttoning and zipping and telling you what I thought . . .

JULIA: (*Packing the music in a carton.*) Gloria, I don't have time to dress you now . . .

GLORIA: You can at least give me . . . your opinion.

JULIA: It's fine. Fine.

GLORIA: Can you manage to concentrate for just a second. Look at me carefully and tell me what you think. (*Julia scrutinizes Gloria.*)

JULIA: There's something wrong . . .

GLORIA: What is it?

JULIA: I don't know.

GLORIA: I need higher heels. It gives me another profile. (*She changes shoes and demonstrates.*)

JULIA: It's okay. (*She continues to pack up her things.*)

GLORIA: But you said something was wrong.

JULIA: I said it's okay.

GLORIA: This is the last chance for me. There are parts you must get to play at least once in your life. And this is my part. I'm ready for it. It's still not too late.

JULIA: And if I'm not ready when Poppa comes, I'll have to drag all this there myself . . . You'll never help me . . .

GLORIA: We'll rent a car . . .

JULIA: Since when do you have a license?

GLORIA: Henrik can drive . . .

JULIA: Everything goes tonight. The cat! Oscar! I have to open the window so he can come in . . . (*Julia goes into the kitchen. She opens the window and calls the cat. She returns with a pet carrier.*)

GLORIA: You have time . . . How many times haven't you sat waiting on the street with your bag packed? Only to come up again and wait by the window. I'll never forget the time Rollie was going to pick you up, and as usual he was late. Charlie and I had to go to the theatre. Afterwards, we went out and had a quiet drink. And when we came home, in the middle of the night, there you were, still waiting with your bag by the window.

JULIA: Poppa was at the hospital with Fanny. She was shivering with fever.

GLORIA: He could have left his new kid for ten minutes to pick you up . . .

JULIA: (*Discovering.*) Now I know . . .

GLORIA: And you were only five at the time.

JULIA: . . . what's wrong with you. (*Pause.*) Menopausal paranoia.

GLORIA: What?

JULIA: Menopausal paranoia.

JULIA: Primitive. That's too crude, Julia . . . (*Proud of the dress.*) This is actually a timeless style. Timeless. Gloria Swanson wore it in the thirties. It'll never go out of fashion. Momma wore it too, although a little tighter . . . I always thought it looked so funny when she walked in it . . . Her legs moved like an eggbeater. (*She imitates the movement.*) And she looked so beautiful. Whatever else she was, she was beautiful. Very young, very beautiful. And so much like Gloria Swanson . . .

JULIA: It looks fine.

GLORIA: I'm happy with my age . . . as long as no one stands in my way . . .

JULIA: I was kidding.

GLORIA: As long as no one tries to torpedo me.

JULIA: I was only kidding . . .

GLORIA: You weren't kidding.

JULIA: That's true. Sorry. I made a mistake.

GLORIA: Unzip me. (*Julia hesitates.*) Unzip me. (*Julia obeys, but the zipper catches.*) . . . *I* made a mistake. Or I simply wasn't thinking. My hand just grabbed a dress. I look like some castoff Hollywood star, one of those Sunset Boulevard types, with her lipstick cockeyed and her heels worn down from begging for one last chance.

JULIA: The zipper's caught . . .

GLORIA: Tear it loose . . .

JULIA: It'll ruin the dress . . .

GLORIA: It's already ruined. (*Julia manages to loosen the zipper with a final tug. Gloria takes off the dress and throws it in one of the trash bags.*) Besides, it itches . . . (*Gloria goes into her bedroom, slamming the door behind her. Julia, watching her mother's door, retrieves the dress, and returns to her room. She holds the dress up to see how it will look on her, then packs it under some other things in a carton. She continues her hectic packing, conscious all the while of the closed door.*)

JULIA: Gloria. Wear the green dress, the one you bought before Christmas. And your red boots. You can borrow my red belt. (*Julia digs into her wardrobe and comes up with a red belt. She crosses to the closed door. Calls "Gloria," gets no answer, then calls again. She suddenly tries to open the door, which at first will not budge, then flies open. Gloria is sitting, on the bed, slumped over, motionless, facing the mirror. She looks naked. She comes to with a jerk.*) Why didn't you answer?

GLORIA: I'm sorry . . . I was thinking of something else . . .

JULIA: I got scared . . .

GLORIA: I got caught up in my body, caught up in Miss Julie. What the hell am I going to wear? Charlie used to say I had the body of a Botticelli goddess . . . But that was long ago . . . (*Gloria goes to the clothesline to take down red underclothes. Julia finds the green dress and red boots, and hangs her red belt around Gloria's neck.*)

JULIA: You're changing your underwear?

GLORIA: I wanted them to match . . .

JULIA: Do you have to show everything to the director?

GLORIA: Yes. (*Pause.*) No . . . are you crazy or something? (*Julia picks up the discarded underclothes and puts them on the bed.*)

JULIA: (*In a sisterly tone as she helps Gloria into the dress.*) Sweetie, you're going to look so *good*. Little Gloria will knock 'em right over.

GLORIA: (*Warding off Julia with laughter.*) Thanks. That's enough. It was just a little black hole I fell into. Now I'm back up again. (*Pause.*) Julia, I love you. (*Julia smiles serenely and returns to the living room. Gloria finishes dressing quickly and efficiently.*) Hope they call soon. Did you know Charlie's in town tonight? I actually thought about going to see Charlie. It's been ages since I saw him . . .

JULIA: Is Charlie in town?

GLORIA: A guest performance. You didn't know?

JULIA: No. I don't know anything about Charlie.

GLORIA: It was in the newspaper.

JULIA: He didn't even send me a birthday card this year.

GLORIA: Did you send him one?

JULIA: He didn't send anything last year either . . . I don't give a shit about Charlie . . .

GLORIA: For six long years . . .

JULIA: When his face pops up on TV I hardly recognize him.

GLORIA: . . . he meant everything to you . . .

JULIA: Except for his voice, I wouldn't even notice him . . .

GLORIA: You're really angry at Charlie, aren't you?

JULIA: No.

GLORIA: Why can't you admit it?

JULIA: "Really." I hate that word, you know . . .

GLORIA: Then who are you angry at. . . ?

JULIA: No one. Stop playing shrink.

GLORIA: I can hear you're angry at someone . . .

JULIA: When I say no one, I mean no one. There's no "really" for you to fish out.

GLORIA: Okay. Never that word again. I'll blot it out. Really. Word of honor.

JULIA: And cut that out too . . .

GLORIA: What did I say?

JULIA: Think about it . . .

GLORIA: You usually know my lines better than I do myself . . .

JULIA: "Word of honor."

GLORIA: But I mean it, honestly and truly. Never again.

JULIA: And never say "never." "Always" is another word I can't stand . . .

GLORIA: Must people stop using words because they can't always live up to them?

JULIA: Yes . . .

GLORIA: (*Jokingly.*) It's going to be quiet around here.

JULIA: And you'll have to keep your mouth shut all the time . . . (*Julia goes to her room, angrily rips the trays out of her closet, and dumps the contents in a carton.*)

GLORIA: (*Following into Julia's room.*) Shall I help you pack. . . ?

JULIA: No, you always screw up everything.

GLORIA: *Always?* I thought you hated that word.

JULIA: Not when it's accurate. Can't you sit down? You're making me nervous.

(*Gloria sits on the sofa. When she discovers that she is too far from the telephone, she moves closer. Julia continues to pack and sort.*)

GLORIA: Am I alright here?

JULIA: Perfect.

GLORIA: You sure?

JULIA: Yes.

GLORIA: The actress and her telephone. A classic picture. It's funny. You never get used to it. You'll see for yourself one day if you keep up your singing. God knows where you got your voice from. It couldn't have been Rollie. Sorry, Roland.

JULIA: Yes, not from you, not from Poppa . . .

GLORIA: Do you remember . . . Surabaya Johnny. . . ? (*Gloria begins to sing in a wobbly voice. Julia picks up the song and helps her mother to stay in key.*)

GLORIA & JULIA:
    Surabaya Johnny—
    Surabaya Johnny—
    Surabaya Johnny—

GLORIA: (*While Julia is singing.*) You practiced with me every evening before I went to the theatre . . .

JULIA: And sometimes you called home and made me sing to you over the phone . . .

GLORIA: Scared to death every time I had to go on and sing. But when I marched in that Viet Nam demonstration . . . we made the whole street echo with our singing. I sang with all my heart, "We shall overcome." And there was a guy with a scraggly beard who yelled in my ear: "Dammit, sister, you sing out of key." I had the right feeling, but it sounded like hell.

JULIA: I'm the only one who can keep you in key.

GLORIA: But now I'm getting my revenge . . . through you. Justice was done, even if it took a while.

JULIA: My voice is mine . . . and it has nothing to do with you.

GLORIA: It's not going to help your singing to move away from home.

Everything's going to be more expensive. You know yourself how tired
you are after your shift at the home. All your energy will go to making
enough money to pay the rent.

JULIA: How many times haven't you said how wonderful it'll be when I
move out . . . so Henrik can move in?

GLORIA: What I said was that one day you'd leave . . . sooner or later.
I don't want my daughter to be an old maid.

JULIA: He will move in, won't he?

GLORIA: Why should it bother you?

JULIA: It doesn't . . .

GLORIA: I just think you should leave under different circumstances . . . I
can't help you much now and Rollie's income is probably what it usually
is: non-existent. Do you have any idea what all this is going to cost? And
then moving into someone else's apartment . . . is that something
worthwile?

JULIA: Anna's parents bought her an apartment. The nicest studio in the
world. With a view over the park. She can do whatever she wants with it.

GLORIA: Why must I be compared with other people's mothers. . . ? Go
ask your father why he doesn't make any money . . . A man who's
going to get somewhere in life doesn't go around knocking up three different women. (*Julia crosses quickly to her room, slamming the door
behind her. Gloria retorts loudly.*) Julia! You've slammed that door for
the last time! That's really the sort of thing you stop doing at thirteen.
(*Gloria checks the telephone, but Julia's closed door is like a magnet for
her.*) It's surely not unreasonable to ask that you leave your childhood
home standing after you're gone . . . (*Pause.*) Julia . . . it wasn't my in-
tention to hurt you. I'd tear heaven down for you if I could . . . You do
the best you can, right? Certain things you can decide . . . others are
decided for you . . .

(*Julia's answer is to begin practicing a musical scale loudly. Gloria goes into
her room, slamming the door behind her. Julia's singing dies out. Pause.
Julia comes out of her room slowly, and positions herself deliberately in the
center of the living room.*)

JULIA: (*Bellowing.*) Gloria . . . forgive me . . . (*Gloria enters quickly from
her room.*) I got so terribly scared . . .

GLORIA: (*Upset, taking Julia in her arms.*) It'll never happen again. Never!
(*Pause.*) . . . You're only going to move some few measly blocks away
and I'm going to start rehearsals for *Miss Julie* and get to play the lead
. . . I'm certainly not going to panic because the phone doesn't ring. I've
reached that point in life where I can see the potholes coming, and I

know how to hop over them . . . You see the quicksand and you go around it . . . calmly and carefully. It's a wonderful feeling . . . you understand?

JULIA: Yes.

GLORIA: You don't believe me.

JULIA: No.

GLORIA: It's been a whole year since I last ripped all the books out of the bookcase . . .

JULIA: (*Irritated.*) That's why they're not in order any more. I stopped putting them back right . . .

GLORIA: That wasn't very practical, but it worked . . .

JULIA: Three times I put them back . . . in alphabetical order.

GLORIA: But if you can't go around beating children or strangling cats . . . what are you supposed to do?

JULIA: The fourth time I asked my teacher and she said, ''Your mother needs help breaking bad habits and learning to accept the consequences of her actions.'' So I just left them there. Lucky for you, you were having people to dinner . . .

GLORIA: Julia, I love you. That's a good story.

JULIA: It's true.

GLORIA: True or false. It's a wonderful story. When I was little, children had no sense of humor. We just had the illusion that everything grownups did was right, followed by the disappointing discovery that everything they did was wrong. My mother had no books to pull down when life got a stranglehold on her . . .

JULIA: Lucky for you . . .

GLORIA: Books can be picked up. That's a small calamity compared with doing something . . .

JULIA: (*Frightened.*) Yes . . . (*Gloria is silent. Julia embraces her hard.*) I love you. Most of all in the whole world. Let's do something together this summer. I know. We'll go far up north, to Lofoten Island. We'll go back there again.

GLORIA: Julia and Gloria on Lofoten Island. We'll never desert each other.

(*Julia breaks the embrace.*)

JULIA: I hate you. Most of all in the whole world. You're forever standing in my way.

GLORIA: I'm sitting by the telephone, minding my own business.

JULIA: In a couple of hours I'll be sitting with Anna in my new place, eating shrimp. This summer we'll travel through Europe.

GLORIA: Anna . . . Anna. Wouldn't it be more fun with a boy?

JULIA: Maybe I'll have a better chance of finding one when I don't have you to take care of anymore.

GLORIA: You're exaggerating.

JULIA: You love exaggerations . . .

GLORIA: True . . . it they're funny . . . and not aimed at me.

JULIA: No, at others, instead. That you enjoy. Admit it.

GLORIA: Have you forgotten all the times we used to laugh together . . . at other people? Why did you want to go every Saturday to the skating rink in the park when you were little? Because you loved to watch those poor innocent Japanese tourists take their first steps on skates and go through terrible somersaults.

JULIA: We went there because that's where you used to turn me over to Poppa . . . I still hate the place. My hands get sweaty every time I walk past it.

GLORIA: But why? You never seemed upset.

JULIA: Maybe my sweater was too hot. I don't know why . . . and I don't care.

GLORIA: But something must have happened . . . which only you can remember . . .

JULIA: I said I don't care!

GLORIA: But I'm curious . . .

JULIA: And I'm more curious what will happen in the future . . .

GLORIA: But if you begin sweating at the sight of a skating rink . . .

JULIA: . . . then I'll take another route. Why should I strain my brain trying to remember everything I've forgotten? There's only one direction that's important—ahead. I get so tired of all this talk about young people not believing in the future. I certainly don't want to go and hang myself.

GLORIA: Why would you want to do that?

JULIA: I just said I didn't want to. I'm planning to live a long life and die a natural death.

GLORIA: (*Increasingly frightened.*) Julia. I don't understand why you have to talk like that. You have everything going for you. You're sweet, talented, smart, sensitive, strong-willed. You know, people have always said there was no future, but the world goes on. And we go on. (*She goes into the kitchen.*)

JULIA: I'll wait till I get old to remember everything that happened up to now.

GLORIA: (*Entering carrying a wine bottle and a glass.*) They've got to call soon . . . any second . . . Skål, Gloria, this is going to turn out well.

JULIA: I musn't forget to take a bottle of wine along . . .

GLORIA: But you told Anna you bought one . . .

JULIA: I was counting on you.

GLORIA: As usual. Sorry. This is the only one there is . . .

JULIA: But Anna and I are going to eat shrimp and this is the first night of my new life.

GLORIA: (*Putting the corkscrew in the bottle.*) I bought it to celebrate my getting the role.

JULIA: Henrik can bring a bottle with him . . .

GLORIA: I don't know anything about Henrik's plans.

JULIA: But you can go out afterwards.

GLORIA: Alone. . . ?

JULIA: Hasn't the bar always been your second home . . .

GLORIA: You're exaggerating.

JULIA: You'd come straight home, you said, but that's not what happened. There was always something you had to discuss afterwards . . . For a while I thought that sitting in a bar was part of your job. Charlie came straight home after his performances. But you threw him out and let that shit move in instead . . .

GLORIA: (*Explosively.*) Most of the time you had a babysitter . . . What the hell does this cork have against me. . . ?

JULIA: You haven't gotten the role yet.

GLORIA: His name is Leo . . . not the Shit!

JULIA: And of course if I got scared, I could always call Jan at the switchboard. It's just that when the performance ended she closed up and went home.

GLORIA: Grandma was here . . . sometimes Rollie . . . and the girls.

JULIA: I could have lived with Poppa . . .

GLORIA: You longed to come home after every holiday with him.

JULIA: I longed for the cat.

GLORIA: I've spent a fortune on babysitters and toys, Julia. Doesn't that count for something? And what about the sweat and tears and the times my heart was in my throat? And the nights when the babysitter couldn't make it and promised to send a friend who didn't come. I stand on stage petrified because the only role I can think of is playing Julia's momma. At the intermission I don't dare to call home for fear of waking you up. And after the performance I'm exhausted and angry. I convince myself you're sleeping like a log, and go out with the others to the bar. Yes, it happened a couple of times. But later you wanted to sit for yourself . . . for pay. Was that also wrong?

JULIA: Can I take the wine or not?

GLORIA: Going to bars isn't fun anymore. It used to be candlelight and expectations . . . Now everything's predictable before you finished checking your coat.

JULIA: Yes or no.

GLORIA: (*Tonelessly.*) Of course.

JULIA: Put the cork back in, then. (*Pause.*) So it doesn't evaporate.

GLORIA: You'll have two glasses each. With greetings from Gloria.

JULIA: You're an angel. Are you sure you'll be all right?

GLORIA: I'll survive. The water in my toothbrush cup will taste like champagne. I'll take my green . . . I mean my yellow cup and raise a toast that'll echo right through the walls . . .

JULIA: I'm sorry I said that about the Shit. It just came out. Forgive me.

GLORIA: I was happy when my mother died. It brought me closer to my own death, but also to my own life. I was free of the disapproval I could always read in her face. It was as if she was at every rehearsal; her face was clearer in my mind than the director's. And at the opening, there she is, right in the first row. She always had to have an opening night ticket. It effects my whole performance. I overact just to feel independent . . . But at the party afterward I can't wait any longer. I have to call her. (*Breathlessly.*) "Well, what did you think?" (*Imitating her mother's thin voice.*) "Yes, it was all right." "But what did you really think?" "Gloria, I just don't understand how you can behave so atrociously." "But it's the character, Momma." "It seemed like you thought the character was right." "But Momma, for God's sake, I have to stand up for my character. I feel differently with each one: I hate her, I love her, but I must defend her. What do you think Gloria Swanson did?" "Well, I feel the theatre should show things that are beautiful in people, things that make you happy."

JULIA: She was my grandmother . . .

GLORIA: She was my mother . . .

JULIA: Sometimes she was afraid of dying . . . and then she'd ask me to sing to her . . .

GLORIA: She had a bad side and a good side. The bad side she turned toward me, the good one toward you. But in the end the two sides came to terms. May she rest in peace. Peace. Skål.

JULIA: Did Grandma die in the hospital?

GLORIA: Yes. When I arrived she was unconscious. She died calmly and peacefully.

JULIA: But the book I got the next morning. . . ?

GLORIA: (*Evasively.*) Yes. . . ?

JULIA: How did you get it?

GLORIA: It was lying in her handbag. Why do you ask?

JULIA: How come she had my present with her in the hospital?

GLORIA: How should I know?

JULIA: You'll have to admit it sounds strange.

(*The phone rings. Gloria rushes frantically to answer it. But she answers in a warm, firm voice.*)

GLORIA: Yes, this is Gloria. (*Pause.*) Yes, it is she. (*To Julia.*) Anna . . . but make it short. (*Julia takes the receiver.*)

JULIA: Hi . . . Poppa hasn't come yet. But I'm almost through packing. And I got the wine . . . (*She is interrupted. She slumps visibly, says "See you" and puts down the phone. She goes into her room, slamming the door so hard that the plaster shakes loose. Gloria opens the door and finds Julia sitting on the bed.*) She can't come tonight . . .

GLORIA: But didn't she promise . . . ?

JULIA: She's at Carl's. He called her and she decided to go to bed with him. They're going at it right now, I guess. So, now I'm alone.

GLORIA: Well, you can still be best friends . . .

JULIA: We were close because we were both virgins . . . The only ones left who . . . hadn't done it.

GLORIA: (*Gently.*) Is that so important?

JULIA: As long as there was Anna, I could go on believing there was so much more that was important. Working, practicing . . . But now . . . what's the point of being a virgin any more?

GLORIA: (*Matter-of-factly.*) Well, call someone up then?

JULIA: You can't do a thing like that.

GLORIA: Why not? "Hi, this is Julia. Want to end my virginity? Name the time and place."

JULIA: But who would I call? Pella . . . Kasper . . . Jonas.

GLORIA: Pick one with a big prick . . .

JULIA: (*Suddenly matter-of-fact.*) That much I know; size isn't important.

GLORIA: That's true. Men with small peckers can be great at fixing meals, finding bargains, cutting the grass, dancing the tango . . .

JULIA: You're disgusting.

GLORIA: . . . they can be loving, sensual, erotic. But since you clearly only want to screw, pick out a proper prick.

JULIA: (*Pause.*) I want to meet someone whom . . . I can love and who only loves me . . . There has to be . . . an understanding between us.

GLORIA: (*Gently.*) Maybe you're taking it too seriously.

JULIA: Now that I've waited this long for someone, it is serious.

(*Gloria strokes Julia's hair. There is a moment of serenity between them.*)

GLORIA: Then maybe you can wait a little longer . . . (*Pause.*) I didn't even have time to wait. Suddenly, there I was, on my back. I became a hero to my friends, but an enemy to myself . . .

JULIA: One thing I know—I'm not going to live like you did. Poppa, Charlie, the Shit, and now . . . is it still Henrik or. . . ?

GLORIA: Why are you so angry at me?

JULIA: Why can't I ever talk about me without you always dragging yourself into it. . . ?

GLORIA: I just wanted to share my experiences with you.

JULIA: Thanks . . . I already know them . . .

GLORIA: Then we'll talk about something else. (*Pause.*) There's not much I can give you, is there?

JULIA: No, not any longer . . .

GLORIA: Why don't you ever call me Momma? Rollie is Poppa and I'm only Gloria . . . Isn't that strange? (*The telephone rings. Gloria pounces on it.*) Yes, this is Gloria . . . (*Pause.*) Just a minute. Anna again. Must be a progress report . . .

JULIA: I'll take it in my room. (*Exits to her room.*)

GLORIA: (*Pouring herself some wine.*) Gloria, get a hold of yourself. If they really want you, they'll call back.

JULIA: (*On the phone.*) It's okay. Of course you should stay.

GLORIA: (*Restless, she picks up a man's overcoat from the clothes Julia has scattered on the floor, tries it on briefly, then drops it.*) Maybe they went out to get something to eat. They'll call from the restaurant. I'll get a meal out of it, too.

JULIA: (*On the phone.*) What brand did he use. . . ? (*Giggles.*) Really? Hello . . . What? . . . Oh. I guess we'll have to hang up then. (*She goes out to Gloria.*) We were cut off because of an incoming call.

GLORIA: Here? (*The telephone rings.*) Hello, this is Gloria. Oh, hi . . . but . . . (*She hangs up the receiver.*) That was Charlie. He's coming up. He placed a call to Greece . . . from this number.

JULIA: Charlie's coming here?

GLORIA: Apparently. He has a house there. Probably calling his family. She must still be there with the kid . . .

JULIA: And he's coming here. After ten years. (*She picks up the overcoat and embraces it hard.*) I know exactly what he smells like. I used to sit by all the shoes in the hall, waiting for him to come back, and smelling the only thing he left . . . this coat . . . But the wrong shoes always came back. It was always the Shit.

GLORIA: (*Pained.*) That wasn't his name, Julia.

JULIA: And then that night you didn't wake up . . .

GLORIA: Julia, you're opening old wounds.

JULIA: I hate Charlie and I'll never forgive him.

(The doorbell rings.)

GLORIA: Typical Charlie. Turns up only to make a phone call.

JULIA: I'm not here. *(She goes into her room. Gloria opens the door. Charlie enters, looking rather shabby, his coat buttoned wrong.)*

GLORIA: You still don't know how to button your coat right. Haven't changed a bit. *(She fixes the buttons.)*

Act II

CHARLIE: And you're just as beautiful. (*Pause.*) I have to borrow the telephone.

GLORIA: (*Coolly.*) I'm waiting for a call. As soon as it comes I have to run. (*Gloria sits with the telephone on her lap. Charlie, his overcoat still on, wanders restlessly about the room. The door to Julia's room remains closed.*)

CHARLIE: It's my son's birthday . . . he's four today. A father has to congratulate his son, right?

GLORIA: Is that why you returned to the scene of the crime? There are telephones everywhere.

CHARLIE: I didn't want to stand screaming into a pay phone at the theatre. . . . Did I commit some crime here?

GLORIA: No.

CHARLIE: You're the one who threw me out, right?

GLORIA: Yes.

CHARLIE: Then we're agreed on the historical facts. That's important for a man my age . . . Even if I still can't understand what was behind them . . .

GLORIA: Whenever I see a comedy, I think: "Charlie would have done it so much better!" I'd really love to see you tonight . . . but I can't. I have an important appointment . . . How's the family? Sometimes I'm really jealous of you. Here we are freezing in Sweden while you're commuting to your house on Leros. I saw it in one of the pictures in her exhibition last year . . . Looks big.

CHARLIE: It's pretty big . . .

GLORIA: Julia's inside. She's moving tonight. Leaving home . . . You won't recognize her . . .

CHARLIE: My son looks like me . . .

GLORIA: Why wouldn't he. . . ?

CHARLIE: Except better . . . He didn't get my nose . . . or hers.

GLORIA: How nicely it all turned out for you, Charlie. You got your son.

(*Charlie pulls Gloria to him in a strong embrace. Julia opens her door slightly and watches them from her room.*)

CHARLIE: Gloria, we smell the same. Do you sense it? A sickly sweet scent . . .

GLORIA: . . . it's Tabu . . .

CHARLIE: . . . a sickly sweet, musty scent of abandonment.

GLORIA: I'm going to play Miss Julie.

CHARLIE: Whatever happened to the Shit? What'd he disappear out in the provinces or something?

GLORIA: Charlie, I don't give a damn.

CHARLIE: Maybe he smells now too. A comforting thought. Admit it. There are more and more of us who smell. And we recognize it from a distance and hate it. Can you sense how I stink? She's down there screwing some young Greek right now. It's so banal you could die laughing. Actually, I don't give a damn either. I never could get used to her nose . . . long and fleshy . . . Gloria, you never should have left me . . .

GLORIA: Then you wouldn't have your son now . . .

CHARLIE: You and I could have had him. (*They embrace. The telephone rings. Charlie breaks the clinch and grabs the receiver. Julia has already picked up in her room.*) It's from Leros . . . hello . . .

GLORIA: No, it's from the theatre.

JULIA: (*Pause.*) Yes, I'll give her the message. (*She puts the receiver down slowly and remains seated where she is. Shouting.*) It was the producer!

GLORIA: What did he say?

JULIA: (*Shouting.*) He called from the restaurant!

GLORIA: So, I'll get a meal after all . . . I'm going to order the most expensive thing on the menu. A big steak . . . rare. You see, I learned my lesson, Charlie. Do you remember what you said when I always came home hungry after somebody else paid the tab? ''People with expense accounts always want you to order a simple omelet or fish of the day, because they're already full. Always do your own ordering! . . . ''

CHARLIE: (*Taking the bottle.*) I need some wine.

GLORIA: (*Retrieving the bottle.*) The wine is Julia's. She's celebrating

the end of her childhood . . . Smells don't last forever, Charlie . . .
Everything is possible again.

CHARLIE: . . . and you and I. . . ?

GLORIA: You can't repeat something like that . . .

CHARLIE: I'd like to see you in that black dress again . . .

GLORIA: Would that have been better? No. It makes no difference what
I'm wearing. (*She is ready to leave.*) Julia! I'm going now. (*To Charlie.*)
Maybe you'll still be here when I get back. Julia! Are you going to say
hello to Charlie? He's going soon . . . (*Julia does not answer.*) Don't
miss your performance, Charlie. (*Exits. Charlie picks up the wine bottle
and goes into Gloria's room. He looks around and opens the mirrored
doors of the closet. Lines from Macbeth come to him, some easily, some
with difficulty.*)

CHARLIE:

"The Queen, my lord, is dead."

She should have died hereafter;

There would have been time for such a word.

To-morrow, and to-morrow, and to-morrow,

Creeps in this petty place from day to day . . .

(*He picks up the receiver, listens, and hangs up again.*)

To the last syllable of recorded time . . .

(*He pulls the cork from the bottle and takes a gulp. Julia stands behind
him, dressed in Gloria's black dress, but Charlie doesn't notice her.*)

And all our yesterdays have lighted fools

The way to dusty death. Out, out, brief candle . . .

JULIA: Don't you want a glass? (*Julia gets two glasses.*)

CHARLIE: Sorry . . . I suddenly got a lump in my throat . . . the kind only
alcohol washes down . . .

JULIA: You going to play Shakespeare. . . ?

CHARLIE: Just a gimmick . . . to keep from going crazy . . .

JULIA: (*Pouring wine into the glasses.*) Skål . . .

CHARLIE: You've grown . . .

JULIA: . . . and you've shrunk . . .

CHARLIE: That's for sure. I'm the most worn-out, bottom step in the
ladder that all women step on to move up in the world . . .

JULIA: You haven't shrunk. I've gotten taller.

CHARLIE: I'm waiting for a call to my son. He's four years old today. Time
goes by so damned fast. Yesterday he was born, tomorrow he's grown up
. . . The days go by so fast your toothbrush won't dry between morning
and night . . .

JULIA: Do you still use a blue toothbrush?

CHARLIE: No, I never had a special color . . .

JULIA: When you lived here you were blue.

CHARLIE: All I know is I lived here.

JULIA: I'm yellow, Gloria is green, and you were blue.

CHARLIE: But I remember that dress. Gloria's so damned pretty in it.

JULIA: *Was* pretty in it . . .

CHARLIE: And now she's going to play Julie. An overrated role. Dreary and musty. But that's what I think of all the roles nowadays. (*Looking at the clock.*) Concocted neuroses. I don't give a damn . . .

JULIA: She's not going to play Julie.

CHARLIE: Sure she is . . .

JULIA: She didn't get the part.

CHARLIE: But you sent her off . . .

JULIA: Yes.

CHARLIE: Why?

JULIA: I don't know. I just did. I felt sorry for her. She was in my way, though I'm almost done packing. I think Julie is a hopeless woman too. The business about her suicide is ridiculous. (*Pause.*)

CHARLIE: I don't think I understand. But of course I'm used to that.

JULIA: (*Quickly.*) What's your son look like? Do you have a picture?

CHARLIE: My God, you've never seen him. I thought everybody had seen him. (*He suddenly comes to life and takes a bunch of pictures from his wallet. Julia sits on Gloria's bed quite close to Charlie.*) Theo, new in the world. My first kid and I'm over forty. You see, he has my birthmark on his cheek.

JULIA: Fantastic. And on the same side too.

CHARLIE: When I first saw it, I . . . Here he is at two years and three months. Maggie went to an artists' colony on Leros, and Theo and I were alone together here the whole summer. We took long walks along the beaches . . .

JULIA: . . . on Sheep Island . . .

CHARLIE: Exactly. It was such a remarkable time. The days were eternities, while the whole summer was a single, brilliant moment. Sometimes, he wiped me out. She never bends down to listen when he talks, but I do, and by the end of the day, my back was wrecked.

JULIA: So, there you walked, hand in hand. Charlie and Theo. You picked up stones and skated them on the water.

CHARLIE: I developed the right arm of a boxer. And this is Leros. She suddenly got it in her head that blue was blue only on Leros. But I can't see any improvement. Her paintings are still just as clumsy. But she got it in her head . . . so I bought the house there and started commuting from Gothenberg. Leros, Gothenberg. It's a haul and it's not cheap. But she promised: "I'm going to paint enough for an exhibition that'll knock the world on its ear. Then we'll come home." For a while I believed her, and I've been tearing back and forth like a madman for almost two years, trying to keep afloat. Road tour after road tour, brewing instant coffee with immersion heaters, and downing enough whiskey to make me an alcoholic. Meanwhile, she's down there, screwing somebody else. Some young, self-appointed genius, who likes to paint on the beach, stripped to the waist. And I pretend not to notice. I gotta hang on . . . Julia, if you knew how much the longing hurts. Then I get that damned lump in my throat. The minute I get on stage I'm scared my throat'll cramp up and I won't be able to make a sound. I get a terrible desire just to scream: "*No!* Life shouldn't be like this." But I gotta hang on. It'll all sort itself out . . . (*Checking the time.*) I should have been putting on makeup exactly ten minutes ago.

JULIA: Poppa's getting a van . . .

CHARLIE: (*Picking up the receiver.*) No, that won't help. It has to come any minute now. I placed a person-to-person call to Theo . . .

JULIA: (*Putting back the receiver.*) . . . and he's going to call to see if I'm ready.

CHARLIE: And what'll you do?

JULIA: Unlock my very own door and lock it behind me.

CHARLIE: What about boys. . . ?

JULIA: I've had a couple.

CHARLIE: Naturally. When a person's (*pause*) over twenty, it'd be strange if you hadn't. And the future?

JULIA: Support myself, sing. I still sing . . . both solo and in the choir.

CHARLIE: (*Suddenly.*) Do you believe in God?

JULIA: Sometimes I do, when I'm singing. Then I believe in God and love . . .

CHARLIE: And when you're not singing?

JULIA: (*After a pause.*) Then I want to believe but . . . I . . .

(*The telephone rings. Charlie pounces on it.*)

CHARLIE: Hello . . . Yes, that's me . . . Hello . . . Theo . . . it's Poppa . . . Hello, can I talk to Theo . . . I don't have time to talk to you now, Maggie. I'm on my way to a performance. I just want to congratulate Theo and hear what he thinks of the presents. (*Pause.*) What? But I sent them air mail. They promised me they'd get there in time. I'm coming down in two weeks. I'm coming down in two weeks. Yes, of course I will. (*Pause.*) Why would he be upset to see me? (*Pause.*) Maggie, I know you've met someone else. It makes no difference. Maggie. You can't afford a divorce. Can I talk to Theo? Maggie, sweetheart . . . I'll kill you! Yes, you're going to force him to. I can hear him crying. He misses me . . . Theo, this is Poppa. Hello. Hello. (*A loud click sounds on the other end. Charlie falls back on Gloria's bed, the receiver lying beside him, squealing desolately. Julia hangs up the phone.*) Theo can't take it any more. He wants to blot me out. Kids don't know how to be faithful; that's why they survive . . . But I can't live with it. This damned smell is suffocating me.

JULIA: But I love you, Charlie. I've always loved you. (*Julia embraces Charlie hard.*) I love the way you smell.

CHARLIE: I stink . . .

JULIA: You smell like Charlie, that's all. You forgot your coat, you know. It's still here. I've been saving your place the whole time. It's all yours, yours alone. I want you to hold me, hard. You must never leave me again. (*Charlie hugs her desperately, and begins kissing her.*)

CHARLIE: Don't ever leave me.

JULIA: Charlie.

CHARLIE: You are mine . . . (*Charlie abruptly halts the intensive embracing and tumbles Julia out of the bed.*)

JULIA: (*On the floor.*) *Pippi in the South Seas* . . . I couldn't find it . . .

CHARLIE: I'm sorry.

JULIA: I want a new one . . .

CHARLIE: I'm sorry . . . it was that dress.

JULIA: I'm eighteen years old . . .

CHARLIE: Why have you got it on?

JULIA: Eighteen and three months. You lived with me for six years and don't even know how old I am. I have pictures from Sheep Island, too. Lots. The first was taken when I was two. I'm walking on the beach. In one hand I have a pail and shovel, in the other, you . . . I have piles of pictures of the two of us together . . . and later there were none.

CHARLIE: You already had a father . . . Rollie.

JULIA: But I always lived with you and Gloria.

CHARLIE: When Gloria kicked me out for that shit, it was like everything we had together turned . . . worthless.

JULIA: But that was Gloria . . .

CHARLIE: I was replaced. How many fathers are you going to have in your life?

JULIA: It took me three years to get him out of the house. One night I waited in the dark for him in the clothes closet. When he stepped out of his shoes, I bit him near the ankle.

CHARLIE: Too bad he didn't die of lockjaw.

JULIA: He got a tetanus shot, and Gloria took me to a psychologist. But I still harrassed him. In a thousand different ways. I had to get rid of his shoes. (*Pause.*) So that yours could come back. Childish, huh? Because you never came back . . . And that night, when Gloria almost died, and I begged you to come, the only thing you could say was "I don't give a shit. I don't give a shit. (*Softly.*) I don't give a shit."

CHARLIE: I have only explanations, no excuses.

JULIA: I don't want to hear them.

CHARLIE: Does it help if I say I'm sorry?

JULIA: No.

CHARLIE: So, you want to get even with old Charlie and Gloria and the whole world?

JULIA: Yes.

(*Charlie puts his arm around Julia.*)

CHARLIE: And justice is so perfect for imperfects like me that I'll get my punishment after all. Won't that be a comfort? (*Taking some bills out of his pocket.*) Here's some money for the phone call. (*Julia gets his coat and drapes it over his shoulders.*) We had fun together those years . . . yeah, damned good fun. Maybe one day all the other stuff will fade in comparison. Say goodbye to Gloria for me.

JULIA: Poppa's coming for me any minute.

CHARLIE: She deserves a better role.

JULIA: It was all her fault, Charlie. Where are you going?

CHARLIE: You want a new copy of *Pippi Longstocking in the South Seas*? I'll send it to you.

JULIA: No. (*Pause.*) Yes. Drop it in the mailbox before you hang yourself. Charlie?

CHARLIE: I'm going over to the hospital. To ask for a bed and some sleeping pills . . . They can take away my tie and belt. A car accident is the best excuse for missing a performance, but a convincing nervous breakdown will also do.

JULIA: (*As he exits.*) If you kill yourself, Charlie, I'll beat the hell out of you. (*Julia tears off the black dress and throws it in a garbage bag. Dressed only in her slip, she frenetically finishes her packing and rolls up her mattress. It is dark out. Gloria enters, wet from the rain. Julia rises, prepared.*)

GLORIA: How could you do a thing like that? (*She crosses to her room and starts undressing.*)

JULIA: How could you do a thing like that?

GLORIA: They were sitting there, in the restaurant. I go straight over to their table. When the great one gets up, I hold out my hand and say in my best English, "Here's Julie."

JULIE: I was only ten years old.

GLORIA: We all sit down. I order a glass of wine. I wave to the waitress as though she's playing Kristine. I order the most expensive thing on the menu, filet of venison with mushrooms. I talk and talk about Julie. They say nothing. "My God," I thought, "I must be talking too fast," so I try to speak slowly and clearly in English. When I stop talking, there's a deadly silence. Then the manager says, "Gloria, didn't you get my message?"

JULIA: I was ten years old and you wouldn't wake up. You just lay there, snoring. Loudly. So loudly that you wake me up. You talked me into sleeping in your bed.

GLORIA: "Yes . . . I was to come . . . right away."

JULIA: (*Crossing to Gloria.*) I tried to wake you.

GLORIA: "I told your daughter you didn't have to come." Then the food arrives. (*Gloria crawls into bed, dressed in her slip. Julia crosses to her and begins to shake her and hit her. The ensuing battle between them becomes violent, and they both end up on the floor in the living room.*)

JULIA: I shook you, rocked you, hit you . . . But you wouldn't wake up. I call Poppa, but he's got his phone unplugged. I call Charlie. He says "I don't give a shit." Who am I going to call? An ambulance? The hospital? The police? Finally I try my teacher. "I'm sorry to be calling this late, but my mother . . . has taken too many pills. Tomorrow she'll be dead . . . so that's why I'm calling this late . . ."

GLORIA: I wanted to die, I just wanted to die . . .

JULIA: And leave me? (*Gloria does not answer. Julia, on top of Gloria, delivers one final rain of blows with her fists. An ambulance can be heard approaching outside. Julia rolls over onto the floor. The ambulance disappears into the distance.*) . . . and leave me?

GLORIA: It hurt so badly. With Leo I'd finally come home. And when he left, there was nothing more to live for. Why should I get up in the morning, brush my teeth, put my clothes on. . . ?

JULIA: (*Interrupting.*) . . . not even for a child?

GLORIA: No. Not even for a child. That's how shameful it was. I was a child myself, forgotten and abandoned.

JULIA: And I was to wake up next to you in the morning and find you cold . . .

GLORIA: (*Breaking in.*) Forgive me.

JULIA: . . . and that it was my fault you counted wrong. Because I hated him as much as you loved him. I was glad when he left you.

GLORIA: Forgive me.

JULIA: I can't believe you did it. I tried, but I can't. All the rest . . . is what it is. But this . . .

GLORIA: Forgive me.

JULIA: A mother can be all kinds of things: flaky, sloppy, unhappy, hysterical. But she can't stop being a mother. (*Pause.* I'll never understand why you can't see that . . .

GLORIA: You don't have to. (*Sitting up.*)

JULIA: . . . and never forgive it.

GLORIA: I said "forgive me" but you shouldn't.

JULIA: Afterwards, I wanted to live with Poppa. But I couldn't leave you alone with your pills.

GLORIA: And I had to promise not to let anyone else move in . . . That it would only be you and me and the cat . . . Why are you packing in those black plastic bags? They look awful?

JULIA: All that's going out.

GLORIA: I wish you'd been born right now. That this wasn't an end but a beginning. I hate seeing my shitty thumb prints on you. I'd like to start all over.

JULIA: I'm my own person.

GLORIA: But I'm the one who brought you into the world. Mistreated you.

JULIA: I don't think that means so much. I believe there's a purpose in me that you have nothing to do with. Something that makes me who I am. And no amount of shitty thumbs in the world can change it . . .

GLORIA: You're not planning to save much.

JULIA: What happened when Grandma died?

GLORIA: Do I have to?

JULIA: Yes.

GLORIA: I never wanted you to call me "Momma." I thought if I avoided the word, I could create something new. So naive. So stupid! Momma called the theatre in the usual way, spaced out on whiskey or pills. She said I had to come over. "Right away," she mumbles, "or I'll die."

  People can't lie to their children and get away with it. She wanted to be a surgical nurse. And no matter what she said, I could feel her hating me for getting in her way. I could never understand how becoming a surgical nurse could be more important than taking care of Gloria . . . That it might be more fun watching Gloria Swanson in a movie house than staying home with me . . .

After the performance, I rode out to her house. All the lights were on . . . Poppa would have been furious, he was so frugal. I go in. On the kitchen table are pill bottles and an almost empty bottle of whiskey . . . I can hear Momma snoring upstairs. I pour out the whiskey that's left and sit in the hall. I drink the whiskey slowly and look around at my childhood home.

So many ambitions, so many failed ambitions. The withered plants . . . (*Pause.*) I know I should call an ambulance, but I don't. I just sit there . . . I must have sat a long time. I don't know. When the ambulance comes I find out what I already knew. She's dead . . . On the hall table is the book she bought for your birthday. (*Pause.*) I take it and come home to you.

Maybe she would have made it if I'd called right away. But at that moment, I wanted her to die. (*Pause.*) Sometimes I suddenly see her. Making an entrance. Young and beautiful in her three-inch heels. She enters and we live our lives over again. And all that rage she has, is turned toward others . . . not toward me, not toward herself . . . (*Pause.*) But she doesn't come.

"Momma" is the loneliest word there is. It's the first word and when you're old enough to say it, you've begun your own life.

JULIA: (*After a pause.*) You know, at night I dream I'm an astronaut, walking on the moon. And I have this great fear that I can never return to earth. It hangs there in the distance, far away, bluish white and shining. Around it, stars are twinkling. It's so terribly fragile. Suddenly I hear the beating of a giant heart, and the sound fills the whole universe. (A car honks below in the street.) Poppa. He's who he is. But sooner or later he comes.

GLORIA: I'm going to play Kristine. That's a good role too. (*Julia runs out of the room, returning with a cat in her arms. Starts toward the pet carrier.*) Julia . . . can I keep the cat? (*Julia hesitates, then laughs. She gives the cat to Gloria.*)

END

Mary Bloom

by

Jussi Kylätasku

Translated from the Finnish by Tim Steffa

CHARACTERS:

Mary Bloom
Otto
Serenity
Cold Cal
Martha
Disabled Veteran
Alcoholic
Blind Man
Deaf Wife

Act I

1

(Dark of night. A bitter wind. Otto on edge of roof.)

OTTO: God! Answer me! This is all the closer I can get! God! Answer me! This is all the closer I can get! God! Answer . . .

MARY: *(Climbing ladder.)* Yoo-hoo.

OTTO: Occupied. Can you wait a moment?

MARY: *(Stepping to the roof.)* It's crazy howling into the night from the rooftops, unless you're drunk . . . A pastor. *(Sits to rest.)* The poor and unfortunate are forbidden to beg and peddle, or step in on the landing to warm themselves when they're numb to the heart with cold. But just watch out when you're the one rigid with a mortal fear of death . . . That goddamn Blacky didn't even give me time to fetch my long johns.

OTTO: God, I've made it this far on my own power. This step leads two ways. Into Your hands . . . Or to hell and damnation. *(Prepares to jump.)*

MARY: If you've got any money, leave it to me.

OTTO: *(Who has already forgotten Mary's presence.)* What being have we here?

MARY: A human being.

OTTO: That is sufficient for you?

MARY: Quite enough.

OTTO: What will remain of you?

MARY: What should.

OTTO: A social security number, and even that they'll forget to strike from the rolls. What on earth has kept you on your feet so long?

MARY: Nothing comes to mind.

OTTO: How rich I am in my poverty beside you.

MARY: What have you got?

OTTO: How powerful in my weakness.

MARY: So go ahead and jump.

OTTO: In faith do I take this step. (*Prepares to jump.*)

MARY: (*Coming to his side.*) That is a power you don't possess.

OTTO: God.

MARY: There is no such thing.

OTTO: God. Answer me.

MARY: (*Stepping to the edge of the roof.*) There is nothing more to your god than to that world down there. *I* will take that step. (*Mary steps from the edge of the roof into nothingness.*) Come on, come on. You won't fall. It's wonderful standing here on nothing but your own two feet. Feel free to rise. What's got you down? Up, man, up.

OTTO: I cannot . . . believe . . .

MARY: And for the rest of your life you'll swear this was mere dream and delusion.

OTTO: Who are you?

MARY: Mary Bloom.

OTTO: Whence comes your power?

MARY: It is *within me*.

OTTO: Who am *I*?

MARY: (*Returning to roof.*) The man of god has no faith in god. The man has no faith in mankind. I have come to you in your great need.

OTTO: I shall follow you.

MARY: Stand me to a cup of coffee?

2

(*Tent meeting. Otto on platform before audience. The handicapped, the afflicted: a disabled veteran, an alcoholic, a blind man and his deaf wife. Mary in wheeled bed upstage.*)

OTTO: In that instant the fair-weather preacher left his sunny prospects and entered upon the materially uncertain but far more spiritually sustaining path of a disciple of Mary Bloom . . . The papers write that we make a fortune at the expense of the disadvantaged victims of society, but this is no big deal. We make ends meet, give or take a little. And if this be an outright swindle, for which we would be answerable in a court of law, let those countless souls whom Mary's power has delivered from both physical and mental pain and suffering bear witness to it. And on this you too, dear visitors, are to render judgment, gathered together with us for the purpose of this meeting. Hark! Silence . . . A silence as profound as eternity. Faded into a distant echo are the city's nerve-wracking grind, stridor, insecurity, depravity, and violence. Relax and receive the sweet peace being offered . . . Indeed! Whence comes this state of peace? (*Turning to audience.*) Can you explain it? An engineer, if I am not mistaken? You there, madam, creased with cares? Can this tattered old threadbare tent, which a mystical tip landed me for one grand at the Circus Mundi's bankruptcy sale, so thoroughly seal us off from the oppressive outside world? I say unto you: the Spirit. It is generated by the Spirit, which even now descends upon us as would a loving father bending to his child . . . "Sleep, my child . . ." We do not sleep! Awake! Arise! . . . Please just sit down and listen closely: I do not intend to rouse you a second time. Will the world be spared, or will mankind, which a thousand times over has earned its doom, be destroyed perhaps this very night? That depends on us here today . . . on you! So do not sleep, friend, but now if ever remain vigilant as Mary Bloom, with all the power of spirit granted her, performs that miracle on which the hope of the World and man depends. My wife there, Serenity, an inno-cent virgin . . . By the power of the Spirit, through sacred vow to us, Mary . . . You cannot falter now! Oh endure! My wife, a virgin, shall bear a child . . . You may behold it with your own eyes! Witness the miracle and make it known to the world!

ALCOHOLIC: (*To Disabled Veteran.*) Have you participated previously? How long does it take before the healing . . . What sort of confession is required? Does one speak into the microphone? (*Hacking cough.*) I don't mean to crowd, but I could conk out any second now.

DISABLED VETERAN: You've brought this situation on yourself. Ten times I've stood in line on these crutches and not a thing has been done for me . . . For the tenth and last time, Mary! I'm no hypochondriac. A direct hit on the Golan Heights. Preventing global war on behalf of human rights . . . The entire lower half of my body is paralyzed, no feel-ing at all. And where there is feeling, it's constant pain . . . Have I got you beat, Mary! Ten long trips I've made on these degrading crutches —on a pensioner's fare in a man's prime—and I'm expected to go back again on these same crutches, the neighborhood laughingstock?

ALCOHOLIC: Isn't it about time something started happening? Have a look at these wrists, have a look at these ankles . . . I've always spoken up for you, Mary! Even back when my word still meant something . . . Mary!

Mary!

DEAF WIFE: (*To Blind Husband.*) Stand your ground. Don't neglect yourself!

BLIND MAN: Mary! My wife is deaf! Not a thing between her ears, but faith like a rock! . . . Nobody ever listens to me.

DEAF WIFE: My husband has been blind from birth! Nothing but hide-covered holes! Mary, release me from this guide dog's life.

OTTO: (*To afflicted.*) Stay! Calm yourselves, dear friends. (*To audience.*) The halt and infirm have been brought forward for healing. Please understand their distress, which leads to selfishness. (*To afflicted.*) This Mary has promised and I guarantee: none of you shall go uncured. The blind shall have sight, the ears of the deaf shall be unstopped, the alcoholic shall be freed of the bottle, and the disabled veteran shall cast away his crutch. (*To Disabled Veteran.*) No, you haven't been forgotten, dauntless Finnish soldier! Ten times—only eight times, to be precise —have you pressed to the fore. Have patience and bear in mind: the first shall be last and time is the great teacher. (*To audience.*) The program will begin very shortly. Here, behind this curtain, my wife Serenity is in spiritual training for a powerful tour de force: here before you this evening she is to give birth, a virgin, to the child whom the Spirit, through Mary, promised to the world. And in that wheeled bed Mary Bloom is concentrating on the performance of her life . . . Mary! . . . Does she wake or sleep? The answer remains beyond us. It is a Spiritual State that she strives so within her soul to achieve. Support her, all of you. Banish doubt! Faithless, be gone! . . . Now with all your soul summon Mary . . . Mary! Mary . . . Mary . . . (*Audience calls guardedly to Mary. Otto approaches her.*)

3

OTTO: Listen to that, Mary. The time is ripe.

MARY: I feel like the devil.

OTTO: Our sole defense against our persecutors is this tiny band of the faithful. If you betray them, Mary! . . . Many have come hundreds of miles on account of you, many have put the last of their savings at stake . . . (*Along with audience.*) Mary . . . Mary . . . How many slaves to the system have given up good jobs on your account? How many have separated from faithful spouses? How many fathers have left their families in the lurch for their souls' sake? How many mothers have spurned their children and in your name demanded freedom?

MARY: You can see for yourself that's not the position I'm in.

OTTO: I begin to apprehend. You, as a woman, envy Serenity. You would rather bear the child yourself.

MARY: Who'd run this show if I skipped out on maternity leave?

OTTO: My god was a bubble you burst. But although I did discard the collar, I didn't escape my skin. All of the miracles I have seen you work with my own eyes, your incredible career, the thousands upon thousands you have brought under your sway . . . none of it has crushed my unbelief. I have waited for this day as for the dawning of Armageddon. Doubt's triumph over faith, despair's triumph over hope, hate's triumph over love.

MARY: I'll go on.

OTTO: You'll do it! I knew you'd do it! You put me to the test and I didn't endure . . . Without faith . . . you can endure . . . Without faith . . . you can't endure . . . (*Babbling fades to silence.*)

4

(*Music—on Otto's cue to musicians. Song.*)

Sweeter than a cherry, that was little Mary.
Evenings on the waterfront she'd hustle up some trade,
Stashing in her garter the sailors' jack she'd made.
Jauntily she set her cap, a rosebud in her tresses;
Sable was the coat she wore, with scarlet silky dresses.
The sailors swarmed around her singing Glory and Amen,
Hey there, Mary sweetheart, what say you and me be friends.

Daddy's little darling, that was little Mary.
She gave her folks the earnings from her amorous soirées,
Just as other little girls take home their factory pay.
They weathered the recession with the money they were given,
Even though it later proved to stink to highest heaven.
The neighbors offered prayers, saying Glory and Amen,
Someone ought to set her on the righteous path again.

Not at all contrary, that was little Mary.
She fell for Captain Blacky, a swarthy bearded chap,
Who left her, when he left her, with a parting dose of clap.
Life is but illusion and all tenderness betrayal;
The flesh is sure to flower, it's the spirit that is frail.
Mary then concluded with a Glory and Amen,
Fighting fire with fire is what this world demands.
(*Music continues softly as Mary speaks.*)

MARY: (*Coming before audience.*) She should've known what those southern banjo-boys were like. So much for that, so long, Mary got dumped ashore and the tub set sail. Wracked with the shakes, I went mooning around the unfamiliar streets in a daze . . . (*She is caught up in her memories. A bitter wind moans maliciously. Music out.*) ''That goddamn Blacky didn't even give me time to fetch my long johns . . .'' But just watch out when you're the one, rigid with a mortal fear of death, knocking at mercy's door, and guarding it, in white robes and with a sword of flame, stands Mary Bloom!

OTTO: (*Shaking Mary.*) Wake up, Mary, to reality . . .

MARY: I'm reality to you.

OTTO: (*Quietly to Mary.*) Are you possessed of the power, Mary, or not? (*To audience.*) We regret this interruption. From time to time the power that possesses her gives rise to unexpected outbursts. (*Lowering limp Mary to bed.*) A moment's rest will so recharge her that, transformed into thermal energy, her power would suffice to solve the western world's entire fuel problem . . . She is sleeping now. And when she wakes it will mean your awakening as well. If anyone faltered in his faith just now, there's time here to pull yourself together. There's been rough going before this. I remember it as if it were yesterday the beginning of the little lady's career. She was like a force of nature seeking an outlet. We toured the country, from town to town and from one cheap hotel to yet a cheaper one . . . Eventually we got stuck with a bill in one of the most miserable of provincial rooming houses, the Patria . . . My nerves were frayed and . . . doubt began to assail me.

5

(*Rooming house. Mary sleeps.*)

OTTO: (*Entering.*) Verily, verily! (*Shaking Mary awake.*) She who would awaken all sleeps most soundly herself.

MARY: (*Waking, grabs* New Testament.) Blessed are the . . . blessed are the . . .

OTTO: (*Relenting.*) Read to yourself in thought. I'll make some chowder. There was that much left over from the price for the overcoat after I'd bought the train tickets.

MARY: (*Eating chocolate.*) So we're pulling up stakes?

OTTO: We'll have to slip out so the old biddy doesn't notice. (*Begins to clean fish.*) This will do fine in soup. I'll make it in the coffee pot. If I stopped by the landlady's to borrow a pot, she'd haul me over the coals.

MARY: I'm not eating that fish.

OTTO: So, fast . . . With a bellyful of chocolate! . . . Who brought you that? Confess!

MARY: I stole it.

OTTO: You, who should exemplify absolute morality?

MARY: I'm the one who brought up "thou shalt not swipe"? (*Reading.*) "Blessed are the meek, for they shall inherit the earth." That is not the case . . . "Blessed are they which do hunger and thirst . . ." What's righteousness?

OTTO: How are you to save a world that until only recently you believed was flat as a pancake? (*Cuts his finger.*) Stop the bleeding. (*Mary stops it.*) Put the book away and get dressed. The train leaves at five thirty.

MARY: I threw all my clothes in the trash . . . You said yourself they stank.

OTTO: Don't you ever do any laundry?

MARY: I'll go naked under a coat.

OTTO: Here endeth your tale, Holy Mary. I've been in touch with every sect and movement possible. Each has its own leaders, and they don't accept outsiders. And the young have their black magic . . . It's all been arranged with prison officials, under the guise of entertainment . . . I told them you sing. The tour begins tomorrow at the state penitentiary. The last possible train leaves at five-twenty-five from platform two. Farewell, Mary. I shared a stretch of the journey with you, and for that I shall thank and curse you the rest of my life.

MARY: There's a diamond ring in the fish's belly. Open it up and take the ring out.

OTTO: Open it up yourself.

MARY: I am not touching that revolting carcass.

OTTO: (*Embracing Mary.*) Poor child, whom the Spirit took for a moment as its own and then abandoned to the tender mercies of the world . . . (*A knock at the door.*) We'll pay up tomorrow!

SERENITY: (*Entering.*) "I will rise now, and go about the city in the streets, and in the broad ways I will seek him whom my soul loveth." Don't be afraid, Otto. There won't be a scene.

OTTO: Serenity, my wedded wife. Our nuptial eve made manifest—suffice it in present company to say made plain—that not even then could I believe in love. Serenity remained a virgin. A rosy country lass born to the village parsonage to provide the world with petit bourgeois preacher's brats.

SERENITY: I have come to inform you that under no circumstances will I ever again allow you to come back to me.

OTTO: Say it in scripture, Serenity dear.

SERENITY: You could have phoned so that I needn't have kept food in the oven for months on end for nothing. (*Opens suitcase.*) I won't be your dog anymore, Otto. I've never even been your kitten . . . I brought your best suit and some shirts . . . (*Shirt tears.*)

OTTO: This girl, whose bloom of youth you view with such bitterness, was a certain way station on my desperate quest. Mary Bloom, child of the Spirit. (*Serenity begins to cry.*) You two may have something to share with one another, but nothing for me.

MARY: Don't cry, Serenity. I used to cry too, but I don't cry anymore. Blessed are those who must bear a heavy heart, for those . . . (*shouting at Otto*) . . . for those who cause their tears shall come to even greater grief! Blessed are the subservient, for they shall see through their master!

OTTO: But, Mary . . .

MARY: Blessed are the crushed and scourged, for their turn shall come to answer blow with blow!

OTTO: Open up . . . open up . . . Resonance! It's on its way, Mary!

MARY: Blessed are those whose level best won't do, for they have something of which their instructors have not the slightest idea! Blessed are those at the mercy of their superiors, for they shall come out on top! Blessed are those who get kicked while they're down, for it is luck everlasting giving them a break!

OTTO: Now that one there was a bit . . . Let it come, just let it all come out! Rage!

MARY: Blessed are those whose mouths are stopped, for their voice shall decide the world's destiny. Blessed are they who must humbly accept their lot, for they shall have dominion. Blessed are the weak and helpless, for from their bitterness shall spring an invincible might. Blessed are those considered subhuman and driven like beasts, for they shall not be taken in by the mask of piety. Blessed are they who pay with labor and toil that the lords and masters may glut themselves at their buffet tables, for bread shall not satisfy their hunger. Blessed are the ruled, for they shall rise up. Blessed are the unemployed, for they shall be given their due. Blessed are those who have lost their land, for to them belongs the world. Blessed are those who can't hold their own, for they shall declare war. Blessed are those who are good for nothing, for they shall have their choosing. Blessed are the broken, for they shall not leave one stone upon another. Blessed are the deceived, for they shall not believe the lies. Blessed are those who do not receive their share of love, for they shall not let the sun go down on their wrath. Blessed are the hopeless and exhausted, for their patience shall cease. Blessed are those who can no longer bear their suffering, for they shall not wait their turn. Blessed are

those who can't go on living, for tomorrow is theirs. Blessed are you
who have no one, for you have me.

OTTO: (*Rummaging through Serenity's luggage.*) Any money?

SERENITY: (*Taking out checkbook.*) What amount do I write it for?

OTTO: Four, five hundred. Go pay the bill. And call a cab.

6

(*Prison dining hall. Otto pushes Mary on stage in a wheeled bed. Serenity with offering plate.*)

OTTO: Blessed are prisoners, for they shall have freedom. (*Inmates burst out laughing.*) On your feet! (*Inmates stand.*) At Mary Bloom's request, there are no guards present in this hall. But no one is to assume that I am not in control of the situation . . . Be seated. (*Inmates sit.*) Mark my words. Although it may appear so, Mary is not asleep. Neither is she awake, as we are in this everyday mundane reality of ours. Her power —which you are about to experience!—is not of this world. Neither is it from god. This she herself denies. He that hath ears, let him hear . . . You may already have heard about her visit to your infirmary. After what she worked there, it will be a little while before crowding is cause for complaint. There isn't but one malingerer left, fighting for his life. (*Otto withdraws upstage. After moderate artful pause, Mary rises from bed.*)

MARY: This place sure is grim. I don't expect the gravy is much to brag about either. It makes the blood run cold just looking . . . Oh, these four narrow walls! Is there any curse they haven't been cursed with, any revenge they haven't been threatened with, any rage they haven't been battered with? Man is fallible. Were your failings so much graver than those of all the money-grubbing, Judas-goat elbow-artists who out of sheer fright keep to that so-called sheltered path along which the majority shuffles, each wheezing down the other's neck? . . . How many of you are just plain thieves? Hands up . . . Uh-oh, you better watch out someone here doesn't snatch the shirt right off your back . . . (*Scattered hesitant laughter.*) By the way, this nightgown is also stolen. I lifted it from a poor-man's shopping center whose owner lolls in Havana with hootchy-kootchy girls turning him every so often to avoid sunburn. (*Unbridled paroxysm of laughter.*) Murderers next. Just raise your hands, I didn't come here to pass judgment . . . Incredible! Have a look for yourselves and consider how each hand stands for one cross in a graveyard. (*Laughter subsides.*)

VOICE AMONG INMATES: Then I'll raise both hands.

ANOTHER VOICE: And me, all my fingers.

MARY: Are you the. . . ? You're the machete man! I had nightmares back when that was in the papers. I was still a little girl then. And here you are, sitting here forgotten, and people have new topics of conversation and terrors . . . Humble your heart and you needn't be in for life for eternity. All of you! Although I've said there is no heaven, there is a hell, and it's within each one of you! (*Pause.*) Someone out there is laughing cold laughter in his soul . . . Just how many gates were opened for me and locked behind me as I was escorted here? Within how many walls do I now stand? At least three stone walls and ten iron gates . . . It makes the skin crawl just thinking about it . . . But I'll be frank with you: one single word, one word from me would shatter all the locks and smash all the walls and you would all be free. I could even say it right this very moment and you would be as good as on your way. The guards wouldn't dare lay a finger on you and the police wouldn't stand in your way. But what good would that do you when walls of wickedness and locks of callousness still remain firm in your hearts? (*Whispers, deep sighs, vague murmuring.*) Someone out there is transmitting a chill from his heart . . . "Mary, Mary . . . smash your own wall . . ." (*Thrusts it away.*) Bow your head before my glory. Bow down your head, press your brow to the stones of the floor and shut your eyes, for the glory of my spirit is entering this room . . . You will stand without batting an eye before society and its justice. Yes, you know the law: "An eye for an eye and a tooth for a tooth." Oh, were you to get right with me, you would weep for joy! Bow down your head, press your brow to the stones of the floor, for now . . . This is the moment of glory! Ah! I can only just bear to look . . . How then can you, in whose innermost souls dwell deceit and violence? Turn your eye inward and look straight at the blackness . . . which was born a blackness and over which each year drew with a huge roller a new blackness . . . A thick blackness. It won't go away by scraping a little at the surface, no . . . (*Inmates are completely in Mary's power. The same for Serenity. Mary nudges her.*) Don't fall asleep at the plate, Serenity. You're about to take the offering. Oh, you murderers, how can you live with your atrocities? Someone just killed I could still revive, but your victims are ashes and dust. And you burglars and thieves. With nothing but the sum of money, ill-gotten and cast to the winds of the world by you here, with that money you could have saved from starvation hundreds, thousands of the Third World's children, provided hospitals with medicines . . . Assist those fighting against their oppressors with your check or money order . . . I don't mean for weapons, but for bandages and food supplies, and for reconstruction when the bombed cities again . . . There would be causes all right if the good will were there. But what does the church do? The sanctimonious and canting keep some small change in their pockets to have a little something to drop in the plate for show, because of the neighbors, not the cause . . . And the church takes its share even of that pittance, on top of tax benefits and real estate . . . (*Lowering her voice, to Serenity.*) Serenity, get a move on.

SERENITY: I am a bad woman.

MARY: Take the plate and get going. It's all set.

SERENITY: All I want is Otto back . . . Behind your back the whole time . . . From the start, outward devotion, inward . . . Condemn me, Mary!

MARY: I have an audience. (*Taking plate to inmates.*) I'm coming to collect the offering. And I'll be frank: pinch your pocket money today, and your days are numbered. Try to get by with the price of a pack of cigarettes, and so shall I too reckon the worth of your soul's blessedness. (*Circulating with offering plate.*) Have your wallets ready . . . Eyes closed and remember the glory! Once the cash is in the coffer you may open your eyes and behold me in all my glory . . . Play cards with those coins, reprobate. You're upping the ante on your only life. Smooth to the touch, the feel of those bills there . . .

OTTO: (*Sings the offeratory hymn.*)
Worms and vermin, like a cancer—
At my soul they suck and gnash.
God, if you exist then answer,
Loose your sword, unleash your wrath.
Begging you on bended knee,
For your judgment now I plead.

I've renounced the cleric's collar,
But I can't escape my skin.
I can feel the pain and squalor;
I can sense the guilt and sin,
Like a knifeblade in my soul,
Brutal, agonizing, cold.

Blindly babbling in anguish
Like a criminal I crawl.
May the enemy the vanquished
Bend beneath his iron law.
Nails and hammer I extend,
Offering a helping hand.

MARY: (*To Cold Cal.*) Pay up. Or meet your doom.

COLD CAL: Lady, that's already behind me.
MARY: What lies before me?
COLD CAL: What lies before us.
MARY: Looking at you makes my blood run cold.
COLD CAL: Same here.
MARY: Is there anything you believe in?
COLD CAL: I don't feel the need.
MARY: Doesn't the past horrify you?
COLD CAL: Not beside the future.
MARY: Have you killed?
COLD CAL: I've had to.
MARY: Follow me.

7

(Meeting continues. Song—"'Sweeter than a cherry . . .'")

> And so our Mary dear set out on her career.
> Soon her private bank account was virtually replete.
> She was prominently featured in the leading scandal sheet,
> Photographed dressed all in white, immaculate and splendid,
> Accompanied by headlines that banner-bold contended
> She should let them have her story, with a Glory and Amen,
> A sensational exclusive sure to sell as hot as sin.

OTTO: (*To audience.*) That was the story of the birth of our fellowship. Ever since that day this convict, whose heart remained untouched by Mary's word, has followed Mary. The epitome of callousness . . . Cold Cal. He has testified as eye-witness to incredible miracles, but he remains unmoved as a mountain in his faithlessness . . . Go have a look, Cal. The doctor should be here soon. (*Cal doens't move.*)
MARY: Go on, Cal. (*Cal exits.*)
OTTO: The moment of birth draws nigh. (*To Serenity.*) Hold on yet, hallowed wife. (*Serenity groans louder, quieting as Otto continues.*) Some of you may perhaps wonder what it's like for me, being the husband here. Mine is a minor sacrifice beside what the world will gain by it. And who can say? Perhaps as the child grows and matures, my turn too will come . . . (*Serenity stifles groans.*) The Spirit willing, he shall have brothers and sisters. But now let Mary kindle in us a mood appropriate to receiving a miracle child. (*Pause.*) Mary.
MARY: Get them shouting more.
OTTO: Not since your revelation of the child have you either stood before an audience or performed your feats of power. Today, Mary! The

greatest miracle since the birth of Christ is expected of you, and you don't even open your mouth!

MARY: (*To audience.*) Oh, you workers, not doing your bit even for solid wages. But on the final day of reckoning your share shall be counted according to how you put your talents to profit. (*To Otto.*) What were these talents again?

OTTO: (*Whispering.*) Get it going!

MARY: Oh, you . . . oh you . . . oh you . . .

OTTO: (*Whispering.*) Oh, you farmers . . .

MARY: Oh, you farmers, planting your field in peas and butchering the cow and braining the little lamb with an axe and slitting its throat and spilling the blood into a basin, not seeing your way fit to selling it cheap to the city's hungry . . . So there's no hunger in Finland? There are those who find the insults of the lot who sit in the welfare offices more than a little hard to stomach. They'd rather go around at first light hefting garbage cans than end up being labeled. The well-fed big-wheel socialist's backside gets stuck in the eye of the same needle as the capitalist's paunch . . . A minor clerical error shows up in the application forms of some needy unemployable gaffer, and it's ruthlessly into the trash bin with them. But let some executive director get nailed for a flagrant misdemeanor, and he's retired on a retainer of going on ten thousand a month clear . . .

OTTO: Mary, are you possessed of the power or not? (*Sob escapes Mary.*) The atmosphere builds! It's so strong a feeling in the bones that you could almost predict the weather by it. Poor Mary. She's had it hard. She's only human after all, flesh and blood, bowels . . . merely a frail clay vessel. Though not bad looking for her ilk . . . Humor along with the text, said old Hieronymus, especially doomsday text. The doctor has not yet arrived, nor is my wife ready. To allow Mary a little time to summon her powers for her decisive effort, we shall recount, to lift the thoughts and strengthen the faith, how Mary received the revelation . . . when the child was promised. For the first time we present it in its entirety, unabridged (with possibly a slight stylistic condensing to save time). Picture a luxury hotel room at night . . . neon lights blaze the bright colors of the spectrum . . . A modern day rainbow like the token of the covenant granted by Old Graddad, that mankind should not perish in a second flood. The muffled beat of a dance band carries from the restaurant . . . (*to musicians*) . . . and stops dead, as if sliced with a knife. And the old bronze church bells . . . Let's leave them out. Mary always slept between us, Serenity and me, one on the right side, the other on the left . . . What are you rattling, Cal? You should be meeting the doctor!

COLD CAL: (*Opening folding bed.*) I was there.

OTTO: And weren't awakened by Mary's glory.

COLD CAL: (*To Mary.*) You told me to keep vigil and I did.

MARY: You kept vigil! Were we asleep? Who told of the dream in the morning?

OTTO: (*To audience.*) And Cold Cal slept in the spare bed like a faithful dog at his post. Good night, Mary.

SERENITY: Please let me sleep.

8

(*Hotel room at night. A wide bed, Mary in the middle between Otto and Serenity. Cold Cal in spare bed. Last waltz heard from restaurant.*)

SERENITY: Our waltz. (*Somewhat along with music.*) Our, our waltz . . . (*Imagining herself in Otto's arms.*) Don't keep looking at my shoulder, my Ottoman. I burned it badly in a hayfield that I can only bear to sleep in the nude. (*Otto hums waltz.*) I may take some keeping in rein, Otto.

OTTO'S VOICE: "I have compared thee, O my love, to a company of horses in Pharoah's chariots."

SERENITY: Who of us would have believed that I would last by your side? In you there was so much of that which met with no response . . . And it's only now, Otto, that we enter a realm where I too may give my all . . . And at full speed too . . .

OTTO'S VOICE: "Thy navel is like a round goblet
which wanteth not liquor:
thy belly is like a heap of wheat
set about with lilies.
Thy two breasts are like two young roes
that are twins,
which feed among the lilies."

SERENITY: (*Along with waltz.*)
"As the apple tree among the trees of the wood,
so is my beloved among the sons." (*A kiss.*)

OTTO'S VOICE:
"Set me as a seal upon thine heart, as a seal upon thine arm:"
(*Squeezes Serenity's arm violently.*)
"For love is strong as death;
jealousy is cruel as the grave:
The coals there are coals of fire, which hath a most vehement flame."

OTTO: (*Whispering.*) Mary.

SERENITY: Please let me sleep.

OTTO: Mary's asleep. That's what I've been waiting for. I knew you were awake . . . because I was awake too.

SERENITY: Mary gave me my own existence.

OTTO: You've come a long way with me. Could we go back again together?

SERENITY: Thus spoke Mary: ''Thou shalt not greet an old friend, for he shall offer you back your old burden. Thou shalt not acknowledge those who call from across the way and the other side of the square: 'Remember back when and where?' Once you were one of them but now you are your own self.''

OTTO: It's a declaration of war.

SERENITY: Oh, future generations. Oh, future generations . . . If only every mother said no.

OTTO: There wouldn't be any mothers.

COLD CAL: Every mother snatches her own son from the flames. But when it's the world on fire, the quicker the better.

OTTO: There is something greater than what you've ever experienced.

COLD CAL: Not a lot.

SERENITY: Love, Cal! (*Embraces Cold Cal.*)

OTTO: (*Drawing Serenity into his own arms.*) For man, Cold Cal. (*Pause.*)

MARY: (*Rising.*) What are you doing while I'm asleep?

SERENITY: His left hand is under my head, and his right hand doth embrace me.

MARY: Otto. Go get some salted peanuts from the bar. (*With great friendliness.*) Serenity, would you care for a glass of milk?

OTTO: I have put of my coat; how shall I put it on?

SERENITY: Stir not up, nor awake my love, until he pleases. (*Pause.*)

OTTO: Asleep . . . That's how far it goes.

SERENITY: Mary's power is gone.

MARY: (*In a trance.*) A message for those of this house.

OTTO: Return to sender!

MARY: Fear not. Good tidings. You, innocent virgin and faithful wife in both the spirit and the letter of matrimony—though without the fleshly fillip—unto you shall be born a child.

SERENITY: The glory is upon her!

MARY: A child of the Spirit.

OTTO: Glory be . . .

MARY: (*Drifting off to sleep.*) Nine months from receipt of this notification. Summon the faithful. And a real doctor. Witness it to the world. It shall be a boy. He shall become the salvation of the world. But if you

betray me and give Mary up, he shall become the child of doom.
OTTO: Amen.
SERENITY: I'm to give birth. A tiny little pure baby. A new life, Otto.
OTTO: He's to be born through you, not of you. He is not your child, he's the whole world's child.

Act II

1

(*As intermission ends. Last seats fill during hymn.*)

Unemployment and inflation
Haunt the old world like a curse.
Mankind, seeking some solution,
Finds no answer in the earth.
Unless you get down on your knees,
There's no hope, Humanity!

You heads of state, you mandarins,
Lay your armaments aside.
The same old story once again:
Evil's forces, like a tide,
Words of peace upon their lips,
Gallop toward apocalypse.

Doesn't anyone still honor
And respect the social norms?
Anarchy triumphs, the victor;
Terrorism, guns and bombs,
Wonders of technology,
Destroy the earth and humanity.

Who still stands and fights for justice
Without expecting first a bribe?
Who is there to cure the sickness?
Who a healing balm prescribe?
Mary Bloom, please set us free!
Save us from calamity!

2

(In section for afflicted.)

ALCOHOLIC: *(To Disabled Veteran.)* Listen, how do you figure this birth business? Will they get it to come out all right? Do you have complete faith in it all?

DISABLED VETERAN: Among the Arabs there were genuine soldiers of the faith. On the strength of the Koran to certain death.

ALCOHOLIC: Did you take that to heart? . . . I've got a bottle on me just in case . . . You do understand, as a man, that if it weren't along, I wouldn't be able to verify if I'm becoming truly free . . . I wouldn't bring another child into such a world situation. Strict control of the birth rate or world war! . . . The white man will pay his dues. Faced with total annihilation, the mongols will rally to their common colors. *(Giggles nervously.)* "Do you read the yellow press?" "I'm no Maoist . . ." Will Russia opt for Europe or Asia? Or will the fuse on the United States' domestic crisis run out before the world has but one card to play? . . . American roulette: anarchy or fascism. The Soviet Union's big guns are loaded for bear.

DISABLED VETERAN: Russia is counting too heavily on tanks in Europe. I've seen beliefs and ideologies face off in this world. I believe in power. I have that behind me too. But first it's Mary's turn to give a show of hers.

ALCOHOLIC: My belief will endure no matter how long the speeches. I'll believe anything as long as it has its own logic. I wasn't a bad speaker myself. Whenever the triumphal march of the forces of the right need obstructing, I was always made to speak . . . Meanwhile, back at the bar . . . No! No more of that, I'd just as soon . . . Have a look at these wrists. *(Significantly.)* The serpent. That which is within each of us . . . *(Becomes muddled.)*

MARTHA: *(Having entered.)* May I look? . . . Didn't you once . . . Four, five years back . . . I voted for you.

ALCOHOLIC: I wouldn't publicize it. Here. *(Suddenly confidential.)* I finally got some feedback, completely unexpected. Those same ideas which brought me your vote back then, suddenly they can be freely voiced—actually, must be! Now I'm the only member of the drop-out generation the young listen to. I dropped out rather than quietly toe the line, and now it's become conscious. (*Slyly.*) Give 'em another barrel-load of serpents, comrade. (*Martha approaches Blind Man and Deaf Wife.*)

DEAF WIFE: Sit here by me . . . A cold hand. Colder than my own.

MARTHA: If only the one whose healing you seek weren't in need of even greater help.

DEAF MAN: Who's that come to make folks falter?

MARTHA: You've lost your faith in doctors.

BLIND MAN: I can sure hear that things aren't right!

DEAF WIFE: Quiet! . . . Will they ever cease their chanting? . . . If you'd go to concerts sometimes and not just stare chin-in-hand at your inner world. The sightless person can still experience a great deal within his soul. I just have to look on.

BLIND MAN: My wife is not a skilled listener. Perfect tin-ear pitch. (*Listens for laughter. Martha approaches the platform.*)

COLD CAL: No admittance to the public.

MARTHA: Has the mass hypnosis already gone so far that a fully conscious person is no longer permitted to make observations? (*Coughs nervously.*) I'm not here as a patient. Are you also one of the saved? . . . Don't you find it claustrophobic, belonging to a closed community and obeying its precepts?

COLD CAL: I was in prison. Mary set me free.

MARTHA: You've never suspected Mary Bloom of being a fraud?

COLD CAL: I am certain.

MARTHA:Faith moves mountains. But pity the lot of those who get caught in the landslide. (*Lights a cigarette.*) Have you seen miracle cures take place?

COLD CAL: I've seen them.

MARTHA: (*Smoking fiercely.*) Absolutely certain cases?

COLD CAL: Do you mean were there healthy ones in with the rest?

MARTHA: What if, let's say, a cancer patient feels himself cured at a meeting, but as the power of suggestion wears off, the disease returns? Who then is responsible for curtailing medical treatment?

COLD CAL: I'm not taking sides.

MARTHA: You don't dare to. On that depend the lives of many people.

COLD CAL: It doesn't depend on me.

MARTHA: Your cold certainty appalls me. What superhuman agonies fanatical faith has produced! Is common sense powerless against it?

COLD CAL: Yes.

MARTHA: (*Stamping out cigarette.*) We'll soon see about that. I was sum-
moned to assist in a birth to take place here.
COLD CAL: (*As if to himself.*) Mary, the doctor is here. (*Pause. To Martha.*)
She says to wait.
MARTHA: Telepathic messages. It is a phenomenon recognized by science.
(*Taking her place as an observer.*) In a virgin birth. If it is unsuccessful,
will that have any effect on your faith?
COLD CAL: If it is successful, will that have any effect on your faith?
MARTHA: Then naturally anything is possible . . . I'll so thoroughly settle
the child's paternity that it will no longer be a matter of faith.

3

(*Otto mounts platform. Cold Cal positions bed in which Serenity groans,
and continues preparations during Otto's speech.*)

OTTO: (*To audience.*) Would you care for some coffee? . . .
A thousand thanks, thank you, thank you . . .
The brand we serve at our revivals in Siesta,
a coffee that is somewhat cheaper.
But this time we are offering Fiesta.
Although it's price is rather steeper,
it has aroma that's beyond compare.
When night's are spent awake and deep in prayer,
it's easy to become a coffee-fiend.
Our book display attracted quite a congregation.
Is anyone still in need of consultation?
Or cassettes, posters, illustrated tracts,
in which you may discover for yourself the facts:
how Mary cured the pains of body and soul.
They're available by mail as well, you know.
To lift the spirits and keep the body fit
I highly recommend our relaxation kit;
our pure white jogging suits all carry
our scarlet-lettered logo: MARY.
But that's enough procrastination!
Let's welcome now the child of salvation!
Doctor, if you please. (*Assists Martha to platform.*)
MARTHA: Am I to examine her in full view of the audience?
OTTO: Observe the situation from the sidelines. It may be that you're
not needed at all. But as this is a first pregnancy and, to top it all off, a
virgin, and the whole thing a total mystery, we're not going to push our

luck.

MARTHA: Has pregnancy been confirmed? Has she had any instruction?

OTTO: She how she whines, she how she whines. (*To audience.*)
Dear visitors . . . more . . . oh, bosom friends!
Now for the birth of the child promised to Mary out of the power
of the Spirit.
The child to lift the curse and break the chain,
rendering humanity humane . . .
in the nick of time! It may be a computer even now—who's to
  say?
—is in the final countdown to launch a missile on its way . . .
I don't follow the news but people show by their expressions
that he is coming none too soon
to restore respect for life's basic values
where affluent well-being is the way
but vanity and self-interest hold sway.
Cal, bring Mary on.

4

(*Cold Cal accompanies Mary to platform.*)

MARY: Do you believe, Cal?

COLD CAL: It doesn't depend on me.

MARY: It all depends on me.

COLD CAL: I don't.

MARY: But if Serenity gives birth?

COLD CAL: Who to?

MARY: Do you have any children of your own?

COLD CAL: Yes, a few.

MARY: I don't know what power I'm possessed of, but you possess its
  counterforce. Cal, my head aches so.

COLD CAL: That's not my headache.

MARY: Can one miracle child save the world?

COLD CAL: (*Laughing.*) If the world believes it can.

MARY: This whole show just to make the world believe!

COLD CAL: It won't believe long in one child.

MARY: It'll work such a solid miracle that even the faithless will believe.

5

(Before audience.)

OTTO: Mary, are you possessed of the power?

MARY: So are you going to take that step, Otto?

SERENITY: Can I keep it? Mary, let me keep the child!

MARY: My mother didn't keep me either.

OTTO: Mary, you *are* possessed of the power.

MARY: *(To audience.)* Every child should have such a reception. You came to see miracles. They do occur in this world, these miracles of birth. Enough to throw away. Whenever a newborn baby latches on to the tit here, on the other side of the world some other baby dies of starvation. Oh, you world powers. You give the children of Africa and Asia such a thin slice of your pie, it's transparent, and then celebrate it with a televised gala concert. We have surpluses too. Doctors in white rubber gloves pluck them out prematurely for chucking into incinerators. These are your ''unwanted persons'' . . . To put it frankly, there is not a single human child on this slip of a planet that was unwanted by Father Life. You . . . you . . . you . . . everyone in this tent and this solar system and all the starry host, each of us is a child of Life, every single sink of corruption. But if you hold that He who made the world and space, that He can go off half-cocked, then what difference does my little miracle make? Think of a tiny baby. The little red ears, the nub of a nose, the eyes crinkling up and the mouth so, so gleeful . . . And the plump little fists and the stubby toes . . . Wonderful. Good enough to eat! When it's hungry it lets out an awful howl and is soon sucking limp with joy at its sweet mother's nipple . . . Was it science that provided the instructions for where to find lunch and how to order it? . . . How to close the little peepers and go to sleep after a burping and a change of diapers? . . . And who informs it how to kick and work the hands and legs to gain strength? For that there is no high school diploma or university gown, but all the same every single human child knows just as well as a kitten in its basket and a calf in its stall how to go about obtaining all of life's basic necessities. Where does it come from, that knowledge? Where do we come from, all the children of this world? . . . I don't know my own father.

OTTO: Mary, by now it's going to take a miracle . . .

MARY: *(As if coming to realization.)* A child of man. A daughter of Life. What's that?

OTTO: Push, Serenity, push! Good lord, Mary, aren't you possessed of . . . Good, Serenity. Good, in the name of the Spirit . . .

MARTHA: Please let me help. She might even die . . .

OTTO: This child does not come from her!

Without faith you cannot endure!

MARTHA: And neither is this woman pregnant. (*Serenity's groans subside.*)

OTTO: Mary!

MARTHA: Oh, lord have mercy. I came here specifically to make certain that the child was not injured . . . You poor woman. It must have been a tremendous ordeal.

OTTO: Mary, if you don't answer for this, I'll take your power! (*Serenity laughs.*) Why did Sarah laugh? But let it pass since they had the promised child. And the scribes laughed at Zacharias, but let it . . .

MARTHA: This woman *is* a *virgin*.

OTTO: A virgin bears the child—listen to her!

Without faith you cannot endure!

MARTHA: Mary Bloom's moment of truth.

OTTO: A virgin needn't necessarily give birth to a nine or ten-pound whopper, which was probably what Barabbas was like . . . A child of the Spirit could be fountain-pen sized . . . It could be a match . . . It could be pinhead sized! While you're all standing here hesitating, He has gone crawling off . . . (*Crawling around on floor.*) Every square inch must be searched! Child, child child child . . . The world's little savior child . . .

6

MARTHA: (*To audience.*) I ask you all to leave in an orderly fashion. We have been through so much that a person can't absorb it all at once. (*Stifles cough.*) As a doctor I have frequently arrived at that frontier at which the resources of science are exhausted. I don't deny miracles. But in Mary Bloom's case the miracles are over now and it is time for psychiatric care . . . A rare form of hysteria that under happier times might have made her a great actress. This same illness has sparked off many a revolution, pitted nation against nation, spawned great cultures . . . (*Fit of coughing.*) Excuse me . . . (*Gently but firmly.*) Come along, Mary. They'll make a healthy person of you.

MARY: Why not heal yourself?

MARTHA: As if you could see right through . . . My illness is incurable. Yours isn't.

MARY: Command the sickness to leave you.

MARTHA: Your powers are gone, Mary.

MARY: You have the power within you.

MARTHA: I know what I have. My work.

MARY: Knowledge didn't give you life and work won't kill you.

MARTHA: That will do. (*Seizes Mary.*)

MARY: You do have a gift for science. Your own life!

MARTHA: We are not going to solve the riddle of life here, Mary dear.

MARY: (*Resisting.*) I just solved it.

MARTHA: Humankind is part of the great cosmic cycle. But each one of us creates our own world through our own work. You have given your all and may now rest.

MARY: Acknowledge one fact: you have *power.*

MARTHA: No, Mary honey, your prescription won't work with me.

MARY: What is electricity?

MARTHA: Energy.

MARY: Love!

MARTHA: (*Laughing.*) The car is waiting, dear child.

MARY: Don't you love life?

MARTHA: I do! (*Fit of coughing.*)

MARY: Louder!

MARTHA: Must I resort to an injection . . .

MARY: Cal, grab her. (*Cold Cal siezes Martha.*)

MARTHA: (*To audience.*) I am being attacked!

MARY: Keep holding on tight. Now, Martha, to fight fire with fire.

MARTHA: (*To audience.*) I am ill . . . Isn't there a single sensible person out there . . . (*To Cold Cal.*) You are committing a punishable offense!

MARY: Leave her, sickness.

MARTHA: (*Receives shock.*) No, no, no . . .

MARY: You're still resisting . . . Out of her, sickness.

MARTHA: A burning . . . A fire in my lungs . . . (*Suffocating.*)

MARY: Out. And don't come back.

MARTHA: A gentle hand . . . swept away the ashes . . . It's gone! The pain . . . The disease is gone!

MARY: (*Very wearily.*) Stop smoking if you want to stay healthy. It doesn't do much for a woman's looks either, for that matter.

MARTHA: A miracle. Simply a miracle. (*Weeping.*) What if the doctor herself sees the X-ray that proves beyond the shadow of a doubt that only a miracle . . . a miracle can . . . save . . . (*Laughing.*) I was a specialist! Authorities in the field! How can I analyze, how am I to explain . . . "I beg your pardon, esteemed colleague, but I am alive!" (*To audience.*) It is not for us to disparage or deny the value of the work that scholars, researchers, specialists carry out in their chambers, shut off from the world in which we live, suffer and die like animals. Every human being owes his origin to a single fertilized egg cell. The mature individual, the thinking, feeling, creative person is composed of hundreds of thousands of cells, not a single one of which we have succeeded in penetrating . . . Physics can't get beyond the black hole without a god-hypothesis, experts admit to being as far from the key to the universe as was the caveman, the inventor of fire, the genius of his age, studying by his fireside the night's starry heavens . . . As far from the key to the riddle of life as the caveman was from splitting the atom. But after a hundred thousand years of diligent toil, he split it nonetheless! It's worth asking if it made him any the happier . . . Did it, Mary?

MARY: (*Irritated.*) Yes, yes.

MARTHA: Did it?

MARY: Okay, no, it didn't.

MARTHA: (*With slight uncertainty to the audience.*) Please forgive me, dear friends, I had a fatal disease, where do we come from, where are we bound! This little girl here just settled that this evening, and I am living proof of it! I will submit myself for thorough examination.

MARY: What examination?

MARTHA: We shall witness it to the world.

MARY: And if they still find something there?

MARTHA: You are testing my faith.

MARY: (*To Disabled Veteran.*) If every cripple that I in the moment of possession put back on his feet still hobbles along on his crutch as before? (*To Blind Man.*) Every blind man whose eyes I opened in my glory goes on groping through the same old perpetual darkness? (*To Deaf Wife.*) Every deaf person hears the old familiar silence in which not so much as a pin dropping breaks the monotony? (*To Alcoholic.*) The alcoholic freed from the bottle slouches in the corner of some smoke-filled bar mulling over the same everlasting thoughts about how the old bag doesn't understand him and the world changed the lock on the door.

MARTHA: I shall be baptized.

MARY: Can you swim?

MARTHA: I believed from the moment I arrived. It was useless fighting it. You were my last hope. I *knew* that I *must not die*! (*Stifles cough.*)

MARY: You can lead a horse to water . . .

MARTHA: Beyond the shadow of a doubt . . . (*Coughs.*)

MARY: There's blood on your handkerchief. You know what that means.

MARTHA: I don't believe it! Mary, I don't believe it!

MARY: Had you cast the disease out yourself, it would have been within your power to keep it away.

7

SERENITY: I didn't want the child. (*Rising from bed.*) Otto, I didn't want the child and there was nothing you could do with me. Because, mister husband of mine, a woman doesn't think from merely the waist up.

OTTO: You have a thick skin, wife. But we'll soften it up.

SERENITY: Hit me. That is one method that hasn't been tried yet . . . Even a goddamn livestock inseminator fondles before he pumps his potion. Since I wasn't allowed to bud or blossom, I refused to bear the fruit. Look, Otto, there really is something in me to cling to. Doesn't that get you thinking? (*To audience.*) Bring me a man!

OTTO: (*Embracing her legs.*) Why were you denied to me?

SERENITY: When my lust was so great that only my skin kept my flesh together, you ordered me to fast. (*To audience.*) I open my pussy to the coming of the bridegroom!

OTTO: I looked into my soul and saw the face of the beast. How could I have brought into the world a child who with your energy would perpetrate those crimes which I buried beneath my vestments?

SERENITY: (*To audience.*) The mare has come into heat!

OTTO: The cold fact is that a bomb there means bread here.

SERENITY: It's a mother's own child that's nearest her bosom. No matter if the child is evil at its worst, just as long as it's your own child.

OTTO: The worst has yet to be acknowledged. When I read of the manifold possibilities of disaster, when I behold the angel of destruction guarding the threshold to the future, my bosom swells with joy . . . For me, it is only right! And for every one of my kind . . . For everyone! Everyone! Everyone!

SERENITY: Not every son dies in war, as every mother knows.

OTTO: If my son becomes the one . . . who shows neither pity nor compassion?

SERENITY: *Our* son.

OTTO: It is his to do. May I burst my banks and sow the beast.

SERENITY: Now, Otto, be a man, and fast. (*Serenity and Otto exit.*)

8

ALCOHOLIC: The spirit that moves in that young lady everyone knows! . . . Every drinker . . . I guess I opened up in the wrong congregation. (*With determination.*) Every drunk! (*Taking bottle from inside coat.*) Just you wait until a little of this opens me up, and soon I too shall break into song . . . (*Can't get bottle open. Summoning will power.*) I need a drink. It's killing me. (*Can't get it open. With renewed concentration.*)

One drink. I've reached my limit. (*Can't get it open. With renewed concentration.*) The people demand a drink.

MARY: (*Having approached him.*) Open. Unaided.

ALCOHOLIC: The end. Everyone leave, that's the end of me. Ten years and I would have . . . five years . . . One election, one term . . . to achieve . . . democracy.

MARY: It isn't democracy until each person is his own ruler.

ALCOHOLIC: (*Summoning will to power.*) Mary. There is much about you of which I approve. Society's deprived, impoverished, handicapped, afflicted, the working class, as I say, need help. It demanded a great deal for me to bring my suffering before you. All the wasted years that would have belonged to the people . . . We belong to the people, Mary, you and I.

MARY: If you want a drink, take a drink. If you don't want one, don't take one.

ALCOHOLIC: You have a charismatic authority, Mary. But you too build your authority on the power of the masses. And when you no longer rule that, you are no longer a power either. (*To audience.*) Man . . . Human . . . Humankind is faced with a challenge greater than any it has ever been presented with heretofore. We are not to surrender or prostrate ourselves, but rather to rally together in the battle for a better life. I neither ridicule nor disparage the hopelessness and anguish that bring people under the sway of Mary's movement of rapture. But the ailing body in need of healing is society. There is no cure for that in the opiate of a blessedness-conferring spirit . . . I'm not placing myself above you. Have a look at my wrists, have a look at my ankles . . . (*Violent shudders. A frenzied outburst.*) How well I know Mary's meteoric flight. When I demanded the people's democratic rights, Mary proclaimed that there was but one true power and authority. When I tore into public health care legislation, Mary summoned the sick and halt to her for miracle cures. Mary Bloom reinforces all those lies beyond the capacities of the media, she generates a terminal apathy mass entertainment cannot achieve, she breaks through that resistance against which the state's machinery of violence is powerless. Resistance from within! . . . Does anyone still remember the proposal for unarmed resistance? That was something other than civil defense! The will of the people versus the armies of the superpowers' blind . . . (*To Blind Man.*) I don't mean to offend you. (*To Disabled Veteran.*) I'll say it right out loud! (*To audience.*) You are a mass of Mary molds! I was once a molder too, but I don't mold anymore! Good riddance down the church's cellar steps and into the bomb shelter to lead a nearly normal life even during global conflagration, with canned food and a well-stocked library, and morning paper deliveries! A chill down my spine . . . The serpent . . . Out, out of me . . .

MARY: Sharper. "Out of me, serpent."

ALCOHOLIC: Out of me, serpent, Mary, out of me, serpent . . . (*Almost hissing like a snake.*) I have fallen, Mary! You will fall too, Mary!

MARY: (*Swiftly drawing snake from Alcoholic's clothing.*) Just look at the viper your democracy feeds in your bosom!

SNAKE: (*In Alcoholic's voice, from deep within and ever deeper.*) The conflict between democracy and authority is irreconcilable! The adherents of democracy babble the slogans of revolution, but as closing time approaches stagger from clique to clique lapping up all the ideological dregs . . .

MARY: Let the venom spew.

SNAKE: The adherents of democracy are the alcoholics of politics! . . . The August Cabinet, that infamous coterie, for which even the supporters of moderation qualified to foot the bill, camouflaged a fear of authority by flaunting the banners of anti-violence . . . (*More wearily.*) To those gentlemen, "popular rule" was the same as "violence rules."

MARY: Is that the lot?

SNAKE: (*Even more wearily.*) When the time came to settle the summit meeting's staggering accounts, democracy's adherents forged the party's signature! But with the dawning of a moral hangover, the telephone lines were humming once more, and there was another batch waiting in line for the doors of opportunism to open for another round of watered-down reforms to be served up . . . May I make a call? It's in the black pages of the phone book . . . Authority. (*Sleeps.*)

MARY: (*To Alcoholic.*) Open the bottle.

ALCOHOLIC: (*Opening bottle with ease.*) Will I ever get it closed again?

MARY: Power preserved in alcohol. (*Slipping snake into bottle.*) Cork it tight.

ALCOHOLIC: (*Closing bottle.*) I won't have any power today.

MARY: You must always carry the bottle in your breast pocket. You'll feel it there, so it won't fall into the wrong hands. But the instant you fall back on authority, no matter how absolute, there will come such an irresistible craving, and with that swig, in swims the serpent.

ALCOHOLIC: It should be repeated each morning. "I won't have any power today." (*Begins to leave, stops, takes bottle from inside coat.*) I have a chance to make a comeback. But I don't have to. (*Puts bottle in breast pocket and exits.*)

9

DEAF WIFE: I've seen a miracle. A miracle happened. A man was saved.

BLIND MAN: Of course you saw how Mary held the snake by the throat, and the snake writhed and spat out the Antabuse? . . . Take me out of here.

DEAF WIFE: I can't hear. I'll just have to keep on observing and concentrate everything on understanding what's behind the words . . . But I saw it!

BLIND MAN: Where's that pisser?

DEAF WIFE: (*To Mary.*) Mary, give my husband the ability to see! He's even making me falter . . . I can't be beautiful if he doesn't see it. And when I want to make our home beautiful, that also hurts his feelings . . .

BLIND MAN: Haven't we been to enough séances and seminars in the spiritually profound life? You get some vibration and you're out like a light. Are you coming along or do I leave without you?

MARY: Try.

10

DISABLED VETERAN: So this is as far as it goes again? Mary avoiding her responsibilities to people just like little Finland wanting to make a good impression on the world but not delivering . . . We weren't allowed to return the fire. We were ordered into the thick of things, with open arms to boot . . . Goddamn it, if this crutch were only a machine gun. (*Mimes firing and is calmed.*) To get to the point. Mary. I gave both my legs for all people in this world, the rich and the poor, all . . . human beings. To be born free and equal in worth and rights. That is more than you can accomplish. Ten times I offered you an opportunity to atone, but that's it. (*Begins to hobble off.*)

MARY: Halt.

DISABLED VETERAN: (*Halting.*) I am not a hypochondriac.

MARY: Throw away your crutches and walk on your own two feet. (*Disabled veteran throws down one crutch.*) Both of them. (*Disabled veteran throws down the other crutch. Falls.*) You didn't dare believe! You threw away your crutches and still didn't dare believe! Is there anybody here who *wants* to be healed? And to go to the little trouble it takes?

DISABLED VETERAN: Where did I drop my rifle? Where in hell did I drop my rifle . . .

COLD CAL: (*Helping Disabled Veteran up.*) Don't surrender.

DISABLED VETERAN: I do have some power.

COLD CAL: Keep a cool head and a close watch on things.

MARY: Cal, should I give in to anger? Yes, I guess I could tour from hospital to hospital and morgue holding revival meetings . . . But whenever I suggest first giving faith a little try, knees start knocking. Should I unleash the fire and brimstone? . . . Cal? (*Cold Cal does not answer.*) Cal, you are to command my headache to go away. (*Cold Cal does not answer. Mary addresses audience.*) Are you for me or against me? (*To sick and handicapped.*) All together and individually: ''Pain, leave Mary's head.''

SICK, HANDICAPPED: (*Mumbling indistinctly.*) Pain, leave Mary's head.

MARY: That wouldn't scare a fly. If you had so much as a flyspeck of faith . . . so much as the lint dug from your own navel . . . Cal, you don't believe. Cal? . . . Wish something and it will happen!

MARTHA: Mary, join the dying.

MARY: You get up from your bed . . . Want something and it will happen! Wish something and it will come true!

MARTHA: I understand you completely. You've set yourself a goal and won't settle for less. I firmly believe that you will encounter a sufficiently powerful opponent. But I want to *know*. Reveal your secret to one who is dying. What is the focus of your power? (*Music.*)

MARY: (*Singing.*)

All alone in the world, here before your eyes,
For all her might and power, little Mary cries.

''What are you griping about? Can't you have mercy on a hapless cripple? When a person believed with all he had, it still wasn't enough . . . What do you want from us? . . . What is there left to believe in? Isn't it enough to acknowledge before the world your faith in one true Mary?'' That was enough for me too. But who's going to look after you when I'm gone?

Soon I'll be killed. It's the name of the game.
And anyone who uses his own power gets the same.

Because he is alone! You've been taught about the wages of sin. Have the good had it any better than the evil? Where were the faithful cringing when Jesus was led away? . . . Then right back to waiting meekly for a second coming . . . Why do you look down on your own power?

Who bears all the sickness? Who is it that strains
To gather all the riches? You, the grieved and pained.

I doubt a single one of you is of the well-heeled middle class . . . at least not if the offering is any indication. I'm just about finished, but it's no use dreaming of a vacation . . . ''Is she looking at me or . . .'' It's each one of you I'm looking at! To each of you belongs the whole world!

Is it really so impossible to dare to believe
What miracles a faith in your power can achieve?
Did anybody ever give me anything for free?
When has any guardian spirit ever guided me?
Although I blush to say it, my secret is, you see,
I love you each and every one so very terribly.

(*Music out.*) So listen. Ever since I was a little girl I've been incurably in love. The guys would deceive me and leave me, hump me and dump me, but I just went on loving my being in love. I acted tough. It was such a good act I was driven like a visiting bishop from the house of correction to reformatory and from reformatory . . . I came to hate those Pharisees and phonies! But I didn't give in. My lifestyle may not be much to brag about, but not once have I ever given in on a single thing . . . And I'm not now either. Does anybody care to try me?

11

DEAF WIFE: This is where we come in. (*They mount platform.*)
MARY: The blind man and his deaf wife. You have traveled a long way together, sustaining each other.
DEAF WIFE: Mary, my not being able to hear puts me in the worst of all situations. But you have also kept me in mind the whole time, haven't you? Maybe I, without understanding a single word, have been the most receptive?
MARY: We're about to put that to the test here on this stage.
DEAF WIFE: My husband uses his blindness. I'm leading him astray and so he doesn't dare abandon himself to the new and the unfamiliar. There is still time for me to experience, to love! But he already wants to retire into his granddaddy days. Oh, if I could only give him my eyes so he could see how beautiful a land can be, how beautiful people are even in suffering! Ahh . . . (*In agony.*) I . . . cannot . . . see . . .
MARY: Your husband has received your eyes.
BLIND MAN: I see with them! . . . The sky . . . filled with stars . . .
MARY: The holes in the tent.
MAN: Beautiful holes! Tiny round bright holes with light filtering through . . . I have eyes! . . . A beautiful woman. Is she my wife? There's one even more beautiful . . . A mirror. I have to see that I have eyes!
MARY: Your wife is now blind and deaf. She's trying to find you. Look.
MAN: Yes . . . That is true. (*Goes to wife.*) Mary . . .

MARY: It was *she* who gave you the gift of love.

MAN: Could she really have had such . . . Faith? But anyway, Mary, wasn't it you . . . in the main . . .

MARY: She gave you her own eyes. Out of love. Do you love her?

MAN: (*Suspecting the worst.*) Yes, I . . . It's so long ago that we . . . I love her.

MARY: Say it to her.

MAN: (*Quieter with each word.*) I . . . love . . . It doesn't get through. (*Becoming wrought up.*) Mary, she wouldn't hear even if I shouted with the voice of an angel!

MARY: You are not returning the gift from your heart.

MAN: May she have my hearing. (*Pause.*) Hello?

MARY: You lack love . . . What do we do now?

WIFE: Eyes . . . my eyes! (*Shrieking with rage.*) You have my eyes! Torn from me . . . in your face . . . my eyes . . .

MAN: I didn't do it! I'm not to blame. I can't stand hearing . . . Mary, I can't stand hearing . . .

MARY: May his ears be stopped. (*Man becomes deaf.*) Open his wife's ears.

DEAF MAN: (*Horrified.*) The pounding of the heart . . . in the temples . . . the surge of blood . . .

BLIND WIFE: A hand . . . (*Taking husband's hand.*) Your hand?

DEAF MAN: You are delicate. How delicate . . .

BLIND WIFE: Rough. Warm.

MARY: Go, sustaining each other. (*Deaf Man and Blind Wife exit.*)

12

DISABLED VETERAN: (*Rising on crutches.*) Mary. A chance.

MARY: You're only damaging yourself, you incurable case.

DISABLED VETERAN: When I threw this crutch away, I still believed. But when a total invalid stands hanging on one crutch, everything hangs on that. I've stood at that point countless times in my shack in the dead of night . . . But that defeat a moment ago put me back on my feet spiritually.

MARY: You might heave yourself up on your haunches, take a few faltering steps and then . . . the final collapse. Don't torture yourself.

DISABLED VETERAN: I no longer want it for myself. I need my legs on the long march on behalf of humanity. To the last ditch. First I'll get right with my neighbor. Then nations will get right among themselves . . . Order me to throw away my crutches and walk.

MARY: (*With indifference.*) Throw away your crutches and walk.

DISABLED VETERAN: (*Faltering.*) Not so fast! . . . Let's take it again from the top.

MARY: Cal, go help him out . . . Cal? Why don't you do what I tell you? Why don't you answer?

DISABLED VETERAN: I don't need reinforcements.

MARY: Throw away your crutches or to hell with them.

DISABLED VETERAN: (*With intense concentration.*) Just like before. The first crutch. The second crutch. I leave on my own two feet or . . . Mary. Take this seriously. As if I were your last chance.

MARY: I have no faith. (*Audience gasps.*)

DISABLED VETERAN: Again.

MARY: I have lost my faith.

MARTHA: (*Rising from bed.*) So we have lost everything. Don't condemn Mary. Rapture and faith work momentary miracles. Up until now I too always lived with hope in my heart. (*To Disabled Veteran.*) But all the same your case may not be quite so hopeless. It's just that with your ordinary poor person not every means is employed . . . Let's have a look at those legs . . . Just make yourself comfortable here. Are you completely relaxed now? (*Tapping.*) Just say if you feel any pressure.

DISABLED VETERAN: The entire lower half of my body is paralyzed. No feeling at all. And where there is feeling, it's constant, unrelenting pain. It usually starts here, grows gradually, and ends with a grown man bursting into tears. In the winter cold, and above all in the autumn when it's damp, and the old shack being as dilapidated as it is, the draft brings on an unbearable neuralgia in the joints. I ended up lying buried in the sand for a day and a half under fire before they managed a truce.

MARY: Your victims in Palestine are in the same straits.

DISABLED VETERAN: It's true I fired. Anyone would have . . . It was either war there then, or war here now.

MARTHA: Have you sought medical attention?

DISABLED VETERAN: Fourteen operations. Twice in Stockholm's Karolinska Hospital.

MARY: Are any of those Charles the Twelfth amputees still laid up there?

DISABLED VETERAN: There are some things I do not joke about. (*Yelps in pain.*)

MARTHA: There's a tactile nerve there. This is the point we'll start from. Soviet geneticists intend to reincarnate an entire mammoth from a single solitary cell frozen alive in permafrost.

MARY: They'll make a soldier of you yet. And then . . . pow! Is it worth it?

MARTHA: These neuroparalyzes have long made a mockery of science.

This too will have to be treated locally. Now we're going to carry out a
neurological operation.

MARY: From that anaesthetic you won't awaken.

MARTHA: (*To Disabled Veteran, helping him up.*) Don't give in to fear.

MARY: What happened last time you conquered your fear?

MARTHA: (*Beginning to lead Disabled Veteran off.*) I give you my word
that you will be treated as if you were a great head of state.

MARY: Refuse.

MARTHA: We'll show the world.

MARY: Throw away your crutches and walk. (*Disabled Veteran halts.*)

MARTHA: The operation will be successful.

MARY: The first crutch. (*Pause. Disabled Veteran throws down crutch.*)
The second crutch. (*Disabled Veteran throws down other crutch. Mary
addresses Martha.*) He's standing.

MARTHA: Not for long.

DISABLED VETERAN: (*Trembling.*) Let me go . . .

MARTHA: Faltering . . . You're faltering. The trembling is spreading
from the feet to the torso. Signals are leaving the brain but they no longer
reach the soles of the feet . . . The knees . . . the center of balance is
paralyzed . . .

MARY: I say stand.

DISABLED VETERAN: (*Producing hand grenade.*) Power. Here it is. Once
the grenade leaves my hand, five seconds . . . Mary, you said pow and
was it worth it? A man's life. Let's put it to the test, Mary. I go out on
my own feet or I don't go out alone. (*To Martha:*) You. You took a person and made a pawn of him. (*To audience.*) Get out. (*Pause.*)

COLD CAL: It won't explode. (*Disabled Veteran falls. Grenade slips from
his hand.*) It won't explode. I didn't allow it to. (*To Disabled Veteran.*)
Get up and leave. Your legs won't fail you. (*Disabled Veteran exits. To
audience.*) We were just shy of a wonder of devastation. This gadget is a
minor wonder of technology. The creativity of countless human brains
and skilled hands was needed to develop it. And it is only the tiniest of
tiny parts of the total destructive might humanity's entire development
has gone into creating. We possess the capacity to destroy all life on the
planet. But not to give life to a single tiny baby. It wasn't a human being
that gave you life either, but nature. And when you buy a packet of
petunia seeds for your garden or to brighten up your window sill, you're
still buying the mystery. You saw how I thwarted destruction. You saw
how I cured a man. Can the miracle of salvation, can healing power also
grow to become universal? Or is that the exclusive right of death and
destruction? Look at the person sitting next to you. Smile. Warmly.

Warmer still. Take his hand. Contact has been established. A miracle required everyone's complete presence. You may go. We will continue tomorrow.

13

MARY: No one is to leave.

COLD CAL: Mary, you were entreated and didn't deliver. People have a right to mercy.

MARY: You saved. You cured.

COLD CAL: You escaped me. I did know that your revelation of the child wasn't for real. But that was an overwhelming move, your not letting it be born. That knocked me for a loop. What is this world-salvation crap? . . . I was keeping a sharp eye on things.

MARY: ''Look at the person sitting next to you. Smile. Warmly. Warmer still. Take his hand . . .'' Why did I go cold?

COLD CAL: Because every person possesses power. Ingenious, but too brutal.

MARY: The only chance! What's wrong with that?

COLD CAL: That it doesn't work. That is a power people don't possess.

MARY: Cold Cal! Cold!

COLD CAL: Have pity on people!

SERENITY: (*Entering.*) Is my husband here?

MARTHA: Are you finally expecting?

SERENTIY: He took me high up on a rooftop.

MARY: No!

SERENITY: His left hand was under my head, and his right hand caressed me. But he fell under the power of a great oppression.

OTTO'S VOICE: (*From distant height, with bitter wind in the background.*) Can it come from man? Can I be true in wickedness as well?

SERENTIY: He kissed me with kisses upon my breasts and stroked my loins with a warm hand. But a great pain ruled his soul.

OTTO'S VOICE: Have I truly been chosen? Am I fulfilling the world's destiny, or only my own?

SERENITY: He laid me naked to my shame and prepared me for admittance. Words of blessed love welled from my lips. My tongue danced with his tongue. The sceptor of his love was as a brimming jar. But he was in the throes of a great despair. He stepped to the edge of the roof.

MARY: No!

OTTO'S VOICE: This far I have come on my own power.

SERENITY: He stepped over.

OTTO'S VOICE: Come. You won't fall. Step bravely over. I'll steady you with my hand.

SERENITY: I . . . could not . . . believe. He disappeared. I didn't see him. He didn't return. Everything in me went cold . . . Hasn't he come to you, Mary? . . . You won't be angry if I look around? (*Begins to search.*) Usually the small harbors the great and the great, the smallest of the small . . . (*Crawls on floor.*)

MARY: (*Trying to get Serenity up.*) It's gone too hard on you. Cal, help.

SERENITY: (*Rising.*) When Otto asks for me, please say that I have returned to my father's house.

MARY: What do you have in your hand?

SERENITY: (*Opening fist briefly.*) Not every girl has a little thing like this.

MARY: I didn't see anything.

SERENITY: It's no Barabbas. Please say to my husband that when he was searching for the head of a pin, the boy was sitting on the point. (*Cooing to her fist.*) I'll put you in a really lovely pot. I'll mix clean soil with my own finger. You can grow on your mother's window sill, mother's pearl, in mother's tender care, in clean country air that smells of flowers and bees. And when the time comes for mother's son to leave the nest, you won't escape your roots. (*Exits kissing her closed hand.*)

COLD CAL: That mother earned her happiness.

MARTHA: (*To Cold Cal.*) You restored the audience's faith. A miracle occurred . . . Everyone got to participate! I followed along so beside myself that I completely forgot my own pain. May I squeeze your hand? It would heal me.

MARY: *You* possess the power. (*To Cold Cal.*) Keep away from my miracles.

MARTHA: (*Taking Cold Cal's hand.*) So much for those few decades. But perhaps I can still learn something new. I certainly still believe in the rational world as well. It's only that our interpretation of it is too narrow. With the latest tools of science it is possible to make observations that do not fit within the scope of our cosmology. And where do we put experience? Where does my pain come from?

COLD CAL: You are well.

MARTHA: I didn't feel anything. . . ?

COLD CAL: My miracle is painless. (*Martha goes off.*)

MARY: Back to her sickness! (*Martha merely exits.*)

COLD CAL: You're out of it. The stakes you played for were too high and you lost everything. I saved the movement's future, Mary.

MARY: It cost the world . . . It cost the world, Cal . . .

COLD CAL: Annihilation is the price of being human.

MARY: You put people out of their misery.

COLD CAL: Man has been prepared for it. It was present at the dawning of creation, death at the cradleside.

MARY: A merciful ending. A beautiful dream.

COLD CAL: From which there is no longer any need to awaken.

MARY: You should be stopped.

COLD CAL: The course of events, Mary: a beginning, a middle, and an end.

MARY: Man chooses.

Man refuses.

Man resolves.

COLD CAL: Even you became human. Try it.

MARY: A small warm human being.

COLD CAL: Become cold, Mary my love.

MARY: I got you, Cal. (*Taking his hand.*) A new strength. A hot power. I'll burn you to ashes.

COLD CAL: You'll burn too.

MARY: There's still a chance. (*A flash. A rumble.*)

END

ON THE EDITOR

Per Brask, who was born in Denmark, has lived in Canada since 1975. He has translated several Danish plays into English, and directed plays in Canada and Denmark. He has written radio dramas for CBC, and has published several short stories, poems, plays, and essays. Recent books include *Power/lessness* and *Duets*. Per Brask teaches in the Department of Theatre and Drama at the University of Winnipeg.